D1215656

New Parties of the Left

Experiences from Europe

Acknowledgements

Resistance Books and the IIRE are grateful to all those who helped in the production of this book. In particular we thank Fred Leplat, Steph Grant, Terry Conway, Rick Hatcher, Carmela Avella, Dave Kellaway, Rob Marsden, Jay Woolrich and the IIRE's director, Marijke Colle.

We also thank Editions Lignes for allowing us to translate "Une idée qui a fait son chemin" from Daniel Bensaïd's 2008 book *Penser Agir*.

New Parties of the Left

Experiences from Europe

Daniel Bensaïd, Alda Sousa,
Alan Thornett and others

Resistance Books
London

International Institute for Research & Education
Amsterdam, Islamabad & Manila

Resistance Books and the International Institute for Research and Education would be glad to have readers' opinions of this book, and any suggestions you may have for future publications or wider distribution.

Our books are available at special quantity discounts to educational and non-profit organisations, and to bookstores.

To contact us, please write to:
Resistance Books
PO Box 62732, London, SW2 9CQ
Email: contact@socialistresistance.org

International Institute for Research and Education
Lombokstraat 40, Amsterdam, NL-1094 AL
Email: iire@iire.org

Published August 2011 by Resistance Books and the International Institute for Research and Education as issue 50 of the Notebooks for Study and Research.

Edited by Fred Leplat

Cover design by Rob Marsden

Cover photograph: Bloco de Esquerda

ISBN: 978-0-902869-51-6

ISSN: 0298-7902

Printed in Britain by Lightning Source

Contents

Contributors

Bertil Videt was director of the IIRE from 2007 to 2011. He is a member of the Red-Green Alliance, which he represented at the founding meeting of the European Anticapitalist Left in 2000.

Daniel Bensaïd was a founder of the Jeunesse Communiste Révolutionaire (JCR), which became the Ligue Communiste (LC). He was a professor of philosophy in Paris. He died in 2010.

Alain Krivine was a founder of the JCR, which became the LC in 1968 and LCR in 1974. He was an MEP for the LCR from 1999 to 2004. He serves on leadership of the Fourth International and the NPA.

Michael Voss is a member of the Red-Green Alliance (RGA) and of the Danish section of the Fourth International (the SAP). He was the RGA parliamentary group's press officer and journalist until 2006.

Alan Thornett is a member of Socialist Resistance (the British section of the Fourth International). He served on Respect's national council until 2010. He worked at the Morris factory in Cowley from 1959 to 1982 and chaired its Joint Shop Stewards' Committee.

John Lister is a member of Socialist Resistance. He served on Respect's national council until 2010 and co-authored *Respect: Documents of the Crisis*. He is director at London Health Emergency.

Klaus Engert is a member of the German section of the Fourth International and writes for its magazine *Inprekorr*. He also contributes to *Avanti* and *Sozialistische Zeitung*.

Salvatore Cannavo was assistant editor of *Liberazione*, the paper of the Partito della Rifondazione Comunista (PRC). From 2006 to 2008 he was a MP first for the PRC and then for Sinistra Critica.

Francisco Louçã is a member of parliament for the Left Bloc. He was its presidential candidate in the election of January 2005.

Alda Sousa joined the Portuguese section of the Fourth International (the LCI/APSR) in 1975. She is a founder member of the Left Bloc and was an MP between February and July 2004.

Jorge Costa has been for many years a member of the Political Committee of the Bloc and was an MP. He is also a member of APSR.

Preface

The political landscape on the left has changed dramatically over the last 25 years. The attacks on the gains of the working class in the early 80s by Reagan and Thatcher, followed by the collapse of the Soviet Union in 1991, also transformed the traditional mass political parties of the working class. Social-democratic parties across Europe, including the Labour Party in Britain, have shifted to the right and have fully embraced neo-liberalism. The Communist Parties have followed in their tracks. The result of this process is that the differences between the traditional parliamentary parties of the left and the right have been dramatically reduced.

This has opened up a political space to the left of social-democracy which the radical left and revolutionary Marxists have a duty to fill. This task cannot be carried out by these currents simply continuing in their traditional forms without seeking new levels of unity. What is therefore necessary are broad pluralist parties embracing both the radical and Marxist left to restore independent working class representation.

In the context of the deepest economic and ecological crisis of capitalism in the post war period and continuing imperialist wars, the need for such parties is urgent.

This book looks at attempts to create new parties in France, Denmark, Britain, Germany, Italy and Portugal. The character of these parties varies from country to country, and this book does not pretend to be a detailed guide for the creation of such new parties.

The authors are members of the Fourth International and activists in the movement. The book relates their experiences as militants who have responded to and encouraged the emergence of these new parties, and who face all of the problems and possibilities arising out of this new situation.

Fred Leplat
London, June 2011

Introduction

Bertil Videt[1]

The European left has undergone major transformations since the turbulent years around 1989. Some former left parties have given up the struggle for socialism and adapted to social-democracy or even social-liberalism. Other parties have ceased to exist. And a number of European countries have witnessed unlikely alliances of the far left that in several cases have turned into stable political actors with a real presence and influence.

These new alliances, or processes of regroupment, among the radical, or sometimes less radical, left is the focus of this book. These processes have drastically altered the political landscape of the far left in several European countries, but have nonetheless received extremely little academic or analytical interest. According to one of the few scholars dealing with the mutation of European left parties "...the assumption was that the radical left in general, and communism in particular, had accompanied it into the 'dustbin of history' (March and Mudde, 2005, p. 23). On the other hand, few Marxist, or left wing, intellectuals do research on political parties. With the basic assumption that social struggles and conflicts shape history rather than electoral politics and parties, it is hardly surprising that most Marxist scholars have focused their research elsewhere.

The combination of these two factors gives us a situation where very little attention has been paid to the mutation of the radical left in Europe in academic literature (Bell, 1993; Dunphy, 2004; Dunphy, 2009; March, 2008; March and Muddle, 2005; Moreau et al., 1998.) This book, published jointly by Resistance Books and the Amsterdam-based International Institute for Research and Education (IIRE), constitutes therefore a needed contribution to the research on the new left in Europe. With its pan-European focus and focus on the role of anticapitalist forces in broader parties, it is a unique analysis of the European phenomenon of regroupment of the radical left.

---

[1]   *Bertil Videt is an international political scientist active in the Fourth International. He is editor and co-author of "Living our internationalism", the history of the International Institute for Research and Education, of which he was director from 2007 to 2011. Bertil Videt has been a leading member of the Danish Red-Green Alliance, which he represented at the founding meeting of the European Anticapitalist Left in 2000.*

Whereas the following chapters will provide detailed accounts of concrete experiences with regroupment in Britain, Denmark, France, Germany, Italy and Portugal, the aim of this extended introduction is to contextualise the discussions, that is to take a bird's-eye view on the development of left parties in Europe by looking at the overall trends, similarities and also differences these parties have. We will see that regroupment is a trend that has been taking place in a number of European countries, and beyond, since the fall of the wall, as an attempt to unite the remaining left forces faced with strengthened neo-liberal attacks.

We can therefore talk about a mutation of the left in response to its decline, but, as we will see, a mutation that in some cases have led to a resurgence of the left that has been declared dead by opponents and mainstream analysts.

Regroupments

Let's first be clear about what we are dealing with when we talk about regroupment or recomposition of the left, two terms that are sometimes used interchangeably. A first attempt to define regroupment of the left was given when the Fourth International, an international organisation of revolutionary socialist organisations, identified it as a strategic objective during its 14th World Congress in 1995. The document *The political situation in imperialist Europe* states that "our political-organisational objective should be to be part of a pole of left regroupment; an engagement in the prolonged crisis of the traditional workers' movement and the dead end of the green current." In the same document it is described that "Practically, it means pulling together (or forming an alliance with) significant fragments coming out of the traditional workers movement, breaking with the social democratic policy of joint responsibility for the economic crisis."

This last sentence contains some important points in its attempt to define regroupment, by stating that it should contain significant fragments of the traditional workers' movement, and that these should break with social democratic policy. In the subsequent 15 years since the adoption of the document, we will see that the different regroupments have taken very different forms,, and some have been quite different from what was anticipated.

The first experience with regroupment took place long before the adoption of the FI document and far from Western Europe. The Brazilian Workers Party (Partido dos Trabalhadores, PT) was founded in 1980 by various left wing groups, with its origins in the radical labour movement that emerged in south-eastern Brazil's industrial sectors by the end of the 1970s. The establishment of the PT, uniting various left wing currents with trade union activists, has set an example, which has inspired socialists beyond the Latin American continent. In his critical analysis of the PT, Michael Löwy, argues that the party "(...) has a more general significance and a broader import as an almost unprecedented attempt to go beyond–within the framework of mass organisation, the usual models of politics within the workers' movement: neo-Keynesian reformism, parliamentary cretinism, bureaucratic centralism, doctrinaire sectarianism, apparatus substitutionism."

Table 1: Year of establishment of European regroupment parties

Year	Party	Country
1986	United Left	Spain
1989	Red Green Alliance	Denmark
1991	Communist Refoundation Party	Italy
1992	Socialist Alliance	England
1996	Freedom and Solidarity Party	Turkey
1997	Scottish Socialist Alliance/Party	Scotland
1999	The Left	Luxembourg
1999	Left Bloc	Portugal
2004	Respect	England
2004	SYRIZA	Greece
2007	The Left	Germany
2009	New Anticapitalist Party	France

However, the general trend, when we talk about regroupment in Western Europe is a process that has taken place since the 1990s. The regroupments have often been a response to a general decline of the left in the wake of the fall of the Berlin wall. Obviously, the pro-Moscow Communist parties were the hardest hit by the collapse of the Soviet *Heilstaat[1]* (welfare state). This seemingly final victory of capitalism, created a widespread sense that capitalism had triumphed, famously articulated by Fukuyama's declaration of the *end of history* and Margaret Thatcher's slogan *there is no alternative* to economic liberalism. The entire left, no matter its stance on the Soviet Union, was badly hit by the ideological surge of liberalism.

It was against this background of a strong ideological offensive of neo-liberalism, and a left that was wounded and confused, that the first attempts to regroupments took place. In Denmark, the Red-Green Alliance was founded in 1989 and got the mocking nickname

---

[1] *Heilstaat is a Dutch word used, often ironically, for a Utopian 'ideal state'. Eds.*

"the united estates of deceased parties", a nickname that would vanish as the alliance grew stronger in the following years. As its name suggests it started as an alliance of three parties to the left of Eurocommunism, including the Communist Party after the more Stalinist parts split out, with the purpose of overcoming the Danish 2% threshold to gain parliamentary representation for the far left. Shortly after, in 1991, the Italian Refoundation Communist Party, with a much stronger organisation and political impact, was established.

As table 1 shows, the bulk of regroupment parties were established in the late 1990s. This is a period that was marked by what we can call a crisis of hegemony of the left. The traditional workers movement, the traditional communist parties and the social democratic parties, are in a crisis as they have lost their hegemonic roles. The communist parties in Southern Europe and the social democratic parties in Northern Europe have played a similar role of setting the hegemony in the workers' movement throughout the cold war. An important part of this role was the existence of counter-cultures where the communist or social democratic party, depending on the country, "cared" for their constituency from cradle to grave with own banking system, media, child care etc. The French Communist Party and the Scandinavian social democratic parties were examples of parties that were very present in the lives of its members. The ideological crises of the traditional left, along with the increased individualism linked to the ideological breakthrough of liberalism, have led to a situation where these parties have lost their all embracing roles.

In Europe, the 1990s were also, at least electorally, the decade of social democracy. By the end of the decade in 1999, the governments of 13 out of 15 EU member countries and all of the 4 major EU countries were led by social democrats. This was thus a unique opportunity for social democracy to show its willingness to make changes and to create a more social Europe. Looking back we do certainly not see the social democratic parties used this opportunity to make more than a few minor reforms here and there, such as the introduction of a 35-hour working week in France under Lionel Jospin. On the whole, there is a broad consensus that this opportunity was missed and that the social democratic leaders, for whatever reason, did not produce explicit left wing policies.

This situation of a crisis of the traditional workers movement, with the collapse of the hegemony of the communist and social democratic parties has created a space for new parties. The creation of such a new space had also been further nurtured by the coming into existence of a number of so called 'new social movements', which are not aligned to these traditional parties or the trade union movements which look to them. These conditions were favourable for the hitherto more marginalised left, and permitted a breakthrough for non social democratic and non Soviet-aligned communist parties. In the period since the early 1990s we have thus witnessed a breakthrough for Trotskyist and Maoist parties in several European countries.

It is against this background of a crisis for the traditionally hegemonic left, combined with a soul-searching among the entire left and a breakthrough of previously marginalised left forces, that the objective conditions for regroupment existed. The Dutch Socialist Party, which differs from the other parties by not being a result of process of regroupment, is not included in Table 1. The SP was established in 1972 and was a rather small Maoist party for most of its life.

The European experiences of regroupment are very uneven, both organisationally and politically. The parties in Table 1 have all progressed organisationally, and are established as parties. In several countries we have witnessed attempts to left regroupment that either have aborted or have failed. Politically, the parties are uneven as some take a clear, anticapitalist stance, whereas others can rather be considered as left social democratic parties. From an analytical point of view this unevenness might cause some frustrations, as it makes it difficult to categorise and compare these parties. But these differences are, on the other hand, a clear indication, that we are dealing with real political movements.

New left parties: differences and similarities

In one of the few analytical articles with a comparative approach to parties of regroupment in Europe, Murray Smith (2007) argues that the process of new political formations on the left is uneven from two points of view: 1) Between countries, as these new political formations have developed very differently according to the different countries and 2) politically, as some of the parties are more radical and clearly anticapitalist. These dividing lines, developed by Murray Smith, is the basis for the below attempt to categorise and compare the different parties.

First, let us have a look at the differences in the organisational strength of these parties. This can obviously not be measured in a simple and scientifically correct way. Nonetheless, with all the shortcomings, we will look at the electoral support to and membership figures of these parties, in order to get an idea of their strength. Table 2 gives us an overview of election results for the new left parties over the last two decades, during general elections.

Several factors have to be taken into account when reading table 2. First of all it does not reflect to which extent there is an electoral competition on the left of the party included in the table. And here, we will, unsurprisingly, find that the parties with the highest scores tend to be the parties maintaining hegemony of the left of social democracy. This is to some extent the case with the Dutch SP, the top scorer in election results: in the Netherlands, the SP has been the only political party to the left of social democracy running for elections since the establishment of Green Left in 1989, which continuously has moved to the right. In Germany, Die Linke, which is another top scorer in the European league, represents a first challenge to German social democracy from the left.

Table 2. Election results in per cent of the vote for general elections

	RGA	PDS - Die Linke	Syriza	LCR - NPA	SP (NL)	RED (N)	Left Bloc	IU Spain	ÖDP Turkey	PRC Italy	SSP
1990	1.7	2.4									
1991											
1992										5.6	
1993			2.9	1.1				9.6			
1994	3.1	4.4				1				6	
1995					1.3						
1996			5.1					10.5		8.6	
1997											
1997				1.4		1.7					
1998	2.7	5.1									
1999					3.5				0.8		2
2000			3.2				2.4	5.5			
2001	2.4	4				1.2				5	
2002				2.5	5.9		2.8		0.34		
2003				3.1	6.3						6.9
2004			3.4					5			
2005	3.4	8.7				1.2	6.4				
2006					16.6					5.8	
2007	2.2		5	3.4					0.15		0.6
2008								3.8		3.54	
2009		12.9	4.6			1.3	9.8				
2010					9.8						

Another factor that plays a role for a radical left party's likelihood to get elected representatives is different political systems, which then affects their access to mainstream media and opens the discussion of tactical voting. Smaller parties will logically score better in systems with proportional representation (Denmark, Portugal, Netherlands, Germany, Luxembourg, Spain, Greece and Turkey) than in systems with plurality voting systems or similar (United Kingdom, France). And again, in systems with proportional representation high thresholds (5% in Germany, 10% in Turkey) discourage the electorate from voting for smaller parties. In other words, we can expect that political systems with proportional representation and a low or no threshold are to the advantage of the radical left. Of the countries discussed here, Denmark, Greece, Netherlands, Luxembourg, Portugal and Spain fall into this category.

In the case of France, results at presidential elections might be more useful parameters than those at general elections. Because of the high degree of power residing with the President of the Republic, the presidential elections are largely considered as the main electoral contest, and the general elections are largely perceived as a confirmation of the power base of the president. The French "run-off" system prevents smaller parties, such as those on the radical left, from obtaining any elected representatives, which might explain the very little media attention these parties get during general election campaigns. In 2002 and 2007, years where France has held both presidential and general elections, the far left (now defunct) LCR performed substantially better in the presidential elections (43% and 4.1%) than in the general elections (2.5% and 3.4%). (For more about the LCR's performance in general elections, see Liegard 2007 and Lemaitre 2002).

The scores of the far left in Britain are not included in table 2, as the national score would be distortedly low, since the regroupment parties in Britain have not stood in all constituencies. As Alan Thornett and John Lister elaborate in their chapter on broad parties and left unity in Britain, both the Socialist Alliance (SA) and its successor Respect have however had some noteworthy election results. In the 2001 general elections SA had an average score of 1.75% in the 93 constituencies it stood, and won 6.8% and 7% in two constituencies. With the establishment of Respect in 2004, which replaced the SA and became a broader coalition, the British far left gained a new momentum in a period marked by a strong anti-war movement and popular dissatisfaction with the Labour government. In the 2005 general elections Respect had its most important elections results, obtaining from less than 1% to 38.9% of the popular votes in the constituencies it stood. The latter score was obtained by George Galloway, who with his election on the Respect platform, was the first MP to be elected to the left of Labour in England since 1945.

Election results might not be as important for anticapitalist parties, who emphasise extra-parliamentary struggles, as for mainstream parties. Nonetheless, it is our only, albeit very problematic, parameter for measuring the broader public support these parties have. Furthermore, participation in elections and having elected representatives markedly increases any party's access to the media and hereby for spreading its message. In his brilliantly clear and still pertinent booklet *Left-Wing Communism: an Infantile Disorder*, Lenin (1912) argues: "Whilst you lack the strength to do away with bourgeois parliaments and every other type of reactionary institution, you must work within them because it is there that you will still find workers who are duped by the priests and stultified by the conditions of rural life; otherwise you risk turning into nothing but windbags."

Table 3. Political systems and impact for far left vote

Country	System	Threshold	Impact
Denmark	Proportional (Sainte-Laguë method)	0.02	Positive
France	Runoff	N/A	Very negative
Germany	Proportional (Sainte-Laguë method)	0.05	
Greece	Mainly proportional	0.03	
Italy	Mainly proportional	0.04	
Luxembourg	Proportional (D'Hondt method)		Positive
Netherlands	Proportional (D'Hondt method)		Positive
Norway	Proportional (Modified Sainte-Laguë)	0.04	
Portugal	Proportional (D'Hondt method)		Positive
Scotland			
Spain	Proportional (D'Hondt method)		Positive
Turkey	Proportional (D'Hondt method)	0.1	Negative
United Kingdom	Plurality Voting System	N/A	Very negative

Membership figures

After having had a closer look at election scores for parties of the new left, across Western Europe over the last 20 years, I will now turn to membership figures. I have chosen to address the membership figures, as this gives us some quantitatively comparable data indicating the organisational strength of the parties. As it was the case for the election results, it is with certain reservations that we can use membership figures as a parameter for measuring the strength of the parties. First of all, there is no clear correlation between membership figures and the, not easy measurable, level of activity of these members. The parties included in this book have very different conceptions of 'membership' and different expectations to their members. The Dutch SP, which is unrivalled in terms of members despite a current decline, does not seem to expect much from their members.

On the website of the SP (www.sp.nl/interact/word_lid/), the party asks visitors to join the party online for a mere 5 Euro per quarter, and mentions among the benefits a free book by the party chairperson and free use of the party's e-mail service. Also, it is noteworthy, that according to comparative research, members of parties on the left do not tend to be more active than members of parties on the right (Weldon: 2006, p 474).

Table 4a. Membership of parties - total

	RGA Denmark	PDS - Die Linke	LCR - NPA	SP Netherlands	Left Bloc	IU Spain	ÖDP Turkey	PRC Italy
1990	1000	150000	1358			70000		
1991	1000		1324			70000		150000
1992	1082			15122		70000		130000
1993	999		1232	15517		70000		120000
1994	1093		1070	15978		70000		120000
1995	1189		1070	16899		70000		
1996	1282	100000	965	17056		70000	30000	100000
1997	1479		1041	19262		70000		100000
1998	2023		1070	21975		70000		110000
1999	1968		1096	25052		70000		80000
2000	1945		1180	26198		60000		85000
2001	1992		1345	26553		60000		
2002	2366	90000	1513	27291		60000		90000
2003	2321	80000	2320	36406		60000		90000
2004	2524	70000	2620	43389	3789	60000		80000
2005	3739	72000	2570	44299	3790	40000		90000
2006	4127	72000	2605	44853	3858	40000		85000
2007	4099	75000	2640	50740	4714	40000		

Above, I illustrate the developments of membership figures in the different parties by three different tables, in order to contextualise the figures. Table 4a represents the membership figures for the relevant parties in absolute numbers. These figures have been obtained directly from the parties in question. Table 4b gives us the possibility to see the membership figures in proportion to the size of the countries, as it represents the membership figures per 10,000 inhabitants (based on 2008 figures for population, provided by the World Bank). Table 4c gives us an insight in how big the party is in relation to the total level of party members in the respective countries.

This is an important factor in order to understand the relative organisational strength of a party within its own country. The ratio of total party membership as percentage of electorate varies strongly in Europe, from 17.66% in Austria to 1.15% in Poland. The extremes of the countries included here are Greece with 6.77% of the electorate being members of a party and France where the figure only is 1.57%. Figures for total membership figures are from the late 1990s and are based on Mair & van Biezen (2001). Reading these figures, we must take into account that the only figures we have for total membership figures are from the late 1990s, and that these calculations thus do not consider the fact that the overall levels of party membership has declined in all long-established democracies in both absolute and relative terms (Mair & van Biezen 2001, p. 11).

The table above, showing membership figures of the new left parties, reflect a marked unevenness among the parties, no matter whether we consider the figures in absolute numbers, in relation to the population or as a ratio of total party membership.

Table 4b. Membership of parties per 10,000 inhabitants

	RGA Denmark	PDS - Die Linke	LCR - NPA	SP Netherlands	Left Bloc	IU Spain	ÖDP Turkey	PRC Italy
1990	1.82	18.27	0.22					
1991	1.82		0.21					25.07
1992	1.96		0.2	9.19		15.36		21.72
1993	1.81		0.17	9.43		15.36		20.05
1994	1.99		0.15	9.72		15.36		20.05
1995	2.16		0.17	10.27		15.36		
1996	2.33	1.22	0.17	10.37		15.36	4.06	16.71
1997	2.69		0.18	11.71		15.36		16.71
1998	3.68		0.19	13.36		15.36		18.38
1999	3.58		0.22	15.23		15.36		13.37
2000	3.54		0.22	15.93		13.17		14.21
2001	3.62		0.37	16.15		13.17		
2002	4.31	1.09	0.42	16.6		13.17		15.04
2003	4.22	0.97	0.41	22.14		13.17		15.04
2004	4.59	8.52	0.4	26.34	3.79	13.17		13.37
2005	6.81	8.77	0.18	26.94	3.79	8.78		15.04
2006	7.51	8.77	0.42	27.27	3.86	8.78		14.21
2007	7.46	9.13	0.47	30.85	4.71	8.78		
2008					5.88			
2009					7.4			
2010					8.19			

It is hardly surprising that parties rooted in very strong communist parties, such as the Italian Communist Refoundation Party, the Spanish United Left and the German PDS, have seen a decline in membership figures throughout the 1990s. Of these, is it only the German Die Linke which has experienced a (moderate) increase in members over recent years, after the election in 2005, when it had its electoral breakthrough becoming the fourth-largest party in the Bundestag with 8.7% of the nationwide vote. Both the Italian Refoundation Party and the Spanish United Left have witnessed an uninterrupted and continuous decline in both absolute and relative terms. In the case of the United Left, this decline in membership has gone hand in hand with a continuous decline in votes. The Refoundation Party did not manage to maintain its level of members, despite having a period of increasing elector support in the mid-1990s.

The new parties, starting from scratch, such as the Danish Red-Green Alliance and the Portuguese Left Bloc have maintained a general trend of an impressive growth in membership figures, despite some minor downturns in the period. The developments of the French LCR/NPA seem to confirm that more people can be attracted when something broader is created. Throughout the 1990s the LCR had steadily around 1,000 members, and experienced a fall in members until 1996. In 1999, LCR ran, and obtained representation, in the European elections on a joint platform with the Trotskyist Lutte Ouvrière (LO). LO refused to continue its unity with LCR, which then decided to present its own candidate, for the first time since 1974, for the presidential elections. The candidate was the then 27 year-old Olivier Besancenot, who won a surprisingly high share of the vote, 4.25%, substantially more than the 3.37% of the French Communist Party. It was on the basis of those events, from which the LCR gained a lot of publicity, that we saw a real surge in its membership figures: most striking was the increase from 1,500 members in 2001 to 2,300 members in 2002: an increase of more than 50% in a single year. As the process of creating a new party developed the LCR continued to have a growth in members, which initially tripled with the creation of NPA in 2009.

Table 4c. Percentage of total membership of parties

	RGA Denmark	PDS - Die Linke	LCR - NPA	SP Netherlands	IU Spain	PRC Italy
1990	0.49	8.43	0.22		6.19	
1991	0.49		0.22		6.19	7.6
1992	0.53			5.14	6.19	6.59
1993	0.49		0.2	5.27	6.19	6.08
1994	0.53		0.17	5.43	6.19	6.08
1995	0.58		0.16	5.74	6.19	
1996	0.62		0.17	5.79	6.19	5.07
1997	0.72		0.17	6.54	6.19	5.07
1998	0.98		0.18	7.46	6.19	5.57
1999	0.96		0.19	8.51	6.19	4.05
2000	0.95		0.22	8.9	5.3	4.31
2001	0.97		0.25	9.02	5.3	
2002	1.15	5.06	0.38	9.27	5.3	4.56
2003	1.13	4.49	0.43	12.36	5.3	4.56
2004	1.23	3.93	0.42	14.73	5.3	4.05

Political challenges

Going over elections results and membership figures, we see clearly that these new left parties are highly uneven in terms of strength, development and presence within their countries.

Politically these parties are equally uneven. Concrete political challenges that the parties have been, and are, faced with, will be thoroughly developed in the following chapters about the cases of

Britain, Denmark, France, Germany, Italy and Portugal. Here the main dividing line is probably not whether the parties label themselves as revolutionaries or reformists, but rather on questions on whether the parties are anticapitalist, that is being clear on the necessity for a break with capitalism, or whether they are anti-neoliberal, merely opposing and resisting neoliberal attacks, without challenging capitalism in systemic way.

We cannot easily put most parties in either category. Again, we are dealing with real movements, with internal dialectics and contradictions, which develop over time.

Looking at the party programmes and their actual policies, we can roughly say that The Left in Germany, United Left in Spain and the Socialist Party in the Netherlands are more in the camp of the anti-neoliberal parties. These parties do not take a clear stance of opposition to capitalism as a system, and these parties are in favour or unclear about participating in a government of capitalist administration. Many other West European parties, which are not discussed in this book, fall more clearly in this category of anti-liberal parties (the Socialist Left Party in Norway, the Left Party in Sweden, the Socialist People's Party in Denmark, The Left and the Communist Party in France). Many of these parties, but not all, are organised at the European level in the Party of the European Left Party, which, however, also count some more radical parties among its members (The Red-Green Alliance in Denmark, the Left Bloc in Portugal and the Freedom and Solidarity Party in Turkey).

This leaves us with a group of parties which we roughly can categorise as being anticapitalist, and still a part of the new broad left: the Scottish Socialist Party, the Red-Green Alliance in Denmark, the Freedom and Solidarity Party in Turkey and the New Anticapitalist Party (NPA) in France. The French should be considered as *sui generis*, as it certainly is not a party of regroupment as defined in the beginning of this chapter (pulling together or forming an alliance with significant fragments coming out of the traditional workers movement), as the initiative has come unilaterally from the LCR, and nonetheless the NPA has become something both qualitatively and quantitatively broader than the LCR was. These parties all consider themselves anticapitalist programmatically and argue, to varying degrees, for the overthrow of the capitalist system. These parties are also the parties which are the most clear on government participation, by either rejecting the idea or making it clear that participation in a government only can take place in a situation where this is considered a socialist government challenging the capitalist powers.

The Italian Party of Communist Refoundation (PRC) has undergone a political development over the past 10 years, which is well described in its own chapter. As Salvatore Cannavo describes, the party kept defending the idea of going beyond capitalism, even while participating in the government of the eighth-strongest capitalist power. In any case the PRC has been considered as moving to the right during the last decade. As a breakaway from the PRC, the Critical Left established itself as a party in 2007, after having operated as a faction with the PRC. The Critical Left is clearly an anticapitalist party, but constitutes neither a broad nor a regroupment party. Similarly, in Spain the Anticapitalist Left confederation has its roots as a current which emerged from the United Left, and is today a clearly anticapitalist, but not broad, political party.

Political parties are of course moving targets, which are difficult to capture and categorise. Any attempt of categorisation can quickly become obsolete, and we have no guarantee that an anticapitalist party will not be tempted by the taste of power and give up on main principles, as did the Italian Communist Refoundation Party, which supported the Italian military intervention in Afghanistan and US bases in Italy. Looking at the European map of the new left, two parties seem to be noteworthy, in issuing from real regroupment of different tendencies of the left, maintaining an anticapitalist perspective and constituting real political forces in their respective countries: The Left Bloc in Portugal and the Red-Green Alliance in Denmark. Despite being at each end of the European map, we witness some important similarities in these two experiences. Both parties have had parliamentary representation for more than a decade and constitute a real political factor, with regular appearance in their national media. Electorally, the Left Bloc has had an impressive surge since its foundation in 1999, and the Red-Green Alliance is stable above the Danish threshold of 2%. Interestingly, both Denmark and Portugal are countries with relative low levels of social mobilisations, which further increase the risk for these parties of being absorbed by technicalities of parliamentary work. The initiative for both parties have been taken by very small revolutionary Marxist groups, which remain loyally active in the parties, and which, helped by a growing organisation (see membership figures above) might explain the fact that the parties have remained fairly clear in their anticapitalist stances.

The history of the new European left parties is a history that is currently being written. This book gives a unique snapshot of the similar, yet different, challenges these parties are faced with.

October 2010

References:

Abers, Rebecca: "From ideas to Practice: The Partido dos Trabalhadores and Participatory Governance in Brazil", *Latin American Perspectives*, Vol. 23, No. 4, The "Urban Question" in Latin America (Autumn, 1996)

Allen, Christopher S.: *"Social democracy, Globalization and Governance: Why is there no European Left Programme in the EU?"*, Paper Presented at the Minda de Gunzburg Center for European Studies, Harvard University, April 3, 2000.

Bell, D.S. (ed.): Western European Communists and the Collapse of Communism, Oxford: Berg, 2003

Fourth International: World Congresses: 14th World Congress, 1995, "The political situation in imperialist Europe". Available online at http://www.internationalviewpoint.org/spip.php?article147 (retrieved 14th June 2010).

Fukuyama, Francis: *The End of History and the Last Man,* 1992.

Lemaitre, Yvan : "Résultats de l'extrème gauche - Crédibilité et division" , *Rouge, No. 1974,* 13/06/2002 (http://orta.dynalias.org/archivesrouge/article-rouge?id=5088, retrieved 2nd June 2010)

Lenin, V.I.: "Left-Wing Communism: an Infantile Disorder", *Lenin Collected Works*, Progress Publishers, [1975], Moscow, Volume 18, pages 132-135. (http://www.marxists.org/archive/lenin/works/1912/jun/24.htm, retrieved 18 September 2010)

Liegard, Guillaume: "Les résultats de la LCR: en progrès, doit poursuivre ses efforts...", Rouge, No. 2210, 14 June 2007. (http://www.europe-solidaire.org/spip.php?article6355 , retrieved 2nd June 2010)

Löwy, Michael: "A New Type of Party, The Brazilian PT", *Latin American Perspectives, Vol. 14, No. 4, Contemporary Issues (Autumn, 1987)*

March, Luke: "Contemporary Far Left Parties in Europe, From Marxism to the Mainstream?" *International Policy Analysis*, 2008, Friedrich Ebert Stiftung

March, Luke and Mudde, Cas: "What's Left f the Radical left? The European Radical Left After 1989: Decline and Mutation", *Comparative European Politics*, 2005, 3.

Mair, Peter and van Biezen, Ingrid: "Party Membership in Twenty European Democracies, 1980-2000", *Party Politics*, 2001; 7; 5.

Moreau, P., Coutois, S. and Hirscher, G.: *Der Kommunismus in Westeuropa. Niedergang oder Mutation*, Landsberg: Olzog, 1998.

Robaina, Roberto: *El gobierno de Lula, Los límites del reformismo*, Edicionoes ¡UníoS!, Mexico, 2004.

Smith, Murray: "The Radical Left in Western Europe", *The Socialist Unity Blog*, April 2007, (http://socialistunity.blogspot.com/2007/04/radical-left-in-western-europe.html, retrieved 2nd June 2010)

Weldon, Steven: "Downsize My Polity? The Impact of Size on Party membership and Member Activism", *Party Politics*, 2006; 12; 467.

World Bank: *Data and Statistics*, http://econ.worldbank.org/WBSITE/EXTERNAL/DATASTATISTICS /0,,contentMDK:20394872~menuPK:1192714~pagePK:64133150~pi PK:64133175~theSitePK:239419,00.html

An idea whose time has come

Daniel Bensaïd [1]

A new party, as loyal to those that are oppressed and dispossessed as the parties of the right are loyal to the owners and the rulers, which does not apologise for being anticapitalist and wanting to change the world, is an idea which has a long history. Today, it is poised to become a significant militant organisation.

At the beginning of the 1990s, the fall of the Berlin Wall and the fragmentation of the Soviet Union marked the end not just of the 'short twentieth century' which had started with the First World War and the Russian Revolution, but also the period of expansion during which the institutional left poured itself into the mould of the Welfare state as if the social contract based on the economic growth following the Second World War was unending. The oil crisis of 1973 (and the recession that followed) was the first warning shot which was immediately followed by a turn towards austerity and stringency. This was accepted by the major currents on the left as if it was a temporary sacrifice, while waiting for the wheel of progress to start turning again.

The crisis of accumulation of capital revealed itself to be of an entirely different scale. In the late 1970s, Thatcher and Reagan launched the neo-liberal counter-offensive. The major social-democratic parties resigned themselves one after the other to go along with these counter-reforms, desperately trying to mitigate their excesses. The current financial, social and ecological crisis is putting everyone to the test. We are constantly told that no-one saw the disaster coming. One does not need to be very clever to understand that a return on investment of at least 15% when economic growth is 3% is nothing but a miracle similar to that of the Biblical transformation of bread. Equally one doesn't need to be very clever to predict that in the real world, with its inflexible logic, the real economy, will, in the end, remind the speculators living on the stars of the trivial earthly realities.

The neo-liberal dream of a "happy globalisation" was always only a dream, as Nicholas Sarkozy admitted in a speech in Toulon. The dream "crashed" and is even turning into a nightmare. But at the

---

[1]   *Daniel Bensaïd was a leading activist in the 1968 student movement and a founder member of the Jeunesse Communiste Révolutionaire which became the LCR. He played a leading role in the LCR and the Fourth International. He was a professor of philosophy in Paris. This article was written in 2008. He died in 2010.*

moment when it is necessary to pay the bill for the disaster, those responsible disappear into an anonymous and mysterious "we": "We hid even greater risks..., we pretended that by spreading around the risks they would disappear..., we left the banks to speculate instead of doing their job...,we financed the speculators rather than the industrialists..., we left the rating agencies and speculative funds operate without any controls...,we imposed on the banks accountancy regulations which provided no guarantee for the management of the risks...." Amazing!!! The allegations are extremely serious. But who is this "we" that is so powerful as to be without a name?? Who is this "we", this killer with a mask which has methodically deregulated the markets and freed up speculation? To achieve this, it was necessary for the political establishment, of both the left and the right, to deploy a lot of effort over the last quarter of a century. "Oddly enough", reminisces this former Parti Socialiste (PS) member and director of the Credit Lyonnais bank, "our country was the first on the continent, as early as the 1980s, to get stuck into the big game of globalisation and of freedom of movement of capital"; as if it was necessary for a socialist president to orchestrate such a game. And it was in 1988, under a socialist minister of finance that disintermediation in banking was inaugurated with the "financial disintermediation". In the United States, it was under Bill Clinton, that in 1999, the Glass-Steagall Act was repealed; this had since 1933 prevented the merger, and enforced the separation, of savings depository banks with speculative investment banks. With its repeal it allowed them to borrow beyond their assets for speculation.

Neither Sarkozy, nor finance minister Strauss-Kahn, proposed to re-establish public control over money/currency and to abolish stock options. Both have constantly supported the making constitutional, and making sacred, the dogma of "free and unfettered competition", even though one of them tells us today that "the all-powerful market is finished", and the other that "the market does not heal the market"! Today both of them call for an "ethical financial market" while rapping the fingers of bosses who put their hands too deeply into the pot of honey. A few scapegoats will be found who will take the blame for the financial delinquency in an attempt to justify the system. Most of those who enriched themselves during these crazy years did it absolutely legally, in accordance with the logic and the laws of a system that should be called by its proper name: a capitalist system, which Sarkozy attempted to exonerate in a suspiciously insistent manner.

All this is to preach the need of a holy alliance, between the left and right in France and between Republicans and Democrats in the United States, in order to socialise the losses after having privatised the profits. But the bailing-out of a bankrupt banking system with hundreds of billions (unlike the deficit of the social security budget), is simply inflicting on workers a punishment twice over. Those, who as workers, sweated surplus value over twenty years by enduring a continuous deterioration (over 10%) of their share of added-value to capital, are now being called upon as tax payers to rush to the rescue of their own exploiters. As far as the measures that are being proposed, whether of the left or of the right, these are symbolic and derisory. To restrict bonuses, or impose more controls on ratings agencies, is the least that should be done but it certainly does not rise to the challenge of the problems. The state comes back to the rescue of capital which is imperilled, but in order to finance the rescue, the counter-reforms continue: privatisation of the postal service, marketisation of the public health system at the expense of the patients and quality of treatment, deep cuts in public sector jobs. And the governmental left has few radical proposals. It is even rather very short of any proposals to respond to the crisis.

During her presidential election campaign, Sègolene Royal was remarking that "the identity of the left is no longer obvious". The author of *the Republic of Ideas*, Pierre Rosanvallon, discovers that social-democracy is "no longer a new idea", as if it was supposed to be in the 1960s. Most of the candidates for a renewal, or 'refoundation', of the Socialist Party agree to the diagnosis that there is a shortage of ideas and the absence of a grand vision. Their party is not short of all sorts of experts and academics. The gravity of their crisis is greater than just a temporary shortage of ideas or squabble between the leaders.

For the last quarter of a century, the social democrats that have been in government, Tony Blair and Gerhard Schröder but also Beregovoy and Jospin, have actively contributed in the destruction of the tools of social solidarity, abolishing the indexation of wages to prices, privatising everything in sight, and dismantling public services. They undermined their own social and electoral base. While doing this, they were developing organic links with the leading circles of banking and finance. The presence of two of them as loyal managers of the main institutions of international capital, the International Monetary Fund and World Trade Organisation, is revealing of the (well earned) confidence that they enjoy from the owners of capital.

As far as the European Communist Parties are concerned, now orphans of an unlikely 'socialist camp', they are the victims of the disappearance of major industrial establishments and are unable to review critically their own history. Almost everywhere in Europe they are undergoing a slow agonising death, or a simple and total disappearance, or even a spectacular dissolution into the centre left which is less and less in on the left, as was the case in Italy.

This drift of the traditional governmental left is evidence of the need for a New Anticapitalist Party able to respond to the renewal of the social movements that have gone through the strikes in France of 1995, the emergence of the global justice movement, the demonstrations against war and militarism, the struggles of youth against social exclusion, the uprisings in the *banlieues*, the mobilisations against relocations of industries or the eradication of public services. Everywhere in Europe, there has been emerging to the left of the traditional left a space, which is not just a social space but also electoral, which attracts the support somewhere between 5% and 15% of the electorate.

During the course of the last ten years, the progression of a radical left has taken different forms in the various countries. In Portugal, it was the creation of the Left Bloc, in Scotland appeared the Scottish Socialist Party, in Netherlands, the Socialist Party with Maoist origins, in Italy the presence of Rifondazione Communista, in Denmark the Red-Green Alliance, and through the movement against the war in Britain the Respect coalition was created. In Greece, following an important strike movement and student struggles, the electoral coalition Syriza which was created around the former Eurocommunist party Synaspismós, is hovering in opinion polls at above the 10% mark. Meanwhile very young Polish Labour Party was born out of the very militant trade union struggles.

The indications of popularity are fragile. The voting shows volatile intentions, but something is undoubtedly changing on the left. It would be naïve to believe that the space that has been freed up on the left is vacant, just like an empty chair that one could just sit on. It is a field of unstable forces, torn between different national and international magnetic fields of unequal strength. For example, in less than three years, the Scottish Socialist Party, Respect and Rifondazione have gone through crises and splits. Frustration and social struggles pull the new forces to the left, but the spiral of defeats is nevertheless not broken. When the electoral moment arrives, there is again a strong temptation to be satisfied with the lesser evil, or with anything but.... (Berlusconi or Sarkozy). This is not a political solution and leads to further demoralisations. That is how we saw Rifondazione Communista, the major force behind the European Social Forums and the anti-war movement in 2003, rally itself loyally to the Prodi government, vote for military intervention in Afghanistan, swallow all sorts of bitter neo-liberal pills on pensions and wages, to eventually end up as an electoral shipwreck.

The new radical lefts in Europe are confronted with two options, represented by the experience of Die Linke in Germany and by the project of an anticapitalist party initiated by the Ligue Communiste Révolutionnaire and Olivier Besancenot in France. For Die Linke, the task is to pressurise social-democracy in order to correct its trajectory. For the New Anticapitalist Party, the task is to create a real strategic alternative to mild social-liberalism.

Those who have been fascinated by the electoral growth of Die Linke want to see it as a model that can be generalised across Europe. This is to misunderstand the specificity of the German situation since the re-unification and the origin of the main components of this organisation, which are a minority split from the SPD in the West, initiated by its former president Oskar Lafontaine, and the PDS, into which a part of the old state bureaucracy from the east found a new home. The emergence of this organisation represents nevertheless, in relation to the hegemony of the SPD, a significant shift to the left. Reality should encourage caution as to its future. With 15% in the opinion polls, 72,000 members, 53 deputies in the Bundestag, 185 regional deputies, 179 mayors, Die Linke is now the third largest political formation in the country and constitutes a potential challenge to traditional social-democracy. In the East, where it is at its strongest (2,000 local branches as opposed to only 260 in the West), the average age of its members, most of whom are former members of the East German communist party (SED), is over 65 years. The work of the party is dedicated much more, if not exclusively, to election campaigns rather than to social struggles and movements.

In his programmatic speech, Oskar Lafontaine defined Die Linke as "the party of the welfare state". He gives it as its priority the restoration of the welfare state. Its strategy of alliances, being consistent with this objective, is a coalition with the SPD, first in certain Landers and then sooner or later at the federal level. At the moment, he destabilises the SPD by proposing an alternative to the great coalition with Christian Democracy. In order to "restore the welfare state", it would first of all be necessary to bury the Agenda 2010 of Gerard Schröder, rebuild public services, re-establish political control over the European Central Bank, break out of the straight-jacket of the Lisbon Treaty; in other words do exactly the opposite what European social democracies have been doing for the last twenty years. However the social composition of Die Linke, its material (and financial) dependency upon the state, its ministerial participation in the government of Berlin, indicate the strength of purpose that such a task requires. In such a game, those that believe they were winning, then find themselves defeated. Die Linke runs the risk of finding itself in a position of having to justify entering into a coalition with the centre right, as was the case for Rifondazione in Italy. We shall see.

In France, the project of the New Anticapitalist Party is that of a slow and patient reconstruction of a strategic alternative on the left. It is sometimes criticised for negativity or even a posture of protest. It is true that to announce what one is against is not sufficient to open up the path for elaborating an alternative. To declare oneself as anticapitalist at least has the advantage of clearly identifying your target: the inherent logic of a system which is more than simply the excesses of unbridled neo-liberalism. In his speech in Toulon, Nicolas Sarkozy was not wrong by insisting in "telling the French" that "anti-capitalism does not offer any solution to the current crisis". This is indeed the dividing line between those who might find themselves in a holy alliance (*union sacrée*) with capitalism on its death bed and those who want to go to the root of the crisis.

A consistent anti-capitalism certainly leads to alternative propositions and the intransigent defence of a programme which includes the project of a social and democratic Europe free of the neo-liberal straightjackets that are the Maastricht and Lisbon treaties, a logic of social solidarity, public services and of the resources common to humanity as opposed to the selfish self-interest of competition, an opposition of the new imperialist wars and a world armed to the teeth, the uncompromising defence of a social ecology which challenges the sacred power of private property, a real participatory democracy as opposed to the permanent system of media plebiscites and bipartisan presidentialism. It requires a rigorous independence towards social-democracy. In the current relationship of forces, any governmental or parliamentary agreement to manage the executive with social-democracy would mean consenting to being held hostage and providing it with a cover, with the disastrous consequences illustrated by the debacle of the Italian left. It requires a democratic functioning to act collectively and to change the relationship of forces, while at the same time guaranteeing total freedom of debate and the creation of currents and tendencies. This is in order to draw the lessons of the common experience and to clarify the questions that remain unanswered by putting these through the test of practice.

It is sometimes said that such intransigence is a sure way for the left to lose. It would forever stop it returning to power. The socialist leaders who peddle this dangerous idea deliberately confuse unity *in action* with unity at the ballot box.

We have never stopped proposing united initiatives to the left such as opposition to privatisations, or against the dismantling of labour protection laws, against the reform of pensions or that of universities, for the withdrawal of troops from Afghanistan, against the Lisbon Treaty. The Socialist Party has systematically refused these initiatives. Maybe it was because it was in disagreement on the form rather than on the content of the governmental reforms. When it voted for the Lisbon Treaty at Versailles, it was burying the majority popular 'No' vote in the 2005 referendum on the European Constitution. It also declared itself for a change in military strategy in Afghanistan but not for a withdrawal.

Unity at the ballot box is another matter. In a local or national election, it is necessary to put forward a project for the country, a region or a town, and to elect women and men who will put this into practice. In a two-round electoral system, the least one can expect is for each party to be able to defend their ideas in the first round. And in the second round, socialist leaders know perfectly well that the anticapitalist left does not equate the parties of the left and right. All research indicates that at least 80% of those who vote for the anticapitalist left go on to vote against the right in the second round. During the council elections of 2008, wherever the lists put forward or supported by the LCR obtained more than 5% in the first round, they proposed to the lists of the plural left (i.e. parties of the then SP coalition government) a fusion for the second round. This was with the proviso that there should be a proportional representation based on the results of the first round and the independence all organisations should be respected. The proposal was rejected by the national leadership of the Socialist Party who preferred instead in most case a privileged agreement with the (centre-right) Modem party. As a result of this refusal, the anticapitalist lists were maintained for the second round, as they are entitled in law, in those towns where they had obtained more than 10% of the vote. The "plural left" consequently lost (or failed to win) towns like Morlaix, Quimperle, Concarneau, or Saint Brieuc. This was not the result of failing to make a unity proposal to the left, but it was a consequence of its decision.

Sometimes it is necessary to take a step back in order to jump higher, and to accept to take an electoral step back in order to be able to take two forward in the reconstruction of the social relationship of forces. The affirmation of independence towards neo-liberal policies and organisations that support them can lead, in the first instance, to the left losing council or parliamentary seats. But to save these seats at the price of the most abject compromises will certainly sow confusion, scramble the front lines, lead to bitter disappointments, demoralise the left and go towards the worst of politics in the name of the lesser evil. Such an attitude is certainly underestimating the determination and the political willpower that is required to confront the forthcoming social and ecological catastrophes.

The project of going beyond the LCR into a new party gained in strength since the 2002 presidential election, in particular during the 2005 campaign against the European Constitution, the struggle of the youth against the CPE (First Employment Contract) in 2006, and the presidential election of 2007. A detailed analysis by Jerome Fouquet for the Fondation Jean-Jaurès concluded that this was not a "media phenomenon", but "a political phenomenon that is long lasting and solid". One should nevertheless not fall in awe with the illusion of opinion polls. Between the 60% who have a "favourable opinion" of Olivier Besancenot in the Ipsos poll, and the 13% of French who have of him an "excellent opinion" (as opposed to 4% in 2004), and the militant presence and real electoral influence, the gap remains considerable and it cannot be filled by the magic of the media. This gap can and must be filled by a presence in the everyday struggles. That is the challenge for the new party.

Among those who are following this initiative with interest, but who hesitate to commit themselves, are some who ask us if our desire for an opening up is genuine, others if we are really ready to "go beyond" ourselves, and others still what does our independence from the Socialist Party really mean.

For our part, we hope that the future party will be as open and broad as possible, without sacrificing, for the sake of openness, clarity on key strategic questions, and without blunting its radical edge which will be its strength. If we have the willingness to do this, then those who are still hesitating will, by joining, shape, as much as us, in its degree of pluralism and openness.

We are determined to "go beyond" ourselves and even to "outdo" ourselves if necessary. We are giving as proof the risk of the dissolution of the LCR into a new organisation which will welcome the best of the diverse revolutionary traditions. This is something unusual in the history of organisations. It would have been more comfortable to manage a (small) capital of militants without knocking over our routines and references. But this would have been to flee the responsibilities and the daring that is required by the gravity of the crisis.

Finally, the independence towards the Socialist Party means that the new party should refuse the invitation from socialist leaders to constitute under their hegemony a permanent co-ordination of the governmental left. It should also refuse to participate in primaries for the whole of the left. These would presume sufficient agreement to abandon independent candidatures during parliamentary or presidential elections and advance commitment to a parliamentary or governmental coalition.

This clarity is the result of twenty years of experiences which bring us today at the birth of a new party.

As the moment gets closer to the ending of Ligue and the creation of the new Party, some ask more and more insistently to the few dozen of us 'veterans' who founded the Ligue in 1969 or the youth organisation (JCR, Jeunesse Communiste Révolutionnaire) which preceded it in 1966 when it was expelled from the communist student movement, if we do not feel nostalgic in our hearts to see it disappear and grow over into a new organisation. We have more the sentiment (with a bit of pride, let us admit) of a job done and of the road travelled. It was much longer than we imagined in our youthful enthusiasm of the 1960s, and it is not easy to remain for such a long time "revolutionaries without a revolution". Few revolutionary organisations have known forty years of continuity and (nearly) uninterrupted legality without going through the test of big events and big political recompositions. We have done it. Without succumbing, at least we hope, to the pathologies of sectarianism and conservatism of small organisations. We can achieve with success a generational transition, a transmission of the inheritance, and an organisational mutation, neither with the conflicts of succession nor of personal rivalries that afflict most organisations.

We have already obtained some modest, but real, results. A few years ago, there was a real and justified worry about the rise of the National Front, and some were going beyond that worry to panic. This rise was for a large part the reflection of the retreats and the resignations of the left in front of a neo-liberal offensive. In less than six years, by giving a different political outlet to social anger and desperation, we have retaken part of the space which was occupied by the far right. Apart from minor electoral considerations, anybody who is on the left should be pleased.

A few years ago, the Socialist Party pretended to exercise an undivided hegemony on the left. The introduction of a new five-year term for the President and with elections just before those to the National Assembly, which was started under Jospin, should have led to a French form of bi-partisanship. The Socialist Party has now set up a committee under the leadership of Daniel Vaillant, a former minister of the interior, to keep watch on the "Besancenot threat"!

Here we are now ready to sail towards new adventures. But the founding of the New Anticapitalist Party is not the end of the story. It will still only be one stage. An electoral and institutional stability lasting nearly half a century can make us forget, at least under our skies, of the periods of crisis when the shifts of militants and electors which were not counted in hundreds or even thousands, but by tens of thousands. These moments of convulsion, "wars and revolutions", we called these in the past, are again approaching with the social and ecological crisis. War is already with us. Revolutions...? The instability and volatility of electorate are only the warnings signs of future realignments. Further recompositions will occur. But the time is well and truly over when revolutionaries were reduced to act by proxy, whispering to the leaders of big parties of the left what they should do, or by publicly demanding of them to do what they would no doubt refuse to do. From now on, we act on our own according to what we think is correct and necessary. The stronger we are, the better we will be able to do it. And the best way to convince those that are hesitating is for us to stop hesitating, and to put our ideas to the test of practice.

During the first national meeting of the committees for the New Anticapitalist Party in June 2008, a female militant from a working class area of Toulon, came up to me and said: "Thanks for waiting for us". The reply was obvious: "Thanks for coming".

This article was first published in August 2008 in the book "Penser Agir" published by Editions Lignes, Paris. Translated by Fred Leplat.

The New Anticapitalist Party

Alain Krivine[1]

In the context of the development of a new radical European left, the French experience is rather special, even if it is linked to the major trends of decomposition-recomposition of the labour movement taking place across the whole of Europe. This must be the only country where there are three Trotskyist groups each with several thousand members, and each with electoral results which exceed one million votes, and, as far as the New Anticapitalist Party (Nouveau Party anticapitalist, or NPA) is concerned, one spokesperson (today Olivier Besancenot) who is always placed first in opinion polls of popularity. It is necessary to try to understand the reasons, the strengths and weaknesses and the future of this phenomenon.

A particular context

The French labour movement has experienced, over a long time period, traditions of radical class struggle through which it has acquired a series of gains such as paid holidays and social security. We can give the examples of the great strikes of the 'Popular Front' in 1936, those after the Liberation or those of 1968 or 1995, not to mention the 'No' victory in the referendum on the draft EU constitution after a large united popular mobilisation. Outside of the period of Nazi occupation, the working class has lost many fights but has never been crushed, and has re-emerged each time in force. Reformists and anarchists were the basis of the construction of the labour movement and, after the war and the Resistance, the Communist Party became one of the biggest parties; for many years providing a framework for the working class from the cradle to the grave through its thousands of local elected councils and councillors, its 'mass' organisations (for young people, women, sports people, pensioners, intellectuals, etc.). Up to 1968, electoral results were around 20%, well ahead of a discredited and marginal Parti Socialiste. However, the PCF was one of the most Stalinist in Europe, both in its methods and in its programme, totally faithful to the zigzags of Kremlin politics and not hesitating to use physical force against its

---

[1]   *Alain Krivine was a leading activist in the 1968 student movement, a founder member of the Jeunesse Communiste Révolutionnaire which became the LC in 1968 and LCR in 1974. He was an MEP for the LCR from 1999 to 2004. He serves on the leadership of the Fourth International and the NPA.*

opponents and Trotskyist activists. Very workerist and having absolute control over the largest union, the CGT, the Communist Party was faced with a labour movement divided into various confederations. Hence the paradox of a labour movement at times very combative but one of the least unionised in Europe (today less than 10% in all the unions together).

The great upheaval in the relationship of forces and the first faltering steps of the radical left originate from the general strike of 1968. In fact, although for the first time in its history the PCF was initially overwhelmed by the movement of students and then a general strike of the working class, it took several years to see the effects of this turning point. At the time no mass rupture occurred in the CGT or the PCF apart from a few isolated individuals. The only break was with the student youth, where there was already an independent far left (JCR, Maoists, Lambertists, anarchists) coming mostly from the expulsions in 1965 that had dominated the first major crisis of a Communist Party organisation: that of students. Not faced at that time by any structures of self-organisation of the working class, the apparatus of the PCF, helped by de Gaulle, succeeded after several weeks in breaking the general strike with little immediate damage except for a widespread lack of understanding and the beginnings of mistrust.

It took several years for the JCR and then the LCR, strongly implanted among students, to begin to benefit from the beginning of the decline of the PCF by starting to establish themselves in the workplace. After '68 it is the combination of several factors that explain the gradual and historic decline of the PCF: the public crisis of Stalinism and the collapse of the USSR, the internal transformations within the working class and the shrinking of its traditional layers (miners, steelworkers), which the PCF did not see coming, its inability to address the new strata (salaried employees, technicians), and above all its participation in government from 1981 onwards which discredited the reformist left and above the PCF with its successive capitulations to the PS ministers.

It is in that context that we must understand both the opportunities for the new anticapitalist left but also the ideological confusion of much of the labour movement which had experienced in the space of less than twenty years the general strike of '68 and the political failure in general elections which had given a majority to the left (including the PCF) in 1981. The signing of a governmental programme, the 'common programme', in 1972 was an attempt by the reformist apparatuses to produce a credible and institutional political outcome to prevent another 68. In this operation, the PS could not but win at the expense of the PCF, and it is that which enabled it to resurface and become the largest party on the left. With the disappearance of the USSR the CP lost all identity. What was the point of voting for a minority party which, in order to get into government and remain there, defended the same programme as the PS? The electoral collapse of the PCF, with a vote of less than 2% in the last presidential election, was accompanied by a collapse in membership in only a few years.

Communist Party and the Socialist Party today

The PCF is no longer a national force even if its history and traditions still inspire hundreds of thousands of people across the country. Its strength (approximately 70,000 activists) is concentrated in the electoral bastions it still retains, fewer than 200 local councils and about 7,000 councillors. It gets around 2% of the vote in most places but can reach 20-30% where it is still implanted (a national average of 6% in the last regional elections). Its average age is very high and its implantation higher among retired people than in the working class. Today many struggles are no longer led by militants of the PCF. Still the strongest militant workers organisation, the PCF has virtually no workplace cells. Its activists prioritise intervention in the unions. Usually the fall of an electoral bastion is accompanied by the irreversible loss of the PCF's control of the local council. PS and Greens now share the spoils in electoral strongholds where there are now more than 60% abstentions. They are forced to have relations with the LCR and today the NPA, most of the time "fraternal" but competitive, with sometimes the emergence of sectarian overtones from the past.

The NPA appears as the bad conscience of the PCF and for many activists Olivier Besancenot says out loud what the PCF should be saying and what they think to themselves. This attraction-repulsion is very unlike the relationship with the PS, the Greens, Lutte Ouvrière or the small groups of the left of the left. In a complete crisis of identity, the majority are hostile to the PS but in electoralist terms believe that maintaining the agreement with the PS is the only way to save their councillors, even though a minority would prefer the NPA.

With the PS it is another world. The party has recovered its electoral health and will undoubtedly win the next election because of disgust with the Sarkozy government rather than enthusiasm for its programme and its record. If you do not abstain, you vote SP today in France to defeat the right at the ballot box, especially if struggles are not succeeding. It is essentially a useful vote in the institutional sense of the term. As a party, the PS is rather discredited by its false internal battles that conceal personal battles, because deep down they all agree on a strategy of sustaining capitalism that brings them closer to the Socialist Party in Spain. Nevertheless they have to have a left discourse in opposition because of the PCF and the NPA. A party of about 150,000 members, it is increasingly an electoral machine rather than a party implanted in the social movement. Essentially its politics and debates are dominated by the tens of thousands of local councillors and by people more or less dependent on them financially or politically.

In this climate the PS has virtually no left wing since it recently experienced a split of its left wing organised around a former Socialist minister Jean-Luc Mélenchon, who created the Left Party, allied structurally to the PCF but sometimes further to the left. With around 2,000 activists the party represents a real left social democratic current with the slogan "The revolution, but through the institutions". Having to constantly choose a strategy between the PCF and the NPA, it appears to be orienting towards maintaining a permanent front with the PCF, especially for elections, and joint actions with the NPA. But all that can break down because the PCF and the PS each want to have the unitary candidate for the next presidential election. This would not be a strategic breach.

Apart from these major parties there are small groups of anti-neoliberal left, often coming from the PCF or the LCR, with a few hundred militants who try to find a place between the PCF and the NPA.

The Trotskyists

The principal force on the far left, after the virtual disappearance of the Maoists, is divided into three organisations.

First there is the Parti Ouvrière Indépendant (Independent Workers' Party, formerly the OCI) created by Pierre Lambert, with about 2-3,000 activists. This is a very sectarian organisation, which specialised in entryism in the PS such as with Lionel Jospin, or in the LCR, it never participates in any united activity and operates mainly through its networks in the unions or freemasonry. In reality it has little political weight.

Lutte Ouvrière (LO) with 2,000 activists, and former spokesperson Arlette Laguiller, is a very tightly-knit organisation, disciplined in the extreme and somewhat workerist. Arlette emerged from the margins with 5% in 1995. Its activists, very dedicated, only intervene in the workplace. Regarding unity with the LCR, its relations have always been all or nothing. In its unitary phase the LO-LCR lists had five members of parliament, including Arlette and Krivine, in the European Parliament in 1996. Very critical of the "reformist" concessions of the NPA, they have nevertheless not hesitated to join the lists of the Union of the Left in the last municipal elections, voting for the budgets of the latter. Declining since the arrival of the NPA and Besancenot (about 1% in the elections) they maintain reasonable relations but refuse any merger.

The birth of the NPA

To understand the process we must remember that it was already the position of the LCR that the French section of the Fourth International did not claim to represent all Marxists, much less all revolutionaries, but was one of the components of a broader revolutionary party still to be constructed. With this approach the LCR participated throughout its history in a series of attempts at regroupment with the OCI, LO and the support committees for the candidacy of the dissident Communist Pierre Juquin. But each time it was a failure. It was not driven by a real social upsurge or the collapse of the PCF. If '68 marks the first steps of a new period, 1995 forces us to deepen our perspectives.

The PCF is in free fall, Arlette Laguiller gets more than 5% in the presidential election and the country is experiencing a mass mobilisation in defence of social security unprecedented since 68. The debate is launched in the LCR to assist in the creation of a new party. In 2002 the success of the candidacy Olivier Besancenot (with over 4% in 2002), still unknown a few months before, is another sign of movement, not to mention the 'No' victory in the referendum in 2005 after a mass united campaign where the LCR plays an important role. In 2007 and 2008, all the leaders of the LCR are discussing the dissolution of the LCR and the creation of the NPA. Only a small minority are opposed, saying the new party is too limited and sectarian.

January 2009 was the founding congress of the NPA. Unlike the experience of Denmark and Portugal, no organisation as such was willing to participate in its construction. However a series of small currents joined them, especially SPEB (about eighty comrades affiliated to the International of the English SWP) and the Spark Fraction of LO (around eighty, excluded from LO), some comrades of Gauche Révolutionnaire (Revolutionary Left), some former Maoists, libertarians, disaffected environmentalists, some members of the Greens, the PCF and the PS. The activists of the former LCR (slightly less than 3,000) found themselves in an organisation of nearly 9,000 members at its formation. Most 'new' members have no political past, many were attracted by the messages and the popularity of Olivier, "a guy like us, who works". They want to fight the right and capitalism and have no confidence in the traditional left.

Programme

In its founding text the NPA stated that it was completely against any possibility of "reforming" or "democratising" capitalism. It declared itself in favour of overturning capitalism and the need to "revolutionise society". Internationalist, feminist, environmentalist, it stands for class struggle and has already developed an "Action Plan" of anticapitalist demands to tackle the crisis. Unlike the LCR, the NPA however does not resolve some issues, it leaves them open for future Conferences. For example all the strategic debates about taking power, transitional demands, dual power, etc. It does not claim to be Trotskyist, as such, but considers Trotskyism to be one of the contributors, among others, to the revolutionary movement. Unwilling, as we had to do under Stalinism, to arrive at policy by the rear view mirror, the NPA has no position on what was the Soviet Union, Stalinism, etc. Policy is based on an agreement on the analysis of the period and on tasks.

Within this general framework, but with the borders delineated enough to make a revolutionary organisation, the NPA has defined some principles for intervention. Today, the tactic of the united front is often decisive in all the unitary structures with the reformists in the battles against the government's social policies: unitary committees to defend pensions, committees to defend the undocumented, immigrants etc, participation in ATTAC, in trade unions, the women's movement and initiatives on the environment; in short, in all the activities of the social movement. It must be recognised that for all militants anti-racism and internationalism are unalterable fundamental principles. Although most militants are union members and undertake responsibilities in the CGT, Solidarity or the FSU, there are some comrades who are not organised in unions because they regard them as "too divided and bureaucratic" and who focus on the activities of the NPA. As for the union leaders, especially the CGT, they do not hesitate to attack publicly the practice of the NPA which they deem substitutionist and factional, although the union members of the NPA have always been very careful to respect the independence of the unions, which does not signify remaining silent on the strategy of the leadership or refraining from trying to promote, both within and between unions, the regroupment of militants and "class struggle" currents.

The NPA has decided against any involvement in co-management of institutions especially with the PS and the PCF (government, regional executive councils and municipalities). It's not a refusal in principle, including participating in government, but only on condition that it is able to carry out its programme, which would mean a different relationship of forces, such as a general strike, alliances with forces other than the reformist Left and another programme. It must be said that these are the subject of internal debates with comrades who think that without participating ourselves we can make electoral alliances with left-wing parties which do themselves participate. In recent elections, it is often on that issue that there were breaks with the traditional left. Today the NPA has a little less than a hundred local councillors, because of the absence of any proportional system for other positions.

Organisation

Structured in branches organised at the local level or in the workplace, and coordinated at the regional level, with meetings often fortnightly, the NPA elected at its founding congress a national political committee of about 190 members who meet approximately every three months and who themselves elected an Executive Committee of about thirty members which meets weekly. At the founding conference parity between men and women was adopted for the leadership bodies, which should not contain more than 50% of ex-members of the LCR. They have been achieved. The various activities are centralised by numerous national committees (women, ecology, business, culture, LGBTI, international, popular neighbourhoods, immigrants etc.). Each year, for four days on the Mediterranean coast, the Summer University brings together over 1,000 participants.

There is a leadership with only a few permanent part-timers (a dozen), a weekly that sells badly and a monthly in progress with the same title 'Everything is ours', and a permanent system of leaflets, pamphlets, posters etc. The NPA is present in all the *départements* with nearly 500 branches. Although the NPA does not claim to be democratic centralist, it is trying to enforce majority decisions, but this is far from being applied. In reality, especially at the beginning of the NPA, many members had a lot of legitimate fear of seeing the emergence of leaders, a bureaucracy, and in short an undemocratic life, hence the fear of any centralisation, the desire of some to give full powers to local branches without creating regional or central leaderships. Experience has allowed things to evolve and now it is more a lack of centralisation and leadership which is being questioned.

Youth

Already in the JCR there had been a debate about whether to maintain the existence of a youth organisation. After difficult discussions it was agreed that, at least initially, there would be a 'youth sector' embedded in the NPA. At the time of the LCR, the JCR had about three hundred militants, nearly half of them in the LCR. Today some young people have established branches of the NPA youth (high school, university) with their own material: leaflets, bulletins, posters etc., but under the name of the NPA. They are represented on the EC of the Party. The others are fully integrated in the local branches. The youth sector participates fully in the youth camps of the Fourth International.

International Relations

Deeply internationalist, the NPA is totally involved in global justice initiatives and its various global and European forums, in ATTAC and in the CADTM. But it also works to set up a coordination of anticapitalist organisations on a European scale. The goal is first to have an exchange of experiences, to try to promote joint initiatives or at least positions, and eventually if possible to participate in European elections with a common acronym, even a common party. Since the creation of the NPA there have already been several meetings with partners and co-organisers of parties, like the English SWP, the Portuguese Left Bloc and the Danish Red and Green Alliance. Present as observers at the beginning the Italian PRC has not taken part since. There are many difficulties, both political and organisational. Let us list the problems. The Red-Green Alliance is against Europe and is therefore against participation in a 'European' list. The Left Bloc is also part of the executive of the Party of the European Left and must take that into account in alliances with anticapitalist parties. That is also the case for the SYRIZA coalition.[1] But in Greece, a country where the extreme revolutionary left is numerically the strongest, there were more than ten organisations very hostile to each other until the regroupment in Antarsia, where the majority of the militants of the Fourth International are. All this shows the difficulty but not the impossibility of arriving at reaching a joint list for the next European elections. In any case, and it is already a success, fifteen organisations from the European radical left have signed a text of resistance to the capitalist crisis and envisage further joint meetings and initiatives in the near future.

With regard to the NPA, the first thing to say is that in addition to the militants of the Fourth International (the 3,000 former LCR members) there are comrades who are members of the International Socialist Tendency (which is led by the SWP) or the International Socialist Organisation of the USA who publish their press without any

---

[1] Although two SYRIZA components, Synaspismós and AKOA, do take part in the Party of the European Left, SYRIZA is not a member.

problem and have special relationships with their International structures which often invite the leadership of the NPA as an observer at their meetings or conferences. For the present, there is no problem.

The relationship with the Fourth International is more complicated to administer given the relationship of forces, the history and the future of the International. The NPA project to build a mass revolutionary party in France corresponds to the FI's project of creating one day a revolutionary Fifth International as a result of phenomena of recomposition of the workers movement. This said, the rhythms are totally different from one country to another and the FI reflects this. Its last Congress saw side by side old and very small Trotskyist cadre organisations, a little 'old-style', rubbing shoulders with new parties with thousands of members, such as those of the Philippines, Pakistan, Portugal or France. In such a situation, where the existence of the FI is still critical but where it cannot compel the new parties to accept in their entirety its history, its references or its programme, it is necessary to find interim solutions tailored to each country. For example, the Danish and Portuguese have retained a section with one or two hundred members in parties with several thousand members. In France it was impossible and would have been manipulative, so there was a unanimous decision to treat the former 3,000 ex-LCR members as members of the FI, continuing to pay dues, and with the NPA invited as an observer to all international meetings.

The World Congress elected to the International Committee a number of French comrades who will report to members of the FI in France in the branches as well as to the national political committee. In return occasional meetings of the FI in France, such as those preparing for the World Congress, are open to all members of the NPA. Given the procedures for establishing the NPA and the weight of the former members of the League, the creation of an FI current or tendency would be meaningless and manipulative towards other comrades, especially since the debates which run through the NPA also run through the former LCR members. As for the debates of the FI, they interest everyone. There remain problems of formal voting arrangements and dues arranged on an interim basis by general consensus.

The balance sheet

The conference of the NPA was held in February 2011. Since its inception, the social situation has changed. Up until the autumn of 2010, we have not seen large social mobilisations for a few years. Many local industrial disputes were isolated by the union bureaucracy and ended in defeat. It is not a series of one day strikes and a demonstration every three months that will restore the confidence of militants. Fatigue, confusion, but nevertheless pockets of local radicalism dominated that period. During these difficult months, hundreds of members have left the party due to weariness or lack of training rather than political disagreements. They had the illusion of an immediate breakthrough of the NPA. Then in the last months of 2010, we saw again a major new social explosion with millions of workers in the street. This mobilisation had a real and exceptional political radicalization in which the NPA activists found themselves like fish in water.

Always present in demonstrations and active in strikes, the NPA emerged as real tribune for the struggles, as a result of which the party recruited hundreds of new members and found an echo in public opinion which had been lost previously. Although this mobilisation occurred without true self-organisation, however its radicalism and its strength forced the union leaders to go along with the movement while avoiding a showdown with the government. The failure to prepare and carry out a prolonged general strike has allowed temporarily the government and the union leaders to get out of a tight spot.

In a situation of social and political crisis where a majority of the population wants to get rid of the government, the NPA has emerged as a significant force which is recognized and valued in the struggles but is hardly credible in electoral terms. Opinion polls show almost 40% popularity for Olivier Besancenot but the NPA would obtain only 5% of the votes in the next presidential election. Besancenot's popularity remains very strong and his visits to the workplaces in struggle or his presence on demonstrations always produces an immense response, out of proportion of that of the NPA.

Strengths and weaknesses, what future?

No one had the experience of running an organisation of this size. With all its problems: how to establish a democracy for all, particularly those who don't have the time or the opportunity to read hundreds of pages of internal bulletin on the internet and still remain active in campaigns? How do we develop a political education for all members, while avoiding demagogy or learning by rote? And how do we use language that is understandable rather than the jargon of insiders?

Setting up a permanent system of education at different levels is not easy. Some super-activist members don't manage to find the time to take part, or they find these educationals too rudimentary. Activism itself is very irregular, depending on the moment, and we do not always find the same comrades at meetings, apart from a network of several hundred militants who provide permanence and continuity.

In the public domain, the NPA is both a victim and a beneficiary of the popularity of its spokesperson. With the new forms of media and television, the personalisation of politics becomes a general phenomenon but depoliticises people and plays a disproportionate role for small parties. In the PS and the UMP, many leaders are well known, while in the PCF, the NPA or LO only one of its members is well known, generally the candidate for the presidency. In the televised debates people remember who was good or bad, but rarely the content. On the television, all the personal qualities of the presenter and the content of the message get mixed together. Arlette Laguiller, the presidential candidate of LO, has been popular because of her message but also because of the fact that she was the 'first woman worker'. Olivier is a star on television because he is young, a postman and he is forceful. But with a different message he would be less successful. The NPA is aware of the dangers of this personalisation but it also benefits from it. We are looking for other spokespeople, but it's not easy when the media tell you "we want Olivier or nobody". But more national spokespeople remains essential if we are to continue to rejuvenate and feminise the leadership. This is especially the case in the context where none of the fifteen former leaders of the LCR remain on the Executive of the NPA.

Another difficulty results from the fact that even if the NPA is not isolated, it is still only a party originating from a single tradition unlike the new parties created from the recomposition from several currents in Denmark or Portugal. Moreover, even if we wanted to, a party such Die Linke would be impossible in France. First, for political reasons as its participation in coalition governments with the Social Democrats in two states, including Berlin where it carries out neo-liberal policies, would not be accepted here by the radical left. But above all, unlike the former SED, the PCF is not interested in a common party with the minority which left the PS. Only the PG (Parti de Gauche) and Mélenchon want a Die Linke type of party in France, where he would play the role of Lafontaine. Trapped between the PCF and the NPA, the PG risks disappearing by remaining alone. But at its 2010 congress, the PCF was very clear as it refused all proposals for individual membership of the Left Front, which has to remain as an electoral bloc run by the PCF with the PG and two hundred activists of the Gauche Unie. It must be said that the creation of the Front de Gauche has been successful in halting the electoral decline of the PCF but it has not added anything more nor has it created a new momentum. In contrast the PCF activists were furious at having seen elected in their place people so unrepresentative.

For now there are no organisations or organised currents ready to build the NPA, and there is no sign of any significant current leaving the PCF or the PS in the near future. The NPA must therefore focus its interventions on the mass of workers and un-organised combative youth instead of inter-organisational regroupment, although this still remains necessary including in terms of political education.

Today, despite all these difficulties, the NPA has reached a threshold of incontestable credibility, but its development is tied to the coming social mobilisations. With the NPA, revolutionaries now have an instrument which is superior to what existed in previously but it is still inadequate compared to the new tasks and responsibilities ahead.

The NPA is an interesting experience of a project that is common to all of the radical left in Europe, but it cannot serve as a model because situations, traditions and relations of force are different from one country to another. The role of revolutionaries is to find in their own conditions the means, tools and tactics tailored to best develop the forces needed to overthrow the old world, and relearn to dream in order to fight for and create another better world.

26 January 2011, Translated by Rick Hatcher

The Red-Green Alliance in Denmark

Michael Voss[1]

Introduction: the present challenge of the Red-Green Alliance

In the coming years The Red-Green Alliance (RGA) of Denmark faces challenges, opportunities and risks that probably are bigger than at any other time since its foundation in 1989. The next elections can be called by the prime minister at any time, but no later than November 2011. According to opinion polls over the last almost two years to January 2011, the present government of the two main bourgeois parties will lose its majority. This will make possible the establishment of a government of two reformist workers parties, needing the support from the RGA and/or a small centre bourgeois party in order to have a majority.

The new situation in parliament, combined with economic crisis, may open a period of increased social and political struggles and political radicalisation. But at the same time the RGA will come under the influence of reformist and populist pressure, externally and internally.

The RGA was probably the first broad and pluralist anticapitalist party in Europe to develop out of the changed political landscape after the fall of the Berlin Wall. It arose organically out of the left wing of the Danish labour movement, merging several established left parties. It has had representation in parliament since 1994.

To understand the nature of the RGA, its development, its positions and the challenges it faces today, it is necessary to make a brief sketch of the Danish labour movement and the Danish left.

---

[1] Michael Voss is a member of the Red-Green Alliance and of the SAP (Danish section of the Fourth International). As a representative of the SAP, he participated in the negotiations that led to the establishment of the RGA. From 1995 to 2006, he worked as a journalist and press officer for the parliamentary group of the RGA. He is a member of the Executive Committee of the SAP.

The Danish labour movement

Social democracy

The Danish Social Democratic Party traces its history back to the 19th century European labour movement, having been part of both the First and the Second International. Its close links to the trade union movement, its reformism and its bureaucratization more or less follows the path of the rest of European social democracy.

Danish social democracy first came into government in the late 1920s and 1930s as part of an alliance with a centre bourgeois party, based on small farmers and city intellectuals, implementing social reform, but always seeking acceptance and alliance with big agriculture and industry.

After World War II, the party was the backbone of building the so called Welfare state, still based on class collaboration and a compromise with the main bourgeois parties and organisations of industry.

During the economic crisis of the 70s the space for class compromise narrowed, and faced with problems of state finances, balance of payment, unemployment and a rising left wing in the trade unions and on the political scene, a Social Democrat-led government gave up power voluntarily in 1982.

Since then, like many other European Social Democratic Parties, the Danish party has developed in a social-liberal direction, outside government (1982–1993; 2001-2011) and as the leading governmental party (1993–2001). Its share of the votes, its standing in opinion polls, and its membership, has all decreased and fierce power struggles have taken place.

Trade Union Movement

The development of the Danish trade union movement has been parallel to that of social democracy, the two regarding themselves as being parts of the same movement. In Denmark the trade union movement has always been unitary. Since the 1950s the percentage of organisation has been very high: close to 100% in industry, less in public jobs and service. The , with the official or unofficial closed shop is normal. During the last two or three decades, union membership has declined, though not as dramatically as in many other European countries.

From time to time, left forces have gained influence at shop steward and branch level. But apart from the CP leadership of the sailors union for a couple of decades and the nursery school teachers union for a brief period, the Social Democratic Party has been hegemonic at the national federation level and in the two confederations LO and FTF. At the moment only the national union of public employees is not headed by a Social Democrat.

The political left

The Danish Communist Party came out of the historical split in the international workers movement and became Danish section of the Third International. Politically it followed the Moscow party line all the way to the end. It had some influence in the trade union movement in the 1930s, especially among unemployed workers. At that time it gained a small representation in Parliament through proportional representation.

It grew during and after World War II because of its involvement in the underground armed liberation movement against German occupation. For ten years, after the World War, it held on to its positions both in parliament and in trade unions. But after supporting the Soviet occupation of Hungary in 1956, it experienced a serious setback and a split.

Its influence grew again from the beginning of the 70s as part of the overall political radicalization of the period. It gained important influence in the movement against Danish membership of EU, the peace movement, the trade union youth movement and the student movement. At that time it regained parliamentary representation.

The CP almost collapsed with the breakdown of the Soviet Union, both for political and financial reasons, and has split into several small factions. As a result of the Soviet invasion of Hungary and the secret Khrushchev speech in 1956, a split in the CP headed by the then chairman occurred leading to the establishment of the Socialist Peoples' Party. The party distanced itself from Moscow, and it positioned itself close to, but still to the left of the Social Democratic Party. A part of the trade union activist base of the CP followed the chairman into the Socialist People's Party, but the party focused almost all its activities on parliamentary work.

In the first election after its establishment (1960), the Socialist People's Party won 11 Members of Parliament (MPs) (6% of national vote). Its number of MPs has since fluctuated, peaking in 1987 with 27 MPs (15%). In two periods in the 60s and the 70s, the party was part of the parliamentary majority supporting Social Democratic-led governments, but never in government itself. From the late 1987 until 2007, the representation in parliament of Socialist People's Party gradually declined.

The radicalisation of the 1960s also led to the establishment of the Left Socialist Party, born as a split of the Socialist People's Party's in 1967. The split was triggered by the Socialist People's Party participation in anti-worker legislation. From the beginning the Left Socialist Party was a mixture of all elements of the New Left: hippies, anarchists, Maoists, Trotskyists, other self-declared Leninists, anti-imperialists and many other shades of anti-establishment opposition. Through most of its existence the Left Socialist Party has had a small parliamentary representation (between two and four percent) until 1987. This representation gave the party a special position on the far left in relation to other groups that either stayed outside or left the Party at different times. Among these were several Maoist groups, several non-Trotskyist, Leninist groups and the Danish section of the Fourth International.

There have always existed one or more Trotskyist groups in Denmark since the 1930s. They have done important political work, especially international solidarity, but never had any real influence in the Danish labour movement. After World War II the Danish section of the Fourth International experienced a period of splits. Some opted for entryism in social democracy, others in the CP. But most of them took part in the establishment of the Socialist People's Party in 1958.

As in many other European countries the Fourth Internationalists grew as a result of the radicalization of the 1960s. They took part in the Socialist People's Party split which established the Left Socialist Party. At the beginning of the 1970s the majority of the Fourth International section left the Left Socialist Party and established its own organisation, which experienced some growth until the mid-1980s. In 1980 it changed its name to the Socialist Workers Party (SAP) and started publishing a weekly paper. It turned its political and organisational focus to industry and the trade unions and collected enough signatures (around 20,000, out of a population of about 5.1 million) to be able to run national lists for the parliamentary election three times in 80s, all on the basis of a membership of no more than 200. The election results were very modest, around 2,000 votes.

The Red-Green Alliance was established in 1989 on the basis of an written agreement between the CP, Left Socialist Party and SAP, and was soon joined by the remaining fragments of the Maoist Communist Workers Party (KAP)

The social struggles and movements of the late 70s and 80s

Established in 1989 the RGA was also a product of the social struggles and movements of the late 1960s, the 70s and the 80s, or more precisely a product of the decline of these movements. Grassroots and left activity in the trade union movement grew in these years, sometimes threatening Social Democratic hegemony. Members of left parties and groups built support committees for wildcat strikes and organised left-wing oppositions in trade unions. It never became a unitary left wing, since the strongest left wing force, the CP was keen not to clash fundamentally with the Social Democratic union leadership.

The highpoint of working class struggle was the strike movement of 1985 against the new union contract and against the government which came close to a general strike and almost forced a government, composed of two bourgeois parties, out of office. The strike movement was led by left wing forces together with oppositional Social Democratic Party trade unionists and it actually bypassed the national trade union leadership.

The strike movement neither succeeded in reducing working week, as was its official aim, nor in ousting the government, but it did put a brake on the neoliberal and anti-union offensive of the Danish ruling class. It prevented the ruling class from inflicting defeats on the working class the way they did in the UK and USA.

In the period from 1967 to 1989, several important grassroots and extra-parliamentary movements developed in Denmark. Some of them, consisting of several hundreds of local committees, were supported by important parts of the trade union movement and mobilised up to 100,000 in demonstrations. These movements were a result of, and gave impetus to, political radicalisation. The most important of them were:

- The anti-Vietnam War movement and other anti imperialist movements, primarily among the youth,
- The movement against the introduction of nuclear power plants in Denmark which was a 100 percent successful,
- The movement against the EU, mostly focusing on the succeeding new treaties put up for referendums and on elections to European Parliament. This Danish anti-EU sentiment was, until the mid-90s, represented almost exclusively by left parties and individuals, though with some nationalist tendencies,
- The peace movement which for several years focused on preventing a NATO plan for new nuclear warheads in Europe and on forcing the government to implement official Danish policy of no nuclear weapons on Danish soil in peace time. The movement forced the government to insist on Danish minority statements in all NATO decisions on nuclear armament for several years,
- The various movements of students against cuts and for democratisation of universities and colleges.

The decline of the late 80s

At the end of the 1980s these movements declined. The left wing was not able to recover its position in the trade union movement after the apparent defeat of the strike movement of 1985. The neo-liberal offensive was weaker and later than that in the UK and the USA, but nevertheless it took its toll and had its effect. This created a mood on the left that "forces of resistance" had to stick together. And, of course, the collapse of the Soviet Union bloc hit not only the CP, but also the non-Stalinist left wing constituency. In this way Denmark did not differ from many other countries of Europe.

In the general election in 1987 the Left Socialist Party failed to pass the 2% threshold and lost its parliamentary representation. It stood in one more election in 1988 with even worse result. The CP had lost representation earlier, and neither SAP nor KAP came near to the threshold. For one brief election period a populist split from the CP was represented in parliament.

For the first time in decades, no party to the left of the Socialist People's Party was represented in Parliament. In a few municipalities common left slates were established. Already before the 1988 national elections informal contacts had been made between individual leaders of the CP, the Left Socialist Party and SAP. The latter two made an electoral agreement allowing SAP candidates on the Left Socialist slate. On election night both representatives of SAP and of the Left Socialist Party introduced the idea of some kind of national electoral collaboration between the three parties.

The basic motivation, of course, was the need of a non-reformist representation to the left of the Socialist People's Party in parliament. At the same time, a maturity had developed in sections of the three parties which wanted to end decades of political infighting on the left.

The CP was also undergoing a decline and fragmentation under the influence of Perestroika in Soviet Union, with people and groupings developing in all kinds of directions.

In the SAP, individual leaders were influenced by the discussions on party building and left alliances taking place within the Fourth International, especially at the IIRE-school in Amsterdam.

The Red-Green Alliance established

Negotiations took place over a long period. There was a deep mistrust in the membership of all three parties towards the other parties. Important political differences existed, especially between SAP/the Left Socialist Party on the one side, and the CP on the other.

Organisationally, the SAP and the CP tended to side together against the deep rooted anti-Leninism in the Left Socialist Party.

Complicating the process was the fragmentation of the CP. One group was rapidly moving to the right, either to social democracy or into business careers. A major group opted for a much broader unity; some kind of peoples' front on an ill-defined platform and with very vague ideas of its components. Another major current wanted to stick with classical Stalinism.

Another issue was the difference of size. The CP had about 4,000 members, Left Socialist Party between 500 and 600 and the SAP not much more than 100, but with a much higher level of activity. Should this be reflected in influence on the political programme and in the leadership? In the pre-foundation negotiations an understanding was developed that all three parties were needed for a balanced alliance.

In reality the issue was settled at a time when the negotiations were in a stalemate because of the factional struggles in the CP. To speed up the process and to put pressure on the CP, the Left Socialist Party and SAP started to prepare to stand in the next elections. This initiative was legitimised by an endorsement from the CP-chairman, though no formal decision in the party had been taken.

According to Danish election law, a party not already represented in parliament must collect around 20,000 verified signatures in support of their participation, to be allowed to stand in national elections. Practically you need 25,000, because many are not valid.

Left Socialist Party and SAP set a target of 10,000 signatures each, while expecting 5,000 from members of the CP and non-aligned activists. For a party of 100 activists it was a huge target, but with the past experience of successful campaigns of to collect 25,000 signatures three times during the 80s, SAP reached its target before the Left Socialist Party, and established itself in that way as an equal partner in the collaboration.

Finally in 1989 an agreement was established between the parties. At that time supporters of the project had won a majority in the CP, though some of them still had the goal of changing it to a much broader alliance on a less developed and not so leftist political platform. A minority left to establish a new but much smaller traditional Stalinist Communist Party.

In December 1989 a founding National Conference was held to declare the establishment of a new organisation which was to be an alliance and not a party.

The conference adopted a preliminary political platform and a set of organisational rules. A national leadership was appointed by each of the three parties and some individuals, but each of the parties could veto any decision.

The name Enhedslisten was chosen. Directly translated it means Unity Slate, stressing the common understanding of the alliance as a corporation for election purposes, while the founding parties continued their separate existence as fractions of the alliance, each with a public face and public activities. Some members preferred the name Red-Green Alliance (RGA). It was incorporated as a "second" name, and soon it was decided to use that outside Denmark, because of the very Danish character of the real name.

The incorporation of "Green" in the party name illustrated that no green party was ever able to establish itself in Denmark. This was partly because the socialist left wing at an early stage manifested itself with a green agenda, beginning with the campaign against nuclear power.

In the next two national conferences the political platform and the organisational rules were developed. The now very small Maoist KAP joined, and the proportion of non-party affiliated members grew, leading to a cancellation of all formal special rights of the founding parties.

Important parts of the political platform which was developed during pre-foundation negotiations and during the first couple of years were:

- To the left of the Socialist People's Party
- Anticapitalist and socialist
- In favour of democratic rights and with an explicit distancing from "experiences of the Soviet bloc" (reflecting real political developments in parts of the CP)
- Focusing on parliamentary activities, but promoting extra-parliamentary mobilisations
- Anti-European Union
- Ecological
- Pro-trade union

The RGA adopted a principle for parliamentary work that originated from the Left Socialist Party which consists of guiding rules for MPs and local councillors. They are expected to:

- Vote for any law or law amendment if it is even a slight improvement (against sectarianism and ultimatism)
- Vote against any law or change of law if it contains any cut-back or set-back in relation to our political platform (against pragmatism and usual parliamentary behaviour of reformist parties)

- Vote therefore against parliamentary deals or horse-trading of packages of law amendments, where all participating parties get a little in their favour in exchange for supporting elements, they don't like (this is a integral part of Danish parliamentary life because of proportional representation, with many parties and none having a majority by itself).

Again in 1990 national elections were called, and for the first time the RGA stood on its own slate. The campaign was not very well prepared: the election manifesto was marked by many compromises, and the majority of the top candidates were "famous" leftist individuals outside the three parties, not all of them very familiar with the RGA-platform and the election manifesto.

The RGA received 1.7% of the votes, below the 2% threshold, and thus won no representation in parliament. Shortly afterwards the ex-CP chairman and a group around him left the RGA and joined the Socialist People's Party, where today he is the Number Two Man!

There was then a period of almost four years until the next election which helped the RGA to mature politically and organisationally. The disappearance of the most right wing CP-group helped in this process. Mutual mistrust diminished, collective experience of political campaiging was gained and a limited political platform on different issues was developed.

Gradually more and more individual members joined the RGA. It changed from collaboration between three parties to a membership organisation. But the notion of an electoral bloc still existed, mostly in the CP, but also in SAP and less so in the Left Socialist Party. All three parties kept their own organisational structure with offices, meetings and publications though KAP quickly dissolved as did the Left Socialist Party some years later.

The question of the European Community/European Union has been a major issue in Denmark since 1972 when a majority in a referendum voted to join. Most other new treaties have been put up for a referendum. Resistance to the EU has been an issue which is popular, working class and of the left. Even social democracy was strongly divided at one point, and they campaigned for a rejection of the Single Market in 1984.

In 1992 a majority voted against the Maastricht Treaty, creating political chaos in Denmark and to some extent in the EU. But soon afterwards a broad group of political parties, including the Socialist People's Party, made a so called "national compromise" leading to the Edinburgh agreement and a new referendum in 1993 incorporating four opt-outs for Denmark in the treaty.

To many members and voters of the Socialist People's Party this was seen as treason, while the RGA was the only left party campaigning for a "No" in the second referendum on the Maastricht Treaty which included the Edinburgh agreement.

This was probably the most important single factor behind the 1994 election result of the RGA. Not only did the RGA pass the threshold, but it obtained 3.1% of the votes securing the election of 6 MPs. The group was composed of two members of the Left Socialist Party, two members of the CP, one member of the SAP and one ex-member of the KAP.

In many ways this was the second birth of the RGA.

Parliamentary watchdog

Since 1994 the RGA has been represented in parliament, shifting from 6 to 5 to 4 to 6 and then again 4 MPs. Until around 2006-7 this was a period with a modest level of class struggle and social and political movements. Of course this has put its mark on the RGA.

In its written programmes and manifestos and whenever asked, the RGA states that it is an extra-parliamentary party supporting the social movements. But in reality the focus has been on parliamentary work, locally and nationally. Though many RGA-members have been active in trade unions, students organisations, tenants organisations, environmental campaigns and social movements, until recently organising the activity of the members in this field has not been regarded as an issue for the RGA-organisation.

RGA has been a radical parliamentary opposition, with some influence from 1994 to 2001 when the Social Democratic party was leading governments. Its brand image has been that of the critical watchdog, getting media coverage for its well-researched single issue campaigns, exposures of big capital, ministers and high-ranking civil servants and the only major party in Denmark with a loosely defined ideal of socialism. Most outstanding have been the campaigns against tax evasion by big multinational corporations.

Politically, the focus has been on the poorest and most marginalised groups in society like immigrants, refugees and people on social benefit and minority groups including youth subcultures and LBGT's. Less importance has been given to the traditional working class. Also ecological issues have had a high priority. In the 90s the RGA called for laws favouring and supporting organic production in agriculture. Support for organic production has since been adopted by most of the mainstream parties, but only the RGA is in favour of 100 % organic agriculture.

Membership has steadily increased from a little more than a thousand members, when the RGA had its first parliamentary representation, to more than 5,500 members in January 2011.

Typically membership increased during and immediately after election campaigns illustrating that it is the work of the MPs that attract more members rather than militant activity. A large part of the membership joined to show their support for the parliamentary group in a more visible and material form than just voting, but does not participate in local meetings or other forms of activity.

After several years of preparation in successive working groups, the RGA in 2003 adopted a formal political programme which is both anticapitalist and socialist. It stresses the need to mobilise the working class and allies to overthrow capitalist society. It even mentions the role of independent working class organisation and dual power organs in the revolutionary process and in the socialist society; plus clear cut internationalism.

The programme may have served as a point of reference for leading layers of the party, but it never played any big role in the political life of the RGA. Only a small minority of the membership has read it, and no organised education in the programme takes place in the party.

A large part of the activists and of the leadership will not agree with the most explicit revolutionary elements of the programme of the RGA. One example is a newspaper interview in May 2010 with an MP who is a young woman and the prime political spokesperson of the RGA. When confronted with quotes from the programme, she honestly defended most of it, but when it came to dual power organs she called it "outdated language".

A democratic and egalitarian culture, with some problems

The internal life of the RGA has for better or worse been marked by the heritage of the left of the 70s and 80s with two important elements:

- The RGA is extremely democratic and egalitarian,
- There is no tradition for open confrontation of different strategic perspectives.

An internal democratic life was important for both Left Socialist Party and SAP, but also for the CP-group that entered the RGA as a reaction to their experience with bureaucratic centralism in the CP.

All issues are decided by the elected delegates at the annual National Conference. Written discussion is open to all members. All individual members can present a proposal for the National Conference and all members can speak at the conference, even if they are not elected delegates.

According to party statutes minorities can withdraw from the general election of the 25 members of the National Leadership and obtain the right to elect their own members proportionally, it they obtain at least four percent of delegates.

Before each National Conference a membership referendum is organised to establish which candidate the members want to head up the election lists. On the basis of the referendum one or more slates, distributing candidates in different constituencies, are presented to the National Conference, which then vote on these slates. In the Danish election system a small party can predict with a high level of certainty who will be elected if it is up to 10 MPs.

It has never been challenged that the elected National Leadership is "above" the RGA's parliamentary group. The MPs must follow the general political line of the National Conference and of the National Leadership, and the parliamentary group must present important and difficult questions for a decision by the National Leadership or the Executive Committee.

In early 2010 the parliamentary group voted to send a Danish war vessel to combat pirates off the coast of Somalia. RGA members protested against this decision. This matter was brought before the National Leadership which decided against the MPs who in turn accepted that they had been incorrect.

The egalitarian culture is reflected by the rules about staff, National Leadership and MPs.

Members of Parliament and staff members can only be in office in for a limited number of years. The details have changed over time, but the limit is between 7 and 11 years. Both former MPs and staff members can return to office only after two year break in another job. They receive a salary fixed to the level of a qualified worker. For MPs, that means that they pay to the party the amount that their parliamentary salary exceeds this level.

Traditionally any tendency towards "the cult of the individual" has been opposed. Until recently election posters would not show pictures of the top candidates on the election list. Grassroots democracy sometimes develops into extremes when for example national committees in charge of a certain area of work are not elected or appointed by the leadership but are free-for-all-members.

On the other hand the organisational culture of the RGA is in some ways not that democratic. Even though the membership has the right to vote on all major issues and elect delegates to National Conferences, they are often not presented with real strategic alternatives.

This is to a large degree a reaction to the sectarianism and factionalism of the Left of the 1960s, 70s and 80s. The RGA was established with a mood of "no more infighting". It certainly was necessary to downplay differences in the first years of the existence of RGA to avoid it all blowing up again.

The first group of six MPs took on themselves the responsibility of keeping the RGA together at almost any price. They decided that they would form a united bloc in public whatever their differences. This was necessary since the media tried to portray the RGA as an unprincipled device to get into Parliament. Journalists looked for any sign of disagreement and predicted a quick dissolution of the RGA.

The consequence of this decision was that the parliamentary group, having a high degree of legitimacy in the party, presented itself as a bloc to the membership. However, this way of acting did reflect a real and deeply felt sentiment in the membership of wanting to avoid splits.

However necessary this was at the beginning, it has created problems. The party never succeeded in overcoming this "together-at-any-price" sentiment, even when it was so well established that it could afford discussions and confrontation between different perspectives.

A tradition of open tendencies around issues that divide the membership and the leadership has never been developed. Instead informal cliques and groupings are formed on the basis of individual leaders and/or of former common activity in youth and student movements. At the same time important leaders usually strive to make a compromise between opposing perspectives inside the leadership, rather than bringing differences into an open democratic discussion among the membership.

Nevertheless, on a couple of occasions important debates on issues of principle have taken place in the RGA. In the second half of the 1990s, the parliamentary tactic was put to a test. The Social Democratic Party minority government had two options when they wanted their proposals adopted in Parliament: either make a deal to the right with one or both of the major bourgeois parties or make a deal to the left with the Socialist People's Party and RGA. The Socialist People's Party and RGA were invited to negotiate major economic packages. In a couple of instances the MPs from the RGA opted for participation in order to help pass important social measures, despite sections of the working class or the youth losing out. The issue of responsibility for bringing down a left government was raised.

It created some heated debate in and around the RGA, and this put a lot of media focus on the party. It is quite unusual in Denmark for MPs to ask their party leadership for advice. The National Leadership of the RGA vetoed a parliamentary deal which the party's

MPs accepted. The MPs returned to the negotiations with the government and had the critical parts of the proposals more or less removed, and a deal was made. The result was that the principle was maintained of voting in parliament for even the slightest progress and against even the least setback.

Over the years, the choice between being a working class party or a party whose purpose is to help the "weak" layers of society has come up several times. This has interrelated with conflicts between sub-cultural layers wanting to realise utopian visions in the here and now, and traditional workers party and trade union layers wanting to promote the struggle on the basis of the material reality and the consciousness of the working class.

For some years this discussion revolved around the proposal of a Citizen's Wage. The proposal was that all citizens should receive a living wage from the state, regardless of being in a job, being available for a job or not, studying or not, young or old. Besides being criticised for being utopian, opponents argued that it would be impossible to mobilise the working class behind such a demand. It was also argued that with a Citizen's Wage, workers would have no objective interest in being part of the union run unemployment benefit scheme, and in that way it would undermine the high percentage of union membership in Denmark. In the end the Citizen's Wage proposal was rejected by the RGA at National Conference in the late 90s.

The fight against the EU has played a major role in the RGA since its beginning. Official policy has been to reject and fight the EU, but the founding parties had very different approaches to the issue.

SAP always tried to fight the EU on a class and internationalist basis, focusing on its pro-capital, pro-neoliberal and anti-democratic character. The CP was central in building and sustaining the cross-party, almost class-collaborationist Peoples Movement against the EU in 1972. In party publications, the CP resorted to very nationalist arguments about Danish self-determination and protecting Denmark against Germany. In the Left Socialist Party internationalist tendencies were in a majority but they co-existed with more nationalist currents on this issue.

In 2002 a formal discussion on these issues was organised because a layer of young activists and party leaders reacted to the self determination line of argument. They argued on the basis of internationalism and wanted to change the party programme which includes the demand for a Danish withdrawal from the EU. A part of this layer moved towards a position of reform of the EU, wanting to change the EU into a tool for pan-European decision making.

The result of the debate was basically to maintain opposition to the EU and the demand for Danish withdrawal but with more stress on the character of the EU policies, such as that they are anti-ecological, anti-social, and anti-worker. This decision has been not seriously been challenged since then, one reason being probably that the Peoples Movement against the EU has moved in that direction, with a member of the RGA and of the Fourth International as an MEP and leading spokesperson.

In 2007 the biggest crisis yet of the RGA erupted when a young Muslim woman, Asmaa Abdol-Hamid, was presented in the internal RGA referendum to be a parliamentary candidate. She wore a religious headscarf (hijab) and she refused to shake hands with men.

Her share of the votes in the internal referendum were so high that she was entitled to a place on the slate, and in case of a successful election result, she could be elected.

This created a huge media interest and protests inside the party. The reasons for this were numerous. A small minority claimed that the RGA is an anti-religious party and that the party should not have candidates that promote their religion visibly. A much larger group reacted because in her statements to the media she was ambiguous on democratic rights, equality of the sexes, the death penalty and Sharia law in general. Furthermore, the opposition against her was due to the fact that she was a fairly new member of the party and her political statements did not go beyond the traditional social attitudes of reformist politicians.

On the other hand a large minority of the party saw the opposition against Asmaa as Islamophobic, which was true for much of the campaign outside the party but not so much inside the RGA. This minority fiercely defended her, and her position on the slate.

In the end, she obtained a position on the list that made her a substitute for one of the MPs. The candidacy of Asmaa no doubt was one of several reasons for a bad election result, reducing the number of RGA MPs from six down to four. It also left the party in a crisis which was overcome a year later. But it was only in 2010, that support in opinion polls for the RGA recovered and went up from around 2% (4 MPs) to 2.5 and still increasing at the time of writing.

Asmaa has not been a candidate in the internal referendum since, but she is still a member and participated actively in the May 2010 National Conference.

The political change of the late 2000s

Since 2001 Denmark has had a government composed of the two major bourgeois parties with support from a rightwing xenophobic party, the Danish Peoples Party. They have implemented neo-liberal policies without head-on confrontations with the working class and the trade unions. They have mostly attacked marginalised groups. Their liberalisation has been sneaking, undermining public welfare and obviously favouring the ruling class and the richest layers of society.

In 2006-8 this process provoked local protests and strikes and national demonstrations against the government, but without the characteristics of an organised movement. National demonstrations were called by trade unions, students' organisations and opposition parties. Related to this movement was a national strike of public sector workers for a better national contract, and some students' mobilisations against cuts.

With no democratic structure and a very weak left presence in the unions, the Social Democratic Party and the union leadership were able to stop actions when the demands and the demonstrations went beyond their collaborationist policies. At the same time a militant youth movement was very visible in the streets of Copenhagen. This movement sometimes isolated itself from broader layers because of its anarchist methods, violent fights with police, the burning of cars and smashing of shops. On other occasions, they gained very broad sympathy.

In comparison with other countries the anti-war movement was weak in Denmark, though a couple of big demonstrations took place at the beginning of the war in Iraq. Smaller mobilisations against racism and in support of asylum seekers have taken place. Finally there was the very big December 2009 demonstration at the time of the Copenhagen intergovernmental summit on climate change.

Compared to the previous period there has been a real and manifest growth of mobilisation, though still modest in size in comparison to some other European countries. It has not resulted in more permanent working class or popular organisation, neither is there any organised opposition within the trade unions. A contract negotiation for the private sector in 2010 resulted in setbacks for the workers, but it was not met with any active opposition from the left.

Nevertheless there is an upward trend in mobilisations which is closely interrelated with an important left wing shift in opinion polls. The Socialist People's Party grew enormously while the Social Democratic Party and the RGA stagnated or grew a little. Although the growth of the Socialist People's Party came at a time when the party was moving politically to the right, the overall tendency is markedly to the left in Danish politics. This leftward process had not peaked when elections were called in 2007, so the right wing government survived. Recently (second half of 2010) the Socialist

People's Party have lost momentum and the Social Democratic Party and the RGA have increased their support proportionally.

The economic crisis which has made it impossible for the bourgeois government to implement rightwing liberal policies without attacking the core parts of the working class has also pushed things to the left. The Social Democratic Party and the Socialist People's Party are openly aiming at taking government after next election, and the majority of the working class is looking forward to a change of government with some expectations of improvement although they are not clearly articulated and vary from one sector to another.

The reaction of the Red-Green Alliance to the new period

The party leadership and parliamentary group have fully supported the movements which have developed during this last period. Lots of RGA members have participated at leadership and grassroots levels. But the level of party involvement has been marked by a general low level of activism in the party, the low level of political education, the lack of well-founded understanding of, and even conscious hostility to, the party's role in organised and developing social movements.

Faced with a new period and new challenges to the RGA, the many years without strategic debates and the fear of political conflict have created problems. It has made it difficult for the RGA to adapt to the new situation fully.

On the one hand the crisis and the mobilisations have helped to shift more members in the direction of an organising, interventionist and activist party.

The first visible internal reaction happened in 2008 when a group of activists and leaders from students', young workers' and other youth movements tried to initiate a discussion about what kind of party the RGA should be. They contrasted the class party with the party of the minorities and the parliamentary watchdog. To a great extent this was a reaction to the party profile in the 2007 elections, and the poor results achieved.

The criticisms of this group provoked much debate and had a positive effect on party priorities.

The positive effects were partly negated because the group ignored the demands of immigrants, asylum-seekers, LBGT's and so on and tended to define the working class as all-white-and-male instead of a working class of both sexes and all ethnic backgrounds. Also they were marked by a very top-down leadership culture in the students' and trade union youth organisations where they gained their political experience.

This informal group helped introduce the idea of organising party members according to workplace, trade unions and branches and have been involved in the slow implementation of this policy. This is an issue that SAP members promoted for many years. Though the adoption of that line of party building is an important step forward, problems still remain. Among the party members actively building these interventionist structures, approaches differ:

- is it primarily for RGA members who are shop stewards, elected trade unionists or trade union employees, or is it basically an organisation of all party members in a particular workplace or trade union?
- is the task for these structures only to support traditional trade union activities or are they also structures to organise the dissemination of party policy in work places and trade unions?
- Here, like in other areas, there is an evident gap between adoption of a decision and the implementation of that same decision.

The reason that some narrow conceptions of party work exist in broad layers of the party is because of very limited working class mobilisation over the last 15-20 years. This in turn resulted in no organised left wing activities at a grassroots level in the trade unions. RGA and other left wing workers were divided into two main groups: the majority who ignored the trade unions as a field of activity and the minority who ended up in elected positions or as employees of the unions. While remaining socialists of conviction they were not free of influence from bureaucratic ways of working. At the same time the layer of young activists wanting to organise trade union activity got most of their experience from organisations of students and young workers where they held leadership responsibility. Another informal group around some party staff members has developed quite another party-building strategy, focusing on a professional communication strategy for the parliamentary work and tending to ignore party members as the most important lever for party decision making, for promoting party policy and for mobilisations. This, too, is a result of decades of left wing activities that are not rooted in mass movements, but focussed on parliamentary activity and media debates.

The first reactions of the RGA to the economic crisis were weak and ambiguous. On the issue of bank saving support packages there was no doubt. The RGA clearly opposed these, and the thrust of the demands was that the rich must bear the burden of the crisis.

On the other hand the RGA explanation of the crisis focussed on greed and a financial sector out of control. Likewise, most of the proposals from MPs for political responses to the crisis were kept inside the framework of a Keynesian understanding.

Left wing forces, among them SAP members, criticized this and succeeded in changing party analysis of the crisis, but are still struggling with the task of developing anticapitalist political answers that can mobilise the working class and its allies.

The most unfortunate result of many years of focusing on parliamentary activity is the development of a right wing tendency in the group of RGA councillors in Copenhagen. The local council system in Copenhagen, capital of Denmark, differs from most other municipal councils in Denmark. In most cities, between 15 and 31 councillors are elected every four years, and they in turn elect one mayor.

In Copenhagen the council elects a kind of Lord Mayor plus 5 or 6 other mayors. Each Copenhagen mayor has special administrative responsibilities: schools, social welfare, environmental issues, etc. They are elected by the council proportionally to the number of councillors from each party. The RGA is the third largest party in Copenhagen and is entitled to one mayor.

Without openly confronting the RGA parliamentary principle of supporting all progressive measures and opposing any drawbacks, the RGA mayor and the group of councillors have defined their task as to have influence and get results, even results in the sense of the lesser evil. They argue that the RGA must show that "we" can manage the Copenhagen economy to the benefit of the people, disregarding the constraints not only of capitalism but also the narrow government limits to local decision making. This parliamentary strategy pushes them towards the lesser-evil policy.

This has led to the RGA supporting cutbacks of municipal administration workers and day care centres with the result that parents and workers demonstrated against a council budget deal that the RGA supported. Fortunately, faced with the demonstrations, the RGA backtracked and pulled out of the political deal a week before local elections. The consequence was that the RGA grew in standing in the opinions polls after losing support for weeks.

The economic crisis and the perspective of a new government

If the Social Democratic Party and the Socialist People's Party form a coalition government after the next election, as expected, it will be the first time in Danish history (apart from the exceptional post World

War II circumstances) that a party to the left of social democracy is part of a government.

For a large section of the working class this will raise hopes for changes and improvements in living standards and public services. But with two reformist parties governing in the middle of a severe economic crisis they are bound to be disappointed by the policies of these two parties if nothing else happens outside parliament.

The tasks of an anticapitalist party in that situation are at least threefold:

- to campaign in trade unions, student organisations, environmental movements, local communities and other movements to place demands on the two parties, to mobilise popular pressure on a new government, behind demands for a policy of social and ecological improvements and of solidarity
- to use the parliamentary platform to transmit this pressure from the working class and its allies and make it difficult for the two reformist parties to collaborate to the right
- to present and make propaganda for those anticapitalist solutions to the economic and ecological crisis that the new government refuse to implement in the name of class collaboration.

These tasks have not been totally clear to the majority of the RGA membership or to the majority of its leadership, and they still are not, though texts that point in this direction were adopted at the latest National Conference.

Tendencies to accommodate to the reformist parties have evolved. Leaders argue that it is paramount that the voters see us as part of the new majority, or else they will not vote for us. Sometimes they argue that we must not be seen as responsible for bringing down a Social Democratic Party/Socialist People's Party government. In itself this is not wrong, but some leaders have argued against attempts to promote the anticapitalist policies of the RGA, and some leaders have been ambiguous in their defence of the traditional RGA parliamentary principles, focusing instead on the necessity to avoid the fall of reformist party government.

These tendencies in a part of the leadership are also supported by sections of the party youth. This is a generation that has only been politically active under the reign of an openly bourgeois government. They have never experienced a Social Democratic Party led government. This makes them naïve towards what improvements the reformists will implement by themselves without any extra-parliamentary pressure. They tend to focus on the pressure that RGA MPs can bring to bear on a new government by way of clever negotiation techniques and refusal to vote for government proposals. They don't realise that a Social Democratic Party/Socialist People's Party government will have no problems in making parliamentary deals with the right, if the two parties think they can do this without being punished by their members, the trade unions and the voters.

If a Social Democratic Party/Socialist People's Party government takes power, enormous possibilities will exist for the RGA. We may get the chance of being part of social and political mobilisations in support of demands for a new government. At the same time we will get the opportunity to make the difference between reformism and anti-capitalism visible to new layers of the working class and of the youth. The RGA can help this education process both by being at the forefront of all movements when Social Democratic and Socialist People's Party-leaders retreat and by presenting an anticapitalist programme of action that combines day-to-day demands of the working class with radical reforms that break with the framework of capitalism.

But such a situation also presents dangers. The pressure of adaptation will be great, for example if the RGA wishes to avoid political responsibility for the fall of a Social-Democratic government, no matter what the reasons.

Taking into the consideration the non-militant character of the membership and the lack of political education it would be irresponsible to disregard the risk of adaptation to reformism, like the majority of the Copenhagen local councillors. This would seriously compromise the hitherto parliamentary principle of the RGA making it part of the failure of a reformist government and part of the disappointment and disillusion instead of a pole of attraction for workers and youth who are disappointed by the Social Democratic Party and the Socialist People's Party.

Debates are going on about these issues. After the May 2010 National Conference the balance is tipping towards the perspective of social mobilisation, against adaptation and for anti-capitalism. The final outcome will depend both of the level of struggles and the political debates inside the RGA.

Evolving SAP perspective for the RGA

The SAP was one of the founding parties of the RGA. SAP members have been actively building the RGA ever since its foundation. In that way SAP has been a part of the life and development of the RGA. Consequently SAP has developed its analysis of the RGA and its strategy and tactics over the years. This has been done openly in resolutions from National Conferences and the National Leadership of the SAP, even in the weekly political statements from the Executive Committee of SAP.

At the time of the creation of the RGA, the SAP supported the model of an electoral collaboration that could also develop common campaign activities and action. We insisted on special rights for the founding parties, and we were reluctant to give these up. We were afraid of losing control and being caught in a right-wing drift of the new organisation. In addition, veto rights for the founding parties could help avoid a split with the CP which felt especially insecure among its new partners.

When the numbers of non-aligned members grew, they naturally insisted in establishing the RGA as an ordinary member-led organisation. They were supported by the Left Socialist Party, and finally the SAP and the CP accepted this.

This development, combined with parliamentary representation, forced the RGA to take positions on more and more issues. The demand for a strategic political programme began to appear.

Members of SAP engaged in the debates on what political positions to take, and in the work of developing a strategic program. But all the time we stressed that the RGA should not adapt strategic positions that might jeopardise the unity of the existing forces. For a long period we worked from the perspective of preserving such a broad unity and at the same time working for a revolutionary regroupment inside the RGA– with parts of the Left Socialist Party in our mind. At the same time we gradually tried to introduce the notion of the RGA as a mobilising force in social struggles and movements.

In 1999 a National Conference of the SAP took stock of the reality that the RGA now was a political party in the ordinary Danish sense of that word. A resolution stated that "Red-Green Alliance is not a revolutionary party in the classical Leninist sense (based on democratic centralism, with a developed programme for a socialist revolution, etc.), and we do not consider it desirable to try to enforce a development in this direction. Neither the subjective, nor the objective conditions for such a development are present at the moment."

But signifying a new SAP-perspective we wrote: "At this stage of development of the Red-Green Alliance we can merely note that there is no pre-set limit as to how far the Red-Green Alliance might develop towards an actual revolutionary party. But, on the other hand, the work of SAP inside the Red-Green Alliance has such a policy as its guiding line."

As a consequence of this 1999 analysis we decided to channel future public political activities through the RGA and through the youth organisation collaborating with the RGA. This meant that the SAP from then on did not engage as a party in organising demonstrations, that we did not organise interventions of the SAP in unions and social movements and that only in exceptional circumstances did we distribute leaflets independently of the RGA. This kind of work we did, if at all possible, as members of the RGA.

The SAP, nevertheless, has continued to publish a monthly magazine, to organise our annual public educational seminar and the occasional public meetings.

In 2006 we confirmed and consolidated this perspective for our work in the RGA and even took it a bit further. In a National Conference resolution we wrote: "The RGA can therefore be the necessary organised socialist force in today's struggles, in tomorrow's struggles and in the socialist revolution; the organisation that can meet the tasks we have described in this text. This is what we wish to build Enhedslisten as, this is what we want Enhedslisten to become, and this is what we need!"

We analysed the weak points of the RGA and the qualities that the SAP can contribute, and we set ourselves the task of introducing "more class, more struggle, more party" into the RGA, that is developing it into a class struggle party.

The fundamental task of the SAP was defined as helping build the RGA (and the youth organisation SUF) in all aspects. The RGA is "our party", and the SAP is a necessary tool for organising our effort in building the RGA, especially necessary and useful because of our historic tradition, our political and practical experiences and our membership of the Fourth International.

12 January 2011

Broad parties and the fight for left unity in Britain

Alan Thornett and John Lister[1]

The need for new left-wing pluralist parties which can embrace a broad spectrum of the left (both those with revolutionary politics and other left wing militants from a social democratic background) has existed now for nearly 20 years, not just in Britain but across Europe. It has been a product of the wholesale adoption of the neo-liberal agenda by European social democracy. In Britain it has been a product of the rise of new Labour, which was on the leading edge of that development. Today the political conditions for such parties remains in full force, yet the left in Britain, in contrast to the wider European experience, is weaker than it has been for many years and the prospects for such parties is in crisis, particularly in England and Wales.

Respect remains today (in 2011) the only left party in England with any electoral substance. It has a small but significant base amongst oppressed migrant working class communities in East London and South Birmingham, where it made an historic breakthrough into ethnic minority support in the wake of the invasion of Iraq. Respect leader Salma Yaqoob, herself, was brilliant gain from the anti-war movement. Respect was strongly anti-imperialist and was a significant gain for the working class. It also made some significant interventions around the environment and climate change at least at some stages in its development.

Respect, however, is now extremely fragile and is locked into an inward-looking orientation which is leading it nowhere. The decision taken at its conference in November 2010 to begin organising in Scotland against the Scottish left and when it has yet to establish itself as a national organisation in England (and which caused SR to leave the organisation) may well be the final chapter.

---

[1] *Alan Thornett is a member of Socialist Resistance (the British section of the Fourth International). He served on Respect's national council until 2010. He worked at the Morris factory in Cowley from 1959 to 1982 and chaired its Joint Shop Stewards' Committee. John Lister is also a member of Socialist Resistance. He served on Respect's national council until 2010. He is director at London Health Emergency. Thornett and Lister are co-authors of Respect: Documents of the Crisis.*

Other formations such as No2EU and TUSC continue on, to some extent, as top down initiatives with little electoral weight and even less democracy and show no signs of changing.

Yet for the last 10 years the basis has existed for a substantial left party in England reflecting the rise of the SSP in Scotland. Not a mass party. But an organisation of fifteen or twenty thousand embracing sections of the trade union left was entirely possible. The failure to establish such a party has been the responsibility both the endemic sectarianism in the British left (with its inbuilt Stalinist legacy) as well as the enduring pull of Labourism, even as it moved to the right. The grotesque first-past-the-post electoral system for Westminster also compounded the problem.

A potted history of left weakness

Ever since the turn of the 20th century, left wing politics in Britain have been relatively marginalised, operating under the shadow of the British trade union leadership, and then the parliamentary political party created in the image of the union leaders. While other European countries witnessed a much more explosive division within working class politics, the relatively new Labour Party in Britain did not face a significant split in the aftermath of the 1917 Russian revolution.

The Communist Party in Britain was always weak both in numbers and in its political theory and approach, and in the 1920s became politically dependent on the line spelled out by the Kremlin: its attempt to organise a large-scale left wing base in the unions, the Minority Movement formed in 1924, was steered almost immediately off course by Stalin's insistence upon an alliance with the "left" trade union leaders who sold out the 1926 General Strike. The British CP and its co-thinkers proceeded to follow every twist and turn of Stalinist policy from the late 1920s (when an ultra-left turn limited its opportunity to exploit the 1931 betrayal as Ramsay MacDonald formed a coalition with the Tories, before the so-called 'Popular Front' period from 1934 led the CP to advocate bizarre cross-class alliances to bolster "liberal" capitalists). This lasted through to the 1950s, where Stalin's notion of a "Parliamentary Road to Socialism" cemented the CP into a reformist political framework, and confirmed the strategy as seeking influence through long-term and opportunist alliances with the trade union leaders.

A disunited far left

In these intervening decades, left wing alternatives to the Communist Party and Labourism have veered between the opportunist and the sectarian, sometimes combining both approaches. In the post-war period this meant that the revolutionary left, which had been vilified and oppressed during the 1940s by the Stalinists, social democrats and fascists alike for holding a class struggle line, was itself subject to repeated splits reflecting its ideological weakness, and the growing problem of individual dominant personalities seeking to gain and maintain political control through bureaucratic and sectarian methods.

Even though some of these organisations professed adherence to the principles of revolutionary Marxism, and the political legacy of the first four congresses of the Communist International, few were able consistently to base their work on any of the concepts of the United Front. Uniting the left was not seen as a priority for people such as Gerry Healy (SLL/WRP), Tony Cliff (IS/SWP), Ted Grant and Peter Taaffe (*Militant*) and later those who copied their methods, such as Sean Matgamna (*Workers Fight*/AWL): instead preserving the separation of each organisation from its rivals on the far left took centre stage, including the use of manoeuvres, opportunist alliances and bureaucratic techniques to control their relatively small memberships.

While Labour retained its political hegemony over the majority of the working class, the left remained fairly much self-contained, a variety of smaller organisations aspiring to become "mass parties", but working separately and having little strategy other than building through one-by-one recruitment, and hoping for a split in the Labour Party that has still never come.

The extent of rank and file trade union militancy and student activism in the 1960s and 1970s meant that there appeared to be a space for the left to organise and the lack of a serious interventionist orientation to the labour movement could appear to be less of a fundamental weakness.

Up until the mid-1980s the Grant-Taaffe Militant group remained within the Labour Party, growing in membership to the point of becoming Britain's fifth biggest party, according to journalist Michael Crick. "Entryism" appeared to have been elevated from a tactic to a long-term strategy, until the nearest thing to a "split" in the Labour Party saw their entire current expelled in a witch-hunt led by Neil Kinnock. The expulsions began on a relatively small scale. In 1982 the Labour conference adopted a list of proscribed organisations: the following year five members of *Militant*'s Editorial Board were expelled.

In 1985-6 Kinnock increased the attack on the group of Liverpool Labour councillors, led by Militant, who had taken a stand against Tory spending cuts, and in 1986 Derek Hatton, who had led the revolt in Liverpool was expelled from the party.

The Bennite movement

Tony Benn called the first of the three Socialist Conferences in October 1987 in response to the defeat of the miners and the rise of the defeatist 'new realism' approach in the unions and the continued rightward trajectory of the Kinnock leadership of the Labour Party. He still had a big movement around him after his leadership challenge in 1981.

The conference was massively over-subscribed, and was refreshingly open and democratic. The Socialist Conferences united a swathe of the left both inside and outside of the Labour Party on what was called a 'twin track' approach, though it was far more inside the Labour Party than out. The Conferences became the Socialist Movement in 1989 and took on much more of the shape of an organisation with a publication, called *The Socialist*. In 1991 it held an impressive trade union conference in Sheffield, which debated the way forward for the trade unions around the theme 'unshackle the unions'. The ISG, then the British section of the Fourth International, was heavily involved in the Socialist Movement, in particular in the trade union conference.

The limitation of the Socialist Movement from the outset, however, was that it was never going to break with Labour, whatever happened within the Labour Party. It was certainly never going to stand candidates against Labour. In any case most of those participating in it, including the ISG, still regarded an electoral challenge to Labour as premature, though this was clearly starting to change.

Militant exits from Labour, and splits

Even though only 250 or so *Militant* supporters were actually expelled from Labour it was by now increasingly operating outside of the party. From 1988 onwards *Militant* ran its successful anti-poll tax campaign largely outside the Labour Party, which clearly questioned entryism in the eyes of many of its members and it would not be long before they would start standing candidates against Labour.

In 1991 Dave Nellist, who had been elected as a Labour MP in 1998, declared that he would stand against Labour as a 'Labour Independent' in his seat of Coventry South East in the general election expected in 1992. Meanwhile *Militant* supporter and Liverpool councillor Lesley Mahmood lost the selection battle for the deceased Eric Heffer's seat to right winger and witch hunter Peter

Kilfoyle. Mahmood went on to stand against Labour as 'Real Labour' in Liverpool Walton.. She received 2,613 votes and beat the Tory candidate. Dave Nellist was expelled from the Labour Party in December 1991 along with fellow Labour MP Terry Fields.

In January 1992 Militant split into two when a majority backed Peter Taaffe's proposal to withdraw from the Labour Party. A minority, following Ted Grant and Allan Woods, stayed in the Labour Party and became Socialist Appeal. Taaffe's proposal was underpinned by the view that the Labour Party was now a straight capitalist party the same as the Tories.

A month later Scottish Militant Labour was proclaimed as an independent organisation in Scotland with jailed poll tax activist Tommy Sheridan as its most prominent member.

In the 1992 General Election on April 9, Dave Nellist and Terry Fields, stood as Independent Labour candidates along with Tommy Sheridan for Scottish Militant Labour north of the border. They did not win but they scored well. Nellist, who had been the sitting Labour MP, stood in Coventry South East and came remarkably close to winning: he polled 10,551 votes against Labour's 11,902. Terry Fields polled 5,952 in Liverpool Broadgreen and Sheridan 6,278.

Labour under Neil Kinnock dramatically lost the election having been convinced it was going to win.

In the local elections the following month Militant took two council seats from Labour in Glasgow, one of them by Sheridan himself, and he won it from prison where he was serving a sentence arising from the anti-Poll Tax campaign.

After these successes the 'Scottish turn' became a model for Militant in England and Wales and by the end of the year Militant in England and Wales had become an independent party called Militant Labour.

The SLP and the Socialist Alliances

After successfully forcing through the abolition of Clause 4 at a special Labour Party Conference at Easter 1994, Blair went on to consolidate his position by trouncing the left and winning every vote at the 1995 Annual Labour Party conference.

After the abolition of Clause 4, the NUM leader Arthur Scargill took the initiative to form the Socialist Labour Party (SLP). The RMT's Bob Crow became a leading member in the early days of the new party. In launching the SLP, however, Scargill did not follow the Socialist Movement's example of democracy and openness, but went sharply in the other direction. From the outset Scargill managed to demonstrate (with the help of former ISG members then organised as the Fourth International Supporters Caucus, FISC, who acted as Scargill's enforcers for several years) exactly how such parties should not be built.

The slamming of the door by Scargill triggered the formation of a number of Socialist Alliances (SAs) and SA type initiatives some of which involved the Militant, for example in Coventry which was its main base. The Greater Manchester SA which was set up by John Nicholson and others was another example. They came together in what became the Network of SAs which also included the Walsall Democratic Labour Party, which was an expelled local branch of the LP. There were also SA type organisations in Lancashire and Kent.

In Scotland many on the left, including Scottish Militant Labour, had discussions with Scargill which broke down when he refused to contemplate any degree of Scottish autonomy.

Some members of organised groups did manage to get into the SLP. Three groups of sectarian leftists all got people in, but were all eventually expelled: the Communist Party of Great Britain/*Weekly Worker*; the Revolutionary Democratic Group and the Bolshevik Tendency (a split from the Spartacists). In 1997 a battle for democracy opened up inside the SLP after an article was published in its name supporting the Chinese government over the 1989 Tiananmen Square massacre!

There was then mayhem at the second conference of the SLP in December 1997 when, having always refused to allow organisations to join, Scargill produced a block vote of 3,000 from the Lancashire and Cheshire Miners Welfare Association from his back pocket and used it to dominate the rest of the conference. Even the FISC was outraged when he used this to abolish Black Sections, which they supported.

This spat with Scargill soon led to the expulsion of FISC itself. After the conference people began leaving the SLP in groups as well as individuals. The only group Scargill built an ongoing alliance with was the pro-Stalin group (serious Stalinists with Stalin t-shirts etc) around the Indian Worker's Association's Harpal Brar.[1]

Scotland shows the way

In Scotland the SSP was formed in 1998 after it became clear that New Labour, elected the previous year, was moving towards devolution including a Scottish Parliament elected by a form of proportional representation.

The forerunner of the SSP was the Scottish Socialist Alliance, a coalition of left-wing organisations (including SML) which had

---

[1] *After several years even Brar's current was expelled by Scargill, forming the Communist Party of Great Britain (Marxist-Leninist) in 2004.*

existed since 1996 and which had drawn on the work the left had been doing in the Scottish Constitutional Convention around the issue of devolution and home rule as well as the poll tax and water privatisation. Even some sections of the Scottish Communist Party were drawn in.

As a result the SSP was able, at the time of its foundation, to represent the bulk of the left in Scotland and become an important model of a broad democratic party of the left at the European level as well in Britain.

The SSP model was based on the idea that an alternative to Labour had to be built as a *party*, with a comprehensive political programme, and that if a serious party was to be built which could challenge the rightward march of social democracy it could not be built by one-by-one recruitment and even less via a single political tradition, even parties which have in the past been as successful in Britain, such as the SWP and *Militant*/the SP, have not been able to do that. The SSP recognized that what was needed was first the unity of the left, and then to reach out to broader forces through the development of a common political experience and culture over a period of struggle.

The first election the SSP fought was the by-election for Glasgow City Council in 1996 where it won a respectable 18% of the vote. It then contested 16 seats in Scotland the in the 1997 general election which brought Tony Blair to Westminster. Tommy Sheridan saved his deposit in Glasgow Pollock and Jim McVicar and Alan McCombes also did well in two other Glasgow constituencies.

The SSP's main breakthrough, however, came in the first elections to the Scottish Parliament in May 1999. Although the SLP polled better in Scotland than the SSP overall, Sheridan was elected to represent Glasgow. The SSP was highly organised, democratic and inclusive and it grew to around 3,000 members.

Socialist Alliances in England

In England the experience of New Labour in office, from 1997, accelerated initiatives towards the establishment of Socialist Alliances. In 1998 a conference was held in Birmingham, after a series of preparatory meetings, which adopted a set of policies, a constitution and a steering committee for a wide and more stable national network of alliances. A number of far left organisations were involved (including the ISG) as well as individual activists. Militant (which had changed its name to the Socialist Party of England and Wales (SPEW) in 1997) were central to it. The SWP was not involved.

The following year the SWP, now overwhelmingly the biggest far-left organisation in Britain following the decline of the *Militant*/SP after its split, took the decision to join the London Socialist Alliance, which had been established by Militant, the ISG and others in order to stand in London in the European elections in June 1999. It was a big break for the SWP to start to work with the rest of the left, and was potentially extremely important for the left as a whole.

The LSA now embraced the bulk of the left in London to the left of Labour outside of the CP tradition, including the SP and the SWP. It appealed to the SLP to come on board to complete a unity slate. Not only did it reject this, however, but announced that the SLP would be standing a full slate in London, with Scargill at the head of it! The LSA offered to put Scargill at the head of a united slate, but this was also rejected by the SLP. It was an isolationism which continues with its full destructive force today.

Faced with a split of this kind in the left vote, the SWP withdrew from the LSA arguing that the LSA candidacy was no longer viable. As a result the LSA withdrew from the election and left the field open to the SLP. The SLP, which stood in the additional members section only, polled 1.7%.

A year later the LSA decided to stand in the election for the new Greater London Assembly, which had been set up by New Labour along with the Scottish Parliament and the Welsh Assembly. ISG member Greg Tucker was now the LSA's secretary. The SWP was also back on board having apparently accepted that the SLP was not going away and was a problem the rest of the left would have to live with.

The LSA launched its campaign with a rally in Camden Town Hall with film maker Ken Loach and journalist and SWP member Paul Foot on the platform. The results of the election were very good, with an average of 3.1% in the constituencies and 74,000 people voting for it overall. The SLP stood for the additional member seats and polled 14,000 votes, 0.8%.

At a conference of the LSA soon after the election, the first structured debate took place on the future and character of the LSA where there seemed to be agreement that the LSA should be an ongoing political organisation building up a record between elections and not just an electoral mechanism to be brought out when an election was imminent.

In September 2000 a conference of the SA Network was held in Coventry to discuss launching an all-England SA for the general election expected in 2001. It was chaired by Dave Nellist and brought together over 400 activists embracing the bulk of the far left organisations in England, including the SWP and the SP.

Independent activists and local campaigning organisations were also involved. The conference adopted a protocol to provide the organisational structure and political framework for the election campaign. A decision was taken to register the name Socialist Alliance as a political party. The conference was a big step forward for the English left.

It meant that the SA now embraced the bulk of the far left including SWP, the SP, the ISG, the AWL, the Democratic Labour Party, Workers Power, the CPGB, Workers International, RDG, Lewisham Independent Socialists, and some important groups and individuals from the Labour Left including former Islington Labour councillor and Labour Party NEC member Liz Davies and journalist and novelist Mike Marqusee

The SA fielded almost 100 candidates for the general election In June 2001 in England and Wales. It polled a total of 55,635 votes in the 93 constituencies in which it stood in England, with an average of 1.75%. It saved two deposits with scores of 7% and 6.8%. The ISG had six candidates in the election, including John Lister in Oxford East.

Party or coalition?

Six months later, in December 2001, the SA held another conference (with a thousand in attendance) to discuss the next stage of its development and to adopt a constitution based on one member one vote. The SP opposed the constitution, however, and when it was adopted they walked out and resigned from the SA.

They had argued for a federal structure, which would have given the component organisations a veto over the decisions of the leadership bodies. This would have rendered individual members who were not members of a component organisation powerless. It would have meant no democratic procedures, just negotiations between the component groups. It meant that, in reality, all political life and debate would take place in the internal meetings of the component groups rather than the broad organisation.

This is not to say that it would have been easy to establish democracy in an organisation where one component organisation (the SWP) had a predominance of members. However the answer was not to demand an undemocratic structure which would exclude independents and hobble political debate. The answer was to fight for democracy in a united organisation and to develop a new culture which would make democracy work. That was what we intended to do.

Despite the SP walk out most of the rest of the far left stayed in the SA at that stage. The SP went on to set up the Campaign for a New Workers Party, which has been for the last 8 years or so a narrow propaganda exercise more designed to build the SP than to create a new broad party. It was and is characterised by the SP's own brand of top-down economism.

A weakness in the unions

The biggest failure of the SA, however, was its inability to win the affiliation or support of any of the left unions, or left union leaders, on a consistent basis. And this was even more important given the continued weakening of shop-floor and workplace organisation, the virtual disappearance of the militant shop stewards' movement that had offered openings to the left in the 1960s and 70s.

The run-down of manufacturing industry in the 1980s, the brutal anti-union laws wheeled in by Thatcher, the defeat of the miners and the political capitulation of many trade union and Labour leaders to "new realism" had helped to reduce the material base, the freedom to act, the morale and the political aspirations of union members.

The key problem, as ever, was at the top, where union leaders were more reluctant than ever to take a political stand themselves, or to separate themselves in any way from the Labour leadership that had won the election and ousted the Tories but refused to reverse the anti-union laws, or carry through policies to benefit the working class.

Even in the days of the so-called "Awkward Squad", few of them were prepared to be awkward enough to break with Labour, and even those who did were not prepared to back left-of-Labour candidates. Even Matt Wrack, who wrote a pamphlet for the SA on the trade union link and the crisis of working class representation, has kept at arm's length from the issue of left parties since he won the leadership of the Fire Brigades Union: indeed the FBU itself, which has for years been disaffiliated from the Labour Party, has still not given any real support to alternative left candidates.

The exception to this was Bob Crow, who after he became general secretary of the RMT in 2002, affiliated the RMT as a national union to the SSP. The RMT was expelled from the Labour Party as a result. Affiliation, however, continued until the SSP was split by the catastrophic decision of Tommy Sheridan to sue the *News of the World* for damages over allegations of infidelity. Soon after the split the RMT withdrew its affiliation.

In an attempt to develop its support in the unions, the SA held an impressive conference of trade unionists, in March 2002, with

1,000 participating, which took up the issue of political representation and the democratization of the trade union political funds. It published the pamphlet written by Matt Wrack entitled *Whose money it is anyway?*

The anti-war movement

The opening of Bush's 'war on terror' with the invasion of Afghanistan not only saw the development of a mass anti-war movement but the radicalisation it produced also laid the basis for a new stage in the development of a broad party of the lefty in England, providing the left could rise to the occasion.

February 2003 saw the biggest political demonstration in British history, with two million people on the streets. Thousands were open to socialist and anti-imperialist ideas, to joining a broad pluralist party and working with revolutionary socialists in that framework, providing they thought it was a genuinely broad and inclusive initiative. This included large numbers of young Muslims who were radicalised to the left by the war and angered by the Islamophobia it generated.

The Stop the War Coalition (StWC) could not itself become a political organisation. It was a single issue campaign, and far too diverse to unite on any more developed political platform than opposition to the war. It embraced the whole of the far-left along with the Green Party, important sections of the trade unions, the Campaign for Nuclear Disarmament, the Muslim Association of Britain (MAB) and a number of left Labour MPs.

A conference of the Socialist Alliance, just after the invasion of Iraq, responded to this opportunity by adopting a resolution calling for a regroupment of the left in the wake of the invasion of Iraq. It discussed with many on the left, including the CPB, and key figures of the trade union left as to their possible involvement.

The SA, however, was unable to do this. The CPB decided not to participate, despite its positive experience of working with other left organisations in the StWC. This was partly due to moves by some of the left union leaders, at that time, to launch a campaign to "Reclaim the Labour Party". This was sharply out of kilter with political reality, of course, but it reflected the CPB's long-held strategy along these lines.

In October 2003 the event which opened the way for something new was the expulsion of MP George Galloway from the Labour Party: the anti-war movement's most prominent and uncompromising leader had called on British troops in Iraq to refuse to fight. Galloway called for a new political organisation to be formed in time to stand in the European (and London Assembly) elections, which were to take place in June 2003.

Galloway was the first Labour left MP in modern times to make a break with Labour in this way. This opened up the possibility of a much broader organisation, based on the radical and radicalising wing of the anti-war movement of which Salma Yaqoob was the most impressive representative. It was a perspective we supported, and the SA merged into Respect when it was launched in January 2004.

In Scotland the SSP had dramatically extended its breakthrough by winning 6 seats in the Scottish Parliament in the second set of elections to that institution on May 1 2003. Frances Curran, Rosie Kane, Rosemary Byrne and Colin Fox joined Tommy Sheridan at Holyrood. The party took a number of important initiatives inside and outside the parliament, probably the most significant was Frances Curran's bill to introduce free school meals for all, but also launched a campaign for free public transport as well as participating in more general campaigns particularly against the wars in Iraq and Afghanistan and the siting of nuclear weapons at Faslane.

The SSP was also making an impact on the left at the European level, and itself becoming influenced by developments elsewhere. It became a founding organisation of the European Anticapitalist Left along with other such left parties which had emerged or were emerging across Europe.

The launching of Respect

Respect came into being via an ad hoc group mostly from the anti-war movement including John Rees and Lindsey German from the SWP as well as George Galloway. Ken Loach played an important role. They agreed an initial draft of a founding declaration which was strong enough in its socialist content to represent a real alternative to new Labour and broad enough to create a wider coalition. Respect was launched from a conference in January 2004. An interim Executive Committee was elected which reflected the anti-war movement in its composition. John Rees was its National Secretary.

The launch of Respect was contentious amongst the far left in the SA since it represented a shift to the right in order to form something which was bigger, broader and more diverse than the SA had been. Some of the smaller groups which had been in the SA rejected Respect and went on to form a plethora of small groupings including a re-launch of the SA with a smaller network of socialist alliances.

Respect replaced what was essentially an anticapitalist party with one which was more left social democratic (at least its key components Galloway and Yaqoob were left social democrats) but with a strong far left, mostly SWP, membership, although the SWP never managed to get anything like the whole of their membership into Respect. From the fringes, the AWL, Workers Power, the CPGB and presented Respect as a betrayal of the politics of the SA. Others denounced it as a "popular front". Respect, however, had the potential, from the outset, to reach out to the anti-war activists (including the young activists and the Muslim activists) and to parts of the wider movement the SA had singularly failed to attract.

In June 2004 Respect stood in both the Euro elections and the elections for the London Assembly, which were held on the same day.

In the Euro elections Respect stood in every constituency in England and Wales and polled 1.7% of the overall vote (250,000 votes). Within this were some very big votes in some places, particularly in East London, and was to shape the development of Respect. In Tower Hamlets in East London Respect polled 21%.

In the London Assembly elections Respect polled 4.5%; just short of winning a seat, which required 5%.

Respect's most important election results were in the General Election in June 2005, when it stood in the limited number of 26 seats, and George Galloway's victory in Bethnal Green and Bow. Respect received votes ranged from less than 1% to the 38.9% won by George Galloway. Nine of the Respect candidates saved their deposits. Salma Yaqoob came a close second in South Birmingham. Galloway was the first MP to be elected to the left of Labour, and in a separate party to Labour, since the Communist Party won two seats (one of them also in East London) in 1945. He overturned a 10,000 majority held by the sitting Blairite and pro-war MP Oona King. Young Muslims, in particular, from the large Bangladeshi community in the constituency, flocked to his campaign.

The debates and battles inside Respect

Although Respect was broader and had a much stronger electoral appeal than the SA, some of the same problems emerged. One of these was the issue of the democracy and transparency of its decision-making and another was the issue of building Respect as a party rather than as a coalition or a network.

These issues were debated at the first Respect conference (the first after the founding conference) in November 2005, which was held in a packed hall with 1500 present. We intervened with both an SR broadsheet and with various resolutions on building Respect.

We were roundly denounced for this by both George Galloway and John Rees for our sins. Afterwards we produced an SR statement which pointed out that although we remained fully committed to building Respect and that it was the best thing to happen on the left in England for a long time the conference had been a deeply worrying event which had "put a question mark over Respect's long-term development as a broad based alternative to new Labour and its neo-liberal agenda." It also questioned its ability to develop as a genuinely pluralist organisation capable of embracing the bulk of the left.

We had pushed for the conference to discuss how to locate Respect firmly in the emerging campaigns against the new neo-liberal offensive of the Blair government, and to confront the assault on civil liberties. But while the conference had adopted some good resolutions problems arose in the session on building Respect, the key session of the conference as far as Respect's future development was concerned.

Faced with resolutions aimed at developing Respect as an organisation which called for better administration, better democratic functioning, better contact with members and branches, more collective policy discussions ... and Respect's own publication, John Rees and George Galloway responded negatively with demagogic speeches and crude appeals to loyalty. The tone of their response was that the proposals were either unnecessary or that they placed unreasonable demands on Respect's resources.

The problem was that the loose coalition model defended by George Galloway and the SWP leadership imposed a narrow organisational framework that could not be a viable model for an organisation which wanted to challenge for political power on the full spectrum of political issues. Nor was it working. Despite important successes Respect remained organisationally weak with a great diversity between its branches as far as their numerical strength and political viability was concerned.

George Galloway's close-of-conference speech continued this theme, despite the fact that the debate had been closed and the votes taken. He said that what John Rees had said had been "brilliant". He said he had always been against Respect having a newspaper and he was now even more against it. Respect was not a party, he said, but a coalition, and that was the way it should stay.

There were policy clashes as well. A supporter of SR who proposed a resolution on LGBT rights was denounced by Lindsey German to the effect that this was not the right time to raise it. The matter of abortion, to which Galloway is opposed, was resolved with the agreement to support a woman's right to chose.

A series of practical measures were adopted by the conference, which, if implemented, would have gone a long way to improving the administration and collective development of Respect. These included:

- Urging local branches develop strong and regular campaigning activities.
- Making Respect as open and inclusive as possible in order to encourage recruitment and keep and consolidate the new members.
- Making a fresh approach to those sections of the left, including the trade union left, which are not currently in Respect.
- Strengthen our political profile at national level by producing further editions of the successful Respect tabloid paper.
- Seeking to strengthen the national office and press and publicity profile between elections.
- Building strong local branches which develop their own political life and culture through regular discussion and debate.
- The National Council should convene consultative groups on specific areas of policy, such as housing, health, transport, drugs, civil liberties etc. drawing on the expertise and specialist knowledge of interested members and supporters of Respect in order to develop policy papers for discussion by the National Council and the party at large and to produce fact sheets and campaign materials for use by party members.
- That the National Secretary should circulate reports on the business conducted at meetings of the National Council as soon as is practically possible after those meetings.
- The publication of a general Respect manifesto which can be available for sale and on the website.

It was a very big 'if' of course, and many in the conference took from the tone of the speeches by George Galloway and John Rees that these proposals would be kicked into the long grass.

The Respect Party Platform

Nor were SR members the only ones to who were shocked by the speeches of Galloway and Rees. This led to the formation of the Respect Party Platform (RPP), mainly from London, particularly Camden and Lewisham. After a few arguments the RPP was recognised as a platform within Respect. Its aims which were published inside Respect were as follows:

"Our priority proposals are:

- Respect has to be built as a mass membership party. This means a new emphasis on recruitment, and a fresh approach to sections of the left currently not in it.
- Respect needs a stronger national political profile, with its own publications, leaflets, pamphlets, and a manifesto for regular use between elections.
- The national office needs to be strengthened.
- The Officers' Committee and National Council need to be more effective, develop greater authority, and improve their connections to the local branches. Minutes of their meetings should be available to branches and members.
- Structures are needed to ensure the accountability of elected representatives.
- Policy groups and special interest groups need to be established to create more membership involvement in Respect.
- We need an internal bulletin and/or website facilities for discussion and debate so that differences can be discussed and ideas developed."

Any progress in this direction, however, was shattered in January 2006 by the decision of George Galloway to go onto the Big Brother show without any consultation within Respect. Respect was rocked to its foundations. It was not only was deeply discrediting event but it raised the issue of democracy and accountability to a new level. The internal crisis it created was compounded by the reluctance of SWP leaders to take Galloway to task over the issue. The crisis eventually passed, but not without damage to Respect and a significant loss of membership.

Respect's electoral appeal was dented but not destroyed, however, and it stood in the local elections in May 2006, winning 16 new council seats, taking its total to 18. Previously Respect only had three councillors, two in Preston and one in Tower Hamlets in London. Respect also stood in a small number (14) other seats in London and a small number of seats (25) in the rest of the country. This made 153 candidates in all. The results in Newham and Tower Hamlets were remarkable by any standards for a left party, with Respect winning 3 seats in Newham and 12 in Tower Hamlets. To get these seats it polled a massive 86,000 votes across the two Boroughs; 23% of the vote.

The only seat Respect won outside of London was in Birmingham Sparkbrook, a deprived inner city working class area with big Pakistani and Kashmiri communities where Salma Yaqoob won with a massive 49% of the vote. The results for her ward were:

Respect 4,339, Labour 2,700, Liberal Democrats 990, Conservatives 343, Greens 309, BNP (fascist) 109.

Despite electoral success, however, Respect continued to decline in terms of members. At the next Respect conference in October 2006 the Respect Party Platform drew focused on this decline in a broadsheet on building Respect, which it distributed. We pointed out that Respect had lost more than half its members, down from 5,000 to about 2,000.

This rather mild intervention received a remarkably over-the-top and hostile reaction. We were given three minutes to articulate an alternative way forward for Respect. After that we were denounced not just by George Galloway but also by Nick Wrack, who spoke on behalf of the SWP leadership. Nick Wrack had been one of the founding group which launched Respect and who we had been working with throughout. He had later joined the SWP.

We were then (once again) completely marginalised by a succession of wildly upbeat speeches by members of the SWP with the blatant distortion of the membership figures, and what proved to be bogus claims of the mass recruitment of students. We were told that Respect had just recruited hundreds of new students in the fresher's fairs which had just taken place. It was complete rubbish of course. The conference was told that Respect was the fastest growing organisation on the left.

In Scotland meanwhile the SSP had been going through a difficult time. In November 2004, 18 months after winning the magnificent total of six seats in the Parliament, Tommy Sheridan resigned as Convenor of the SSP. This was the outward sign of what would eventually lead to a split in the party; Sheridan's demand that the SSP support his decision to sue the News of the World, demanding £200,000 in damages, for allegations that paper had made about his sexual behaviour some of which he had admitted to fellow party members were true. Sheridan and his supporters walked out to form Solidarity in Autumn 2006. The split and what had preceded it led to disastrous results in the 2007 elections for the Scottish Parliament. The SSP vote collapsed and they lost all six seats, including Sheridan's. It is true that the rise of the SNP and the squeeze it exerted was also a factor not the main one.

Galloway's letter and the split in Respect

In September 2007 the issue of democracy came to a head in Respect in an extremely unlikely way. George Galloway wrote a letter to the Respect NC which implicitly challenged the SWP's control of the apparatus of respect and called for a broader-based leadership with a

position of 'national organiser' created which would be in parallel to
John Rees as National Secretary.

We, as SR, supported the letter (as did a large majority of the
non- SWP Respect members including Ken Loach and Salma Yaqoob)
not because we had confidence in George Galloway, which had been
severely shaken by the Big Brother affair and his attitude towards us
in Respect conferences, but because we agreed with what the letter
said. In fact much of it could have been written by us.

The reaction of the SWP leadership was to brand the letter as a
'declaration of war on the SWP'. After that a split between the SWP
and most of the rest Respect was probably inevitable. We (Alan
Thornett in particular, working most closely with Nick Wrack)
became a part of the organising group for the non-SWP side of the
argument from then until the conference which launched Respect
Renewal in November 2007.

There was a huge political debate around the split and the
politics it reflected. Those members of the SWP who supported the
letter (Nick Wrack, Rob Hoveman and Kevin Ovenden) were expelled
from the SWP early in this process. However a majority of the
members of the NC supported the Galloway letter and were strongly
opposed to the response of the SWP leadership. SR NC members
signed a statement along with 21 other members of the NC which
included the following passage:

> "On the ground many SWP members have worked alongside
> other members of Respect to great effect. However, it has
> become clear ... that the actions of the SWP leadership imperil
> the very existence of Respect as a broad, pluralistic and
> democratic left alternative to New Labour. Since the letter from
> George Galloway, which echoed some of the criticisms others
> had been making earlier, was sent to the members of the
> National Council on August 23, the SWP leadership have
> demonstrated that they are incapable of engaging in open and
> frank discussion with those who have disagreements with them.

> "The chain of events in this crisis is contrary to the ethos which
> Respect has been seeking to develop and which is reflected in its
> constitution: 'Respect is a broad, open and inclusive
> organisation. It is politically pluralistic and will encourage all its
> members to participate in its campaigns and activities'."

SR subsequently produced a book, *Respect: Documents of the Crisis*,
so that the lessons would not be lost. We (John Lister and Alan
Thornett) produced a discussion paper, which included the following
passage:

> "Even their very worst enemies could not have hatched up a
> scheme half as destructive as the one the SWP Central

Committee has imposed upon itself. It must be the first time such a large-scale left current effectively launched a witch-hunt on itself, driving towards a split which, if they were to go to a stitched-up Respect conference and win the vote, would be a Pyrrhic victory, leaving only a downsized SWP and a wafer thin layer of hangers-on in Respect. Such a formation would never attract any broader forces, many of whom will instinctively recoil from the SWP for years to come as the reality becomes more widely known.

"The SWP leadership have also broken from most of the well-known figures who could draw a crowd for Respect, notably Galloway and Salma Yaqoob, but also Victoria Britain and Ken Loach.

"In other words the SWP leadership's tactics have driven off virtually all of the independent forces that made Respect a genuinely broad-based coalition. After three years of work they now stand to walk away from the project weaker and more discredited than they were before it launched: their track record is one of politically hobbling Respect, under-selling it and failing to tap its potential in a period uniquely favourable to building a left alternative. And having failed to build it to its potential, rather than face up to any of the errors that have been made, or correct them, they have embarked on a suicidal policy of polarising Respect for and against the SWP."

Respect Renewal was launched at an impressive and upbeat conference in November 2007. Nick Wrack was elected national secretary and prominent FBU member, Linda Smith as chair. It was to have monthly paper, facilitated by Socialist Resistance which closed down its own paper and handed the resources to Respect in order to have a paper of its own.

The launch was a great achievement in the circumstances, given that it involved challenging the strength of the SWP. There was a bitter battle with the SWP over the ownership of the name, which was eventually resolved in Respect Renewal's favour.

The leadership bodies functioned well the early stages. The NC was initially well attended, and the officer group (which Alan Thornett was on) met every week and ran the organisation.

There was, however, a very strong challenge right from the start, led by Mark Perryman who comes from a Eurocommunist tradition. He argued, against Respect Renewal becoming anything resembling a party, or having what he called 'traditional, out of date' structures. He was opposed not only a newspaper but a policy making conference. Although his line was not openly supported by many in

Respect at that time it would in the end be supported by the main players around George Galloway and Salma Yaqoob.

It was a similar story when the economic and banking crisis broke in 2008. Attempts by ourselves (Alan Thornett and John Lister) to even discuss the crisis and Respect's response to it were ridiculed on Respect's National Council Mark Perryman, Andy Newman and others, as the usual far left mantra. Even after the crisis hit them in the face the issue of Respect relating seriously to the crisis was never resolved. We were told at one meeting of the NC by George Galloway that 'people are not interested in what we have to say about the crisis.

An equally important (and related) difference as far as building Respect was concerned, was to emerge over the issue of electoral work as against wider campaigning activities. No one was against electoral work: it was and is clearly essential for any party presenting itself as an alternative the establishment parties, you can't surrender the electoral territory to the enemy. There were those, however, around George Galloway's office in particular who would accept little less than a dominance of electoral work virtually over all else.

This came to a head over the October 2008 Respect Renewal conference, when Galloway's office called for the conference to be postponed in favour of a Saturday afternoon of election work for an election (in Tower Hamlets) which was still 7 weeks away. The move against the conference satisfied both those who saw electoral work as above all else as well as those who were opposed to 'traditional' policy making conference. In the end there was a 'compromise' with an early finish, but the issue caused ongoing resentment, even though the conference itself was well attended and very successful.

Another walk-out weakens Respect

After that tensions increased on the leadership bodies, although they continued to function quite well. We had worked closely with Nick Wrack and Will McMahon throughout all this, although there was some tension developing around the fact that Nick himself was refusing to call meetings of the EC because he did not want to debate with his political opponents. Our view was that this approach undermined the democracy of Respect, and thus could not be supported however frustrating it was to have seemingly pointless debates some of the time.

An important turning point came with resignation of Nick Wrack and Will McMahon, as National Secretary and Treasurer, and others, over the issue of supporting 'No2EU' in the European elections.

This new mini-split took place just before the 2009 conference, and it altered the relationship of forces on the leadership bodies. One of the consequences was the collapse of *The Respect Paper*. It also had a demobilising effect on many of our supporters inside Respect, with some of them partially or completely dropping out

The 2009 conference itself, held in Birmingham, was well attended and had some good debates. However the intervention of Galloway, who implied that whatever the conference decided would make little difference to him, was a throwback to 2005 and the speeches he and John Rees had made in the past. It did not bode well for the post-conference internal situation.

A half-hearted 2010 election campaign

Respect's objective in the 2010 general election was to extend its one seat in Parliament to three. George Galloway would stand in Poplar and Limehouse (in Tower Hamlets) Abjol Miah would stand in Bethnal Green and Bow and Salma Yaqoob would stand in Birmingham Hall Green. All three were regarded as winnable.

However in the run-up to the election Respect more or less ceased to function at all as an organisation. Suggestions of a monthly publication of a newspaper were dropped without discussion, leaving the organisation with only a rudimentary means of communicating with members or publicising its views. An election manifesto commissioned by the National Executive and written by Alan Thornett on the basis of agreed policies was vetoed by an obscure process with no meeting of the officers or National Council to discuss it, and a bowdlerised version with little content was published in its stead.

Astonishingly for an election campaign, no appeal was even circulated to members for an election fund or resources to help build the party's campaigns.

The eventual results, further skewed by a last minute anti-Tory swing to Labour in London and other urban areas, were almost universally disappointing, with Galloway and Abjol Miah losing heavily in East London, although Salma Yaqoob increased her vote in Birmingham Hall Green. She secured an 11.7% swing from Labour. Simultaneous council elections in London saw most of the Respect councillors lose their seats

The period since the election has seen no evidence that Respect can pick itself up from these setbacks. This was illustrated by the fiasco in the power-base of East London, where Respect, having campaigned (controversially) for an elected mayor, and succeeded in securing an election, then decided it was not strong enough to stand its own candidate, and instead wound up supporting Lutfur Rahman, a Labour nominee. Blushes were spared somewhat when the Labour bureaucracy intervened and deselected him and installed another candidate, giving respect at least a fig-leaf of supporting a left challenge to Labour, who went on to win the election.

No2EU and TUSC

In 2009 and 2010 there were two closely related attempts to launch electoral initiatives. The first was the No2EU campaign which was launched in 2009 as an intervention into the European elections. Its driving force was the Socialist Party with Dave Nellist as the central figure. It also included the Communist Party of Britain and the rail union the RMT. Bob Crow, General Secretary of the RMT, was centrally and actively involved. Also involved were the Alliance for Green Socialism, the Indian Workers Association and the Liberal Party (not the Lib-Dems). The second was the Trade Union and Socialist Coalition (TUSC) set up in 2010 in order to stand candidates in the general election. This no longer involved the Communist Party or the RMT as a union, which had also withdrawn, although Bob Crow was central to it in an individual capacity.

Neither organisation had any significant electoral impact, but the test would be whether anything might come out of them as far as uniting the left was concerned. Both organisations emerged as electoral fronts from secretive and exclusive processes, and each set itself up as a self-appointed top-down structure (or core group) with the powers to keep out anyone they did not like. The lesson of the long struggle for broad parties to the left of Labour, outlined above, is that organisations set up in this way have nothing to offer, and in the end will only be an obstacle to the process itself.

Other organisations, including SR, which applied to join were rejected, both by No2EU and TUSC. These also included the CPGB, the AWL and Workers Power. SR wrote to Dave Nellist and received no acknowledgment or even a letter saying that we had been rejected. By contrast Nick Wrack, as an individual, was given a place on the core group of both bodies!

With No2EU we were told that the lack of democracy and transparency was the result of 'practical difficulties', not a preferred method of operation. Its late emergence of, just before the European elections, we were told, simply did not allow for democratic structures to be put in place. At numerous public meetings of No2EU, assurances were given that after the election there would be a conference in which everyone could participate and at which the next stage of the project could be democratically discussed, including whether No2EU would develop into a party.

These 'commitments' were coming mostly from SP members, however. The direct representatives of the RMT such as Bob Crow and Alex Gordon were much more circumspect about it and stressed repeatedly that No2EU was "not a party" or a future party, but an electoral arrangement for the European elections.

Despite the high hopes among some, after the European elections and the disappointing results for No2EU, nothing happened. The RMT organised a conference in November, at which the SP floated the initiative which eventually became TUSC. This, however, was not a No2EU post-election conference. It was organised as a result of a series of decision of RMT conferences to organise conferences on Labour Representation and was the third such conference in four years.

TUSC then emerged fully formed in the same way as No2EU, after it had been decided behind closed doors what it was, how it would run and what it stood for. All others could do was deciding whether or not to support it: there was not even a facility to join. This was now clearly a consciously chosen method of operation and not an unfortunate necessity. In fact what TUSC has ended up as was very close to what the SP advocated at the 2001 SA conference.

We have to reject this kind of method. It contributes nothing to the formation of the kind of party which is required. We do not defend democracy as an abstract concept. We defend it because it is the only effective way on which to build a political alternative to right wing social democracy and tackle the crisis of political representation.

During the TUSC campaign we were again told that after the General Election there would be a conference and the whole thing would be opened up. Again it did not happen and looks unlikely to happen. Nothing changes.

Recent events and initiatives

Not only have all the initiatives towards a broad pluralist party of the left failed over the past 10 years but new initiatives are still taking place and not just the SP project via the CNWP.

At the end of July 2010 a meeting was called by Pete McLaren who leads one of the fragments left over from the SA and who was involved in N2EU and TUSC, to discuss the setting up another new organisation of the left. The meeting was a predictable combination of his particular brand of a top-down approach and a dangerous tendency to localism which has arisen in recent years. There was a nasty antipathy to the socialist organisations present, which went alongside a heavy bias towards various politically disparate and ill-defined local groups, which were seen as the key to the future of the left.

The main discussion was around Pete McClaren's proposal to set up a new network of organisations with a name and officers with the aim that it would 'become a political party on a federal basis within a year'. Nothing was said as to what its political basis would be When it looked like the vote would be lost Pete McClaren proposed that a new network be established on an 'interim; basis and with 'interim' officers and this was agreed with a few votes against. He was of course the 'interim secretary'.

There was a lot of talk in the meeting about building from the bottom up, which seemed to be code for getting round the SWP and SP and building something without them. We have to start, however, from the need for left unity and fight to establish the right political basis for it. None of the organisations which we look to as useful models at the European level were built from the "bottom up" in that way. They were built out of the unity in practice of the left organisations and their leaderships, as well as a multiplicity of individual activists.

It is the same with localism. We have to relate seriously to local electoral initiatives where they spring up, not least because they reflect the failure to build anything at the level of national politics. It would be a mistake, however, to see this as a strategic way forward towards a party of the left at the national level. The extreme diversity of the local groups represented in Rugby, some were explicitly non-socialist, only reinforced that view. Unfortunately there are no political shortcuts.

Moreover the decision taken at Respect's conference in November 2010 has seriously compounded the problem. We were faced with the situation of a late amendment from George Galloway's office to the effect that Respect would abandon a long held policy and begin organising in Scotland. Not only that, but Respect would stand George Galloway for the Scottish Parliament in 2011!

This was completely unacceptable to us in SR for a number of reasons. First because we have always supported and continue to support the SSP. Secondly because in general we are opposed to English organisations organising and standing for election in Scotland. And thirdly because of the way it was pushed through, with no discussion prior to the conference on this proposal and under conditions where Respect has never discussed Scottish politics.

It was also under conditions that not only has Respect failed to build itself as an organisation in England at the national level we have always been opposed when we have proposed that it do so. Now with no discussion on Scottish politics and even less resources, it has decided to organise in Scotland as well.

Having been outvoted on this at the conference SR has withdrawn from Respect and is no longer involved. It is a defeat for us (and for Respect in our view) since Respect started with real potential and had achieved things both at the electoral level as well as its impact in minority migrant communities which no other organisation of the left has been able to achieve.

Unfortunately Respect has succumbed to the problems traced in this article since the mid-1990s, the top down domination by powerful organisations or individuals who are only prepared to be part of such an organisation providing it turns around their own individual needs. Until we are able to break from such conceptions the left will remain marginalised.

Conclusion

There has been a common thread running through the failures and missed opportunities since the early 1980s when can be summed up as follows:

- The failure to organise the various formations to the left of Labour as *political parties,* with their own political life, communication systems and culture of debate, to offer a convincing alternative for those who had been part of, or been attracted to the Labour Party.
- The failure to establish genuine democracy. Time and again this is supplanted by some form of top-down domination by domineering, self-seeking individuals or groups, which offers no real political alternative to the bureaucracy of social democracy and no opportunity for activists to play a leadership role and feel they have a genuine voice.
- The continuing failure to establish the right relationship between the far left organisations which join such parties and the leadership structures of that organisation. An example of this was the decisions being taken in the structures of the SWP rather than the structures of Respect and the lash-up which allowed the SP with its various partners to rebuff attempts of other left currents and groupings to join No2EU and TUSC.

As the ConDem government drives through the biggest public spending cuts in recent history, to be met with a pitifully ineffective, timid-Blairite opposition from Ed Miliband's New Labour front bench and by the empty words of a stridently vocal but largely passive trade union bureaucracy, the need for a political alternative to the left of social democracy is as great as it has ever been.

But unless these basic lessons are learned and the left breaks from its sorry history of sectarianism, demagogy and opportunism, the working class movement in Britain seems doomed to repeat the cycle of false start and failure that has marked the last 30 years.

13th November 2010

The rise of Die Linke in Germany

Klaus Engert[1]

Introduction

After World War II the division of Germany created an exceptional situation for the left. In East Germany, the unification took place of the Social Democratic Party (SPD) and the Communist Party (KPD) to form the SED (United Socialist Party) which ruled until 1989.

In West Germany, the KPD was marginalized and banned in the 1950s. It re-emerged as the German Communist Party (DKP) at the end of the 1960s during the 1968 movement. But it never achieved a mass influence. It acted as an instrument of the East-German SED leadership and was financed and guided by them.

The dominant political force among the workers and the trade unions for several decades in West Germany remained the SPD. This changed in the 1990s with the neo-liberal turn of the SPD which implemented a brutal programme of cuts in public services, deregulation and privatisation. The SPD also committed Germany to join the illegal war against Serbia under the SPD/Green Party government coalition between 1998 and 2005.

The long march of the SPD to become a bourgeois party which started in 1959 with the so-called Godesberg programme in which the SPD removed the label of "workers party" and claimed instead to be a "people's party", has now been completed. This was the starting point for the rise of Die Linke.

But to explain what Die Linke represents, we have to go back in history.

A brief history of left parties in Germany since the seventies

Without looking at the 1970s, it is not possible to understand the role that Die Linke is playing in German politics today, which is quite

[1]   *Klaus Engert, is a member of RSB and of the Fourth International since 1974. He is also a member of the scientific board of the Foundation SALZ (Soziales, Arbeit, Leben, Zukunft - Social affairs, Labour, Life, Future), and of the Ecosocialist International Network. He writes for "Avanti", "Sozialistische Zeitung" and "Inprekorr". He is the author of the book "Ökosozialismus-das geht" (Ecosocialism - it works).*

different to that played by other parties such as the Left Bloc in Portugal.

Die Linke is not the first attempt of the radical left in Germany to create a party to the left of social democracy. At the end of the 1970s, the Green Party emerged from the social movements of those times, in particular the movement against nuclear power stations. A large part of the radical left, which had emerged from the 1968 movement, joined the Green Party.

But with an amazing speed, the Green Party integrated itself into the bourgeois mainstream. The forces of the radical left which had taken part in its foundation, either adopted bourgeois politics like the former minister of foreign affairs Joschka Fischer, or were marginalized and left the party.

Die Linke is therefore the second attempt[1] in the history of post-war Germany to establish an alternative to the left of social democracy.

The Green Party was a completely new formation with a crude mixture of bourgeois forces (in the beginning there were even right-wingers who eventually left the party), ecologists, former anarchists and Maoists and members of the anti-nuclear and peace movements. In contrast to the Green Party, Die Linke was a merger of one big party, the PDS (Party of Democratic Socialism) and a new formation, the WASG (Election Alternative for Social Justice). The Green Party never had much of a base in the workers' movement, but represented (and still represents) mainly petit-bourgeois layers of the population. However the parties that formed Die Linke had strong roots in what was left of the German worker's movement.

The foundation of the PDS

After the fall of the Berlin wall the SED, which had been the ruling party in East Germany, was completely discredited. But the SED did not dissolve in December 1989 although the transitional East German parliament changed the constitution to remove the article about the "leading role" of the SED. An extraordinary congress of the SED in the same month decided to change the name into SED-PDS and agreed to an "irrevocable break with Stalinism as a system".

In February 1990, it changed its name to PDS (Party of Democratic Socialism) and by then there had already taken place considerable changes in personnel and political positions. Before the fall of the wall the SED had about 2.3 million members, but this was dramatically changing:

---

[1]   *There were a couple of other minor attempts, but none of them really managed to get a real mass base.*

Members of PDS after 1989
(figures for West Germany in brackets)

1990:	285,000	
1991:	172,579	
1992:	146,792	(617)
1993:	131,406	(891)
1994:	123,751	(1,871)
1995:	114,940	(1,905)
1996:	105,920	(1,943)
1997:	98,624	(2,074)
1998:	94,627	(2,917)
1999:	88,594	(3,773)
2000:	83,478	(3,959)
2001:	77,845	(4,172)
2002:	70,850	(4,708)

The PDS also tried to establish itself from the very beginning in former West Germany, but as we can see from the figures above, this was not very successful.

A paradoxical development was taking place: in East Germany the PDS was stabilizing itself and getting a regular electoral score of up to 20%, entering local and regional governments and rapidly adopting classic social democratic policies (and even in some cases, like in Berlin, neo-liberal ones). In West Germany, a part of the remaining, much-splintered, radical left entered the PDS and took more radical positions. The outcome of this process was that in the western part of the country the PDS usually did not get more than 2% of the votes and only managed to get a few token councillors elected because of special local conditions. Not even the fact that the PDS took a clear distance from its former partner, the West-German DKP, allowed it to break out of its marginalized position in the West.

This generated a problem for the PDS. The votes in East Germany could not compensate on the federal level for the weakness in the very much bigger Western part. The result was that in the elections of 2002 the PDS did not manage to get more than two deputies elected, both from East Germany, into the federal parliament.

The shrinking of its membership after the first big blood-letting directly after the fall of the Berlin wall (the membership declined by almost 90% which revealed how many members had been opportunists or were forced to enter the party) was mainly caused for "biological" reasons as the remaining members were quite old. At the time of the formation of Die Linke, the average age of the 60,000 members of the PDS in 2005 was 70. In 2005, the 72,000 members of the new party had an average age of 65 .

In the meantime, Die Linke had recruited about 78,000 members. But the growth had only taken place in the Western part. In the East, the membership was still shrinking because of the reasons mentioned above.

The SPD, PDS and WASG

At the beginning of the new century, the PDS was confronted with the problem that it had not succeeded in becoming a nationwide party. It was de facto an Eastern-based party with a small group in the West. This was a threat to its future existence. In the West the PDS was still identified with the former SED, which was a major problem to be able to pass the 5% threshold of votes necessary for entering the federal parliament.

Despite the accelerating degeneration of the Social Democrats, they were favoured by the German bourgeoisie because they guaranteed that for the first time since World War II, the German army could take part in wars of aggression without major resistance. The first was the war against Serbia, the so-called "Kosovo war", the second was in Afghanistan. The latter was classified as a "peace mission" to avoid legal problems, as under the Constitution German forces are only allowed to take part in defensive actions. With the Green Party in a coalition government with the SPD from 1998 to 2005, a potential major movement against the participation of the German Army had been neutralised.

The second bit of "dirty work" the SPD and Green Party had to carry out, was the brutal cuts in the social security system justified by the economic crisis at the beginning of the century. The measure taken was called "Agenda 2010" with at its centre the "Hartz IV" clause. This was enigmatic: Peter Hartz was the former staff manager of Volkswagen and a personal friend of the former chancellor Gerhard Schroeder. Volkswagen had always been the main example for the traditional post-war co-operation between trade unions, social democracy and industry. Hartz worked out a new system for unemployment benefits, which became a federal law. This new law limited the wage-based benefits to 18 months and reduced them afterwards to a standard amount of a little over 350 Euros (plus rent and heating). Those who had savings had to spend these first before receiving benefits.[1] Furthermore the retirement age was raised from 65 to 67 (which was a disguised cut in pensions).

---

[1]   *The swamp that Hartz was working in was later exposed when Hartz and Klaus Volkert (a member of the metalworkers' union IG-Metall who chaired the*

These radical anti-social measures generated a mass movement against Agenda 2010 with the "Monday demonstrations" taking place in numerous towns. These were in the tradition of the Monday demonstrations during the last phase of the East German opposition before the fall of the wall.

It is in this context that a part of the middle layer of the trade union bureaucracy, mostly members of the SPD, opposed the course of their party and took the initiative to found the WASG (Electoral Alternative for Social Justice) in 2004. This organisation emerged mainly from two different initiatives, one northern-based, the other southern-based, but both united a very broad spectrum of forces, such as disappointed social democrats, radical leftists, Christians, greens and members of social movements like ATTAC. From the very beginning there was a discussion in the WASG about the relationship they should have with the PDS.

There were different organised currents that opposed co-operation or merger with the PDS. The radical left criticized the PDS for taking part in regional governments like in Berlin and orientated themselves to the construction of a party clearly to the left of the PDS. There was also a right-wing current, which vanished after the merger, which was strictly against any co-operation with Communists. A third current was pushing forward the concept of a left socialist party like Rifondazione in Italy or the Socialist Party in Netherlands.

The WASG was growing quite fast. Most of the remaining small groups of the radical left and Trotskyists joined the WASG. These included the SAV, Socialist Alternative Forward (Committee for a Workers International section in Germany), "Linksruck" which was close to the IST (International Socialist Tendency) and the ISL (International Socialist Left, one of the two groups of the Fourth International in Germany). The SAV, mainly based in Berlin, strongly opposed the merger with the PDS. This was because in Berlin the WASG was founded as a left opposition to the SPD and PDS regional government which was pushing through a programme of privatisation of public services and brutal budget cuts due to the enormous debts of the Berlin city budget.

When the WASG had been established and consolidated, Oskar Lafontaine, a charismatic populist and political "truffle-pig", reappeared. He had been the former chairman of the SPD and a

---

European Volkswagen works council) were charged with corruption. Volkert not only received high amounts of money from Volkswagen, but he received money for his girlfriend, a Brazilian prostitute, and had orgies organised for him and others, in which Hartz also took part. Volkert went to jail and Hartz got a very high fine. Today "Hartz IV" is still a word everybody uses in Germany as synonym for the 350 Euro unemployment benefit.

minister of finances in the first Schroeder government. He had resigned from all his posts shortly after entering the government in 1999. In 2005, Chancellor Schroeder called for early federal elections (originally scheduled for 2006). The WASG was not prepared for such an early election, but Oskar Lafontaine offered to lead a common election slate between WASG and PDS with Gregor Gysi, the former chairman of the PDS. Legally this was not possible, so members of the WASG ran for parliament on the ticket of the PDS, which changed its name to "Linkspartei-PDS" (Left Party-PDS). Lafontaine joined the WASG in June 2005 and was put at the head of the list for the PDS in North Rhine-Westphalia. This gave another impetus to the WASG and the PDS, with many former Social Democrats joining the WASG, including a regional deputy. These elections were a success for the PDS which gained 8.7% of the votes and entered parliament with 54 deputies. Lafontaine and Gysi, along with one of the founders of the WASG, the IG-Metall (metal workers' union) full-timer Klaus Ernst, pushed for a rapid merger of the two parties.

The foundation of Die Linke

Lafontaine, Gysi and Ernst succeeded in merging the PDS and the WASG. This was despite the resistance of a few right-wingers and the SAV-dominated Berlin-branch, but also some of the radical left forces who feared that the PDS, with its membership ten times greater than the WASG and its huge financial backing (although most of the money of the former SED had been confiscated by the state after 1990), would just swallow the WASG. As a first step membership of both parties was officially allowed and the leading figures like Lafontaine and Gysi were among the first ones to do so. Already in the election campaign of summer 2005, Gysi and Lafontaine publicly claimed they did not want to miss the "historical chance" to establish a genuine left party in Germany.

In a ballot of the WASG members at the beginning of 2006, 78% of those voting agreed to further negotiations with the PDS with the goal of a new left party. A co-operation treaty was agreed by a party conference in April 2006. In March 2007, parallel conferences of WASG and PDS were held which both agreed to the merger and adopted programmatic principles. The new party gave itself the name Die Linke (The Left).

Since then, Die Linke has consolidated itself and managed not only to reach its best result ever in the last federal elections in 2009 with 11.9 %, one percent more than the Green Party, but in recent years entered most of the regional parliaments, won numerous mayors in East Germany and is part of two regional governments.

In 2010 a proposal for a political long-term programme was presented, in which the goal of a "democratic socialism" was incorporated.

Die Linke today

Its membership

The overwhelming majority of Die Linke members were also members of the former SED and subsequently the PDS. They can be divided into a smaller (but growing) layer of younger members, who are quite pragmatic and are involved in politics on the basis of moderate social democratic ideas. These are the people who dominate the daily life of the party, who sit in parliaments and councils, co-operating with the SPD on the local and regional level and who are on the whole not involved or interested in strategic debates about a vision of a post-capitalist society. This does not mean that they do a bad job under the circumstances, but these are the people who try to carry out a classic reformist strategy. This is one (but just one) of the reasons why the SPD in East Germany never really succeeded.[1]

At the same time in the western part of the country, a growing number of those joining Die Linke see it as a big chance to succeed in getting seats in parliament and whom we can characterise as pragmatic careerists.[2] Others who joined the party are also victims of the crisis such as people who have lost their jobs. The sociological composition of the membership of Die Linke in the West is therefore considerably different from that of the East.

A broader layer of quite old communists or "traditionalists" exists, but they are not very active in daily politics. Among them,

---

[1] *This is a complicated debate which cannot be dealt with here. Just a remark: one has to consider for instance, that the SED/PDS after the fall of the wall kept its influence especially in institutions like the "Volkssolidarität" ("People's Solidarity") which still exists. At the time of the GDR, this was an official organisation doing social work in the community. Today it is one of the big competitors in the market of social services against Red Cross, Church-linked organisations, etc... But they kept the links which the newly formed SPD did not have. People, especially the elderly, needed an organisation to help them through the completely new jungle of the free market economy after reunification.*

[2] *On this point, one must take into account that the number of members in the Eastern part of the country is about 60,000 and the population about 16 millions. In the West there are about 12,000 members and a population of about 65 millions. With the current rise of Die Linke, the chance of becoming an elected official or obtaining a job with an organisation is quite high. One has to consider that the overwhelming majority of votes for it are still won in East Germany: Die Linke has got 36 full time-mayors nationwide, but all of them in the East. Out of 155 part-time-mayors only three were elected in the West. Altogether Die Linke has got at the local and regional level almost 6,000 members in elected positions.*

there still remains the belief (mostly not openly expressed) that the former GDR (German Democratic Republic) was not at all bad but "mistakes" had been made. In one sense the foundation of the PDS for them was a socio-psychological measure that enabled them to keep their identity. Furthermore, the former active cadres of the SED in reality had no other choice but to keep their own party because they were not welcome in the West German parties which had opened branches in East Germany after the fall of the wall.

The organisational expression of this layer is a platform inside Die Linke, the so-called Communist Platform (KPF). One of its protagonists is the former MEP Sahra Wagenknecht, who publicly defended the former GDR. But they paradoxically also keep to their old-fashioned Stalinist understanding of "the party", i.e. they do not openly oppose the elected leadership. The former federal deputy of the PDS (from 1994 to 2002), Winfried Wolf, a former member of the Fourth International, who joined the PDS in the nineties and left it disappointed after 2002 after failing to build a left current inside the party, described this platform once as a "Sozialistische Wärmestube".[1]

Another small layer of the party is composed of the former members of the old Western-based DKP who joined Die Linke individually. They are organised in different platforms but are not to be considered as a separate current inside Die Linke.

Then there is a layer of disappointed old Social Democrats, such as the ones who founded the WASG. They argue the SPD has changed into a neo-liberal party and they claim to be the "real" Social Democrats. A leading figure of this layer is the trade unionist Klaus Ernst, one of the founders of the WASG and new co-chair of Die Linke. At the very beginning, he described the WASG as a pressure group to push the SPD back to the "right way". Klaus Ernst recently got into problems because of his life-style as he drives a Porsche and accepts a salary of 3,500 Euros from the party in addition to his salary as a deputy, while the other co-chair, Gesine Lötzsch, refuses to do so.

The numerous small groupings of the revolutionary left who "survived" the backlash of the 80s and 90s, entered the party in two "waves". A first wave entered the PDS at the beginning of the 90s and then into the WASG/Die Linke over the last six years. A big part of the post-68 left (mainly the Maoist and spontaneist groupings) had already vanished into the Green Party. The remainder, that is the Trotskyist currents such the SAV, Linksruck and the ISL, joined either

---

[1]   *Wolf argued that they used this platform only to keep their own identity cooking, but were not willing to develop a real political activity together with other left forces to change the party in the direction of real socialist policies. – KE. A Wärmestube is heated common rooms which charities in Germany provide to shelter the poor from the cold, rather like a soup-kitchen. – Eds.*

the PDS or more recently Die Linke. Some of their members managed to secure very quickly high positions: two members of the former Linksruck[1] are in the federal parliament since 2009, a member of the ISL (International Socialist Left) was until 2010 member of the national council of Die Linke Another member of the ISL is chairperson of the regional branch in North Rhine-Westphalia and since the recent elections in May 2010, leader of the parliamentary group in the regional parliament. But these are exceptions. In North Rhine-Westphalia, the leadership is radical left in its majority because these forces entered the WASG at the very beginning and built the party. But in the meantime, after the first successes in elections, a wave of new members is entering who in their majority are moderate or right-wingers. So it is to be expected that this situation will change. It should be noted that in an interview for a big German newspaper Gregor Gysi, referring to the radical forces inside Die Linke, said, "every party has got its 10% percent of crazy people".

In conclusion, the vast majority of the active members (there is a high percentage of inactive members because of the age profile) have got a more or less developed social democratic, reformist approach to politics and part of them just want to try to "administer" the system. One of the decisive points is their parliamentary orientation. Only a small layer of the radical left participates in the organisation of extra-parliamentary initiatives or even takes the initiative for such things as the Social Forums. For the majority of members, politics is what happens in meetings , although the party will from time to time call public actions such as the traditional demonstrations for the anniversary of the assassination of Rosa Luxemburg.

Youth

Die Linke has got a youth organisation (called "Solid") and a students' organisation called the SDS (reviving the name of the SDS, Socialist German Students League, a leading organisation of the 1968 movement). In the recent students' movement in Germany, which generally did not have a high political level as the demands were quite pragmatic and moderate, the SDS played an active and mobilising role. But generally the main base of the youth work is in the East.[2]

Solid was founded in 1999 and officially has got 1,800 members. The SDS, founded in 2007, does not have a strong base in

---

[1]   *The organisation "Linksruck" was dissolved officially against the advice of the SWP-leadership in Great Britain and now exists as under the label "Marx 21".*
[2]   *And this would be another interesting discussion because the willingness to organise generally seems to be higher in the East, which could be explained by the respective history - which as we know generally works on the long run....*

the East, but obtained excellent results in the elections to the student parliaments in the West. Both organisations keep a relative independence from the party, but are financed by it. The SDS for example, receives 100,000 Euros a year.

Ecology

There is an ecological platform inside the left party, which is producing a quarterly magazine called "Tarantel". Its influence in the party is low and the platform itself regrets in its publications that when in doubt, the deputies of Die Linke neglect ecological questions in favour of economic necessities. There have recently been local attempts to build up ecosocialist networks and the education institute SALZ, which is independent but sympathetic to Die Linke, organised a conference in March 2010 on Ecosocialism which had quite a good resonance. But generally the question of ecology is underestimated inside the party. In the anti-nuclear mobilisations of 2011, Die Linke played only a marginal role. In the regional elections in Baden-Württemberg in 2011 where ecological questions were a key issue, the party got only 3.9% and did not get into parliament.

International relationships

Currently Die Linke has eight deputies in the European Parliament and is a member of the European Left Parties group. The latter was created to obtain subsidies from the European Parliament and its constituent organisations are mainly Communist Parties from different European countries, although there are some exceptions such as the Left Bloc from Portugal. Since the former leading force in the European Left Parties group, Rifondazione Communista from Italy, collapsed dramatically, Die Linke has taken up that role. Die Linke still maintains links with many Communist parties across the world.

The programme of Die Linke

Until now there has been no party programme, but only programmatic guidelines. Looking at the proposal for a programme for the party, currently under discussion and comparing it with the daily politics of Die Linke, one might come to the conclusion that the SPD prior to the 1959 "Godesberg" programme has been reborn. This is because it is possible to read in it the classic social democratic minimum/maximum strategy.

The programme claims to be for democratic socialism. It describes correctly the central challenges of the present period, which is the crisis of the capitalist economy, the inequality at the national and international level, the ecological crisis and especially the question of climate change, the question of war and women's oppression. But it does not refer to the class structure of the bourgeois state, nor does it outline the way forward to a new society. The chapter about the demands is labelled "left reform projects; steps to the remodelling of society" and it speaks about " democratising society" and "social-ecological re-modelling". This chapter contains the central points and gives a very general answer: "democratic socialism". But it is classically reformist in its approach with regards to the question of class society and its description of a step-by-step transition to socialism. This is roughly what the SPD supported until 1959, with the difference that the SPD considered itself at that time a workers' party while Die Linke does not.

One has to compare this kind of programme with the politics that the party actually carries out. Die Linke clearly prioritises parliamentary work and has kept some of the bourgeois parliamentary rules of the former PDS. For example, when in 2002 the US president George Bush spoke in the German Parliament, two deputies of the PDS protested publicly during his speech. After this protest, the speaker of the PDS group in parliament delivered an official apology!

In the two regional parliaments in which Die Linke is part of the government, Berlin and Brandenburg, there is little difference between its politics and that of the bourgeois parties. Die Linke generally argues for a neo-Keynesian economic policy, but extra-parliamentary actions and mobilisations, as proposed by the radical left, are not accepted by a large majority of the party and especially its leading figures.

At the moment, the proposals for the new party programme are heavily criticized by the left wing.

Some analytical remarks

As we can see, the rise of Die Linke is a product of several factors. Some of them are more general and led to comparable changes in the landscape of political parties in some other European countries. Others are more or less specific to the German situation.

The first factor, which has to be considered as a general one, is the continuous change of classical social democracy. This is a phenomenon that we can observe in several western European countries. Due to the ongoing capitalist crisis, these parties adopted more or less neo-liberal policies, reduced social services, privatised public services and have agreed to treaties that are clearly imposing the free market economy as the only basis for the European Union. This has led to a growing distance between the trade union movement and their traditional partner, the Social Democrats, such as in the case of the Labour Party in Britain. The fact that the initiative for the foundation of the WASG was taken by a layer in the trade unions, illustrates this ongoing dissolution of the links between the latter and social democracy in Germany.

The second general factor is the dissolution of the Eastern European Bloc. The former ruling Communist Parties in Eastern Europe had to adapt to the new situation. In some countries they took up the role of the Social Democratic parties where these did not exist and renamed or relaunched themselves under a different label. In Germany this was the case with the SED that renamed itself PDS and used its remaining organisational strength and roots in society to refound itself as a reformist party.

The third general factor is the impact of the crisis of the capitalist economy. It is producing a growing layer of casualised and unemployed workers who are confronted with the anti-social policies of the ruling parties, including social democracy, are looking for alternatives and mobilising to a certain extent. In Germany the demonstrations against the so-called Agenda 2010 were one of the catalysts for the creation of the WASG.

The fourth general factor that we can identify is the opposition against the different wars which the ruling class is fighting in Afghanistan, Iraq and elsewhere. In Germany, the Green Party lost its former position as the party of the peace movement by agreeing that Germany could take part in the wars in Serbia and Afghanistan while it was in the government coalition with the SPD between 1998 and 2005.

But there are also some German peculiarities.

The first one is the fact that Die Linke is neither a formation that is just a former Communist Party with a reformist turn, like the MSZP (Hungarian Socialist Party) in Hungary nor a completely new formation, like the Left Bloc in Portugal. It is a mixture of both. This is a result of the exceptional situation caused by the unification of the two German States which produced both a former Communist Party that changed its character in the former German Democratic Republic and an alternative party to the SPD in the former Federal Republic of Germany.

The second peculiarity is the fact that the rise of Die Linke is neither the result of a broad social movement to the left, nor of a radical mass movement, but of the movement of traditional social democracy to the right. So Die Linke fills the space that the SPD had opened by adopting neo-liberal policies.

And finally, you have to take in account the extremely low level of class struggle in Germany in the last decades. The "Monday demonstrations" mentioned earlier were an exception in this period and were not, as some people had hoped, the beginning of a rapidly growing self-organised mass movement.[1]

The politics of the revolutionary left

The breathtaking rise of Die Linke in Germany generated big hopes in the radical left all over Europe. But in analysing the situation, we have to say that this party is not a new, broad, radical anticapitalist party like the NPA in France. It is also not comparable with parties like the Left Bloc in Portugal or the Red-Green Alliance in Denmark. Because of the specific situation in Germany after the reunification, it represents a completely different socio-political formation. A possible comparison to other similar parties in Europe would be to a certain extent Rifondazione in Italy. Rifondazione also emerged as a result of the breakdown of the traditional Communist Party, incorporating a part of the revolutionary left and then changing rapidly into a Social Democratic parliamentary type of organisation. The forces that adhered to anticapitalist politics in Rifondazione were marginalized or resigned from the party.

In the German revolutionary left, nobody has big illusions about the character of Die Linke as a social democratic formation. The question is whether it is useful to work in it, or whether it as an obstacle for building up a real, radical left alternative. The major part of the radical left took the first option that is in the long run such an alternative has to be built, because Die Linke itself is not this alternative and will not change into it. This is more or less a common view among the revolutionaries. But the fact is that at the moment most people, especially the youth who are radicalising, are attracted by Die Linke. So if you want to have an influence on the formation of this new generation of activists, you have to be with them and that means taking part in Die Linke.

In brief, Die Linke represents the stage of consciousness that the advanced forces of the working class have reached. It is a giant task for the revolutionaries inside Die Linke to build a credible common current to prepare for the struggles inside the party. These will certainly emerge after the next elections when the question of forming a government at the federal level is posed.

The problem is that until now such a common strategy of the radical left forces inside Die Linke did not exist nor did it seem likely to. Some, like the CWI current, are quite sectarian and just use the

---

[1]   *The WASG in one sense channelled this movement and its parliamentary orientation was the mirror image of that of the German population itself.*

party for building their own group. Others adapt to the mainstream and are affiliated to different platforms inside the party.

It is an urgent necessity for the radical left not only to develop a common strategy for working inside the party, to gather the radical forces and to attract new young activists, but also to develop a consistent exit strategy in the (likely) case of participation in government. But unfortunately such a step forward seems unlikely to be taken at the moment. This could change when the general ecological, economic and political situation worsens, as it is expected to do in the coming years.

It should at least be mentioned that with the rise of Die Linke, the SPD has lost dramatically its share of the vote in elections and seems to be trying to change course. A merger between Die Linke and the SPD in the future may be possible and there are leading figures in both parties who take this possibility into account.[1] It is therefore even more necessary for the revolutionaries to prepare for different possible scenarios.

Conclusion

Die Linke is on the one hand the result of the fall of the Iron Curtain, as it represents the remaining forces of the former East German ruling party, the SED and on the other hand the result of the shift to neo-liberal positions of the German Social Democrats. It fills the space left by the SPD.

Die Linke is therefore the (logical) historical reflex to these changes and expresses the stage of consciousness of a certain layer of the German working class.

Die Linke in its broad majority is not an anticapitalist, but a social democratic party, integrating a traditional communist and a radical left wing. The first does not influence the politics of the party to any great extent, while the latter remains splintered and at the

---

[1]   *An interview with Gregor Gysi before the 2009 elections already pointed in this direction:*

"Question: Social justice, equal chances: all that the SPD is demanding as well, but in spite of that, it is losing voters who vote instead for Die Linke?

Gysi: So what? I tell you, what must happen. The SPD needs a defeat, that there takes place an internal rebellion and the party will re-social-democratise internally. This is their chance and this is also the chance for a co-operation with us. To reach that, this may sound arrogant, the SPD has to move a lot towards us, but we have to move only a bit towards them."

The former chairman of Die Linke and deputy in the European parliament, Lothar Bisky, argued in December 2009, that a merger with the SPD could be possible in "the next generation". A similar opinion was expressed by Wolfgang Thierse, SPD Vice-President of Parliament, who argued, that "in the long run" a fusion between SPD and Die Linke might be possible.

moment seems unable to develop a consistent strategy to confront the ongoing integration of the party into the "normal" bourgeois political process.

What is necessary is a debate and co-operation between the forces of the revolutionary left inside and outside Die Linke, to organise the struggle for a radical, anticapitalist course of the party on one hand and to develop an exit strategy on the other.

2 December 2010

Italy: A Failed Refoundation

Notes for a History of the Communist Refoundation Party (PRC, Partito di Rifondazione Communista)[1]

Salvatore Cannavo[2]

What have we done to deserve all this?

2008 was the year when the Italian left disappeared from parliament. It has been reduced to an historic minimum of scattered, smashed and divided remains. This book aims to answer the question: "How could this have happened?" What did we do to try and avoid it? What have we done to keep an alternative project alive? Finally what can we do now to recover from the defeat? We have to understand that the recovery will be a long-term one without shortcuts or 'clever', immediate solutions. Furthermore it is precisely the big bang strategy (looking for new openings at all costs), that has created further weakening, leading us to the current dead end.

This writer has been a protagonist of sorts in these events. I want to state this now, not because I want to glorify a role that at the end of the day was quite modest, but rather to inform readers that this is a personal account written by somebody who has a specific point of view. Nevertheless it can be useful to have a story told by someone who has had direct experience of these key political events.

Return to the Bolognina Conference

It was already clear that a political cycle had ended during the Prodi government, when the attempted political project of the so-called radical left oscillated between ridicule and incompetence, resulting in

---

[1]   This text is the first and final chapters of the book "La Rifondazione Mancata" [The Failed Refoundation], published by Edizioni Alegre in 2009. Translated by Carmela Avella and Dave Kellaway.

[2]   Salvatore Cannavo is a journalist by profession and was assistant editor of Liberazione, the daily newspaper of Rifondazione Communista. From 2006 to 2008 he was a member of parliament, first for the PRC and then represented Sinistra Critica of which he was founding member. He is an executive of the Edizione Alegre publishing house and contributes to the Fatto Quotidiano and other publications. He is also the author of "Porto Alegre – Capitale dei Movimenti" [Porto Alegre – Capital of the Movements] (Manifestolibri, 2002).

a series of failures. The political cycle had begun at the end of the 1980s with the fall of the Berlin Wall and the so-called Bolognina Communist Party conference led by Achille Ochetto, which led to the formation of the Democratic Socialist Party (PDS) and the Communist Refoundation Party (PRC). This new phase, which spanned the 1990s, nearly came to a complete halt in 1998 with the fall of the first Prodi government. It continued however into the first years of the new century, riding the rising and falling tide of the Anti-Globalisation movement and then ended in the formation of the Union of the Left which led to the formation of the second Prodi government. The establishment of the Democratic Party (PD) and the failure of the radical left, not only the PRC but also its split-off group the PDCI (Democratic Party of Italian Communists) and the Greens, marks the end of this political cycle. The leaders of the left have not wanted to come to terms with this political journey and have continued on their way as if the objective, subjective, social and political contexts have remained unchanged. It is as if they thought their political support, built up over the years through their electoral success and from the internal dialectic of the centre left, could not be undermined.

As we will see there were many errors and a blindness to reality. There were obvious analytical failures such as the superficial way in which they evaluated the potential impact of Berlusconi who, in 2006 after five years of real political and social disaster, only lost the general election by twenty-four thousand votes. All opinion polls had predicted a clear win for the centre left parties. Social reality and the relationship of class forces were analysed in a very shallow way. They jumped to the conclusion that a series of successful demonstrations and a general mass mobilisation between 2001 and 2003 in Italy would hold back the country's deep-rooted drift to the right. There were also errors of leadership and organisation, utter incompetence, crude judgements, overbearing arrogance and ignorance. In turn this is related to the actual people involved, to a particular type of person selected over the years for their loyalty and not for their intellectual quality. What did this look like? Bureaucratic methods driven by base ambition; an inclination to compromise and to adapt to the world as it is, justifying 'theoretically' their own personal comfort zone; and small- scale personal enrichment isolated from any concrete political analysis.

Herein lays the roots of such an obvious failure, of a personal defeat and a political disaster affecting millions of people and involving tens of thousands of militants, members and leaders of the shipwrecked parties. We never envisaged this evolution of the left and we still scarcely comprehend it now, a left divided between a poor, opportunist and compromising leadership and a naive, sentimentally generous and therefore easily manipulated base. Since the electoral disaster of 13th/14th April 2008, Fausto Bertinotti has become the main person held responsible for the disaster. For twelve long years he had been the most admired leader of communist supporters. He lost the vote at the July 2008 PRC congress but he was acclaimed triumphantly, reflecting a schizophrenia which maybe needs analysing on a psychoanalytic level. So no-one is free of guilt or responsibility. The last political turn of the PRC, the one in 2005 at the Venice congress, carried through by thousands of members and leaders, brutally imposed a political line against the internal opposition. They were indifferent to the hurt inflicted and the irreversible blows made against nearly half the party.

But these errors are not just related to the Prodi government period, to the suicidal choice of governing the eighth strongest capitalist power while defending the idea of going beyond capitalism and the cloud cuckoo hypothesis of making a turn to the left in government with people like Dini, Mastella or Padoa Schioppa (bourgeois centrist politicians/bankers/ex DCI). Although we are talking about the end of a political period, the errors were made throughout the period and are emblematic of its contradictions, its painful conflicts that just grew and grew without being seriously dealt with and were therefore never resolved. It is a question of cultural vices, a limited political strategy and the illusion of a 'refoundation' that would supposedly mature and grow on the basis of a hypothesis validated by self-proclamation rather than concrete results. We needed a real life advance of the party within the social struggles and its affirmation as a tenacious political subject able to resist and struggle in the longer term. What we got was a slow negation of its original positive purpose and usefulness expressed in the founding congress.

In Bertinotti's PRC a 'great illusion' was built on an immense speculative/political bubble that, like the sub-prime mortgages, self-inflated. It was like a shimmering mirage, a fantasy constructed by putting opposites together and twisting concepts according to the event and the occasion. The illusion amounted to the idea that you could defeat a Stalinism stuck in a nostalgic past without settling accounts with the 'human material' who followed turn and counter-turn without any real conviction. It was claimed the government question was resolved when half the party wanted to stay in government. Later the leadership had to bring them back again when this time they did not want to go. There was an Enlightenment, even Jacobin, leadership style, leading the membership from on high through sheer charisma and unscrupulous political manoeuvres.

However, PRC members were resilient and were ready for the long haul, but from split to split they had never really come to terms with their sense of loss, repressing the shock of 1989 (the fall of Berlin Wall). In the PRC we kept moving all the time, from emergency to emergency, from election to election and from turn to turn without ever really stopping to look at who we really were, where we came from, what we had been and what we wanted to become. A pick and mix politics, a bit like Milan in the 80s under Craxi.

In many ways, even given the variety of rich personal histories and the motivation of militants, this unforeseen collapse of Refoundation and the radical left is very much the dissolution of that experience. No other party in Italy has gone so quickly from the heights to the depths, no leadership group has fallen so quickly. This even includes the PSI (Italian Socialist Party) which was the first to make tactics and manoeuvring the keystone of its politics. Over and beyond the obvious real differences, both political projects had to come to terms with a political system dominated by two big blocs. For Craxi it was the DC (Christian Democrats) and the PCI (Italian Communist Party). For Refoundation it was the Polo (Berlusconi/Fini/Bossi) and the Ulivo (Olive Tree, social democratic alliance between ex-PCI, Democratic Socialists and other left centre forces). It is as if both projects had to carefully watch over a fragile porcelain dish in a china shop selling tin plates. Such a situation was used to justify, once again leaving aside the different political content of the two projects, a bold, volatile political line. Bertinotti was in charge of Refoundation in a period of Italian bi-partisanship where the strength of the two ex-mass parties had been artificially pumped up by an electoral law that had achieved a false two party system. It constrained the PRC to come to a deal with the obligatory ally, the centre left, whether in the form of the Olive Tree bloc or the Democratic Party. However this was uncomfortable and unwieldy. Above all from the point of view of its own history and its "raison d'être" it was unnatural. From this flowed the need for rapid, but disorientating changes in its political 'tactical' line, which were both artful and ill-judged: first going into alliance with Prodi and then breaking with him; the turn to the movements and then to government; anti-Stalinism and then non-violence. It was a patchwork of attempts to bring the party away from its minority position and from the orbit of the majority factions of the PCI which had set up first the DS and then the PD. Just as Craxi needed to go beyond the 10% of the De Martino PSI to at least 16 to 18% (which it never achieved), so the PRC needed to go from its historical scores of 5-6% to double-figure results. This also explains the confused, muddled Rainbow Coalition project, the electoral slate on which the whole government Left stood in the 2008 parliamentary elections. It was a way of trying to operate in the context of the imperfect two-party system which Berlusconi and the PD had opted for; , of gaining a breathing space to limit the damage and trying to get a winning strategy. Deemed a vital necessity in fact it led to too much haste and improvisation, to 'acrobatic' politics driven at a speed never seen before.

We could perhaps end the analogy here, having emphasised that you cannot assimilate two such different political processes. Nonetheless there is something else that connects the two across time. It is the fact that the Socialist Party had helped initiate the process of decomposition of the Italian workers movement and that Communist Refoundation tried to get a grasp of that degenerative process at the end but let slip it through its fingers. Craxi and the PSI intervened quickly and greedily in a context in which defeats that had been accumulating since the 70s, from the historic compromise to the out and out betrayal of the 35-day FIAT struggle, changed the workers movement. It produced a backwards ideological step in terms of the Marxist definition of a 'class for itself' and an embarrassing turn to support the savage liberalism emerging under the banner of the Thatcher-Reagan duo. In the 1980s we saw economic/industrial restructuring and a reduction in the labour force concentrated in the big factories. We had a move away from the centres of class power which meant above all more division and a weakened identity leading in turn to weaker organisation. Temporary and flexible working became more prevalent. The PSI was implementing its strategy when the weakening of the organised working class permitted its leaders to effectively develop a line we could summarise as 'sort you out'. A line particularly aimed at the younger generations dealing with the difficulties of universities and a rapidly changing workplace. Organisational and structural weakening and the overall ideological crisis allowed Craxi to ride the back of these forces, intervening negatively in its objective transformation. Craxi took advantage of and further nourished the disaggregation of, the Italian workers movement to further his political project (which ultimately failed).

These crises then led, in a much more serious and devastating way, to the crisis and the name change of the PCI. Ten years later the latter *de facto* followed in the footsteps of the PSI and threw itself into its own genetic mutation. The leadership group did this in a style and arrogance of people who had learnt their politics in the 'bread and Togliatti' period of the party. They did it with the requisite ritual, with tears shed from the stage and internecine conflicts. They did it for the good of the country and the party, they did it for democracy and they did it better than anyone else could have done. But they did it. Exactly in the same way, without the ritual and the 1989 pantomime, as Craxi had done more prosaically and pragmatically at the end of the 1970s with the famous Midas congress, or yet again in 1990 when they changed the name of the PSI to Unita Socialista (Socialist Unity) in the course of a secretariat meeting.

The PSI was the harbinger of the land-slip which became an avalanche in the 1990s and the first decade of the third millennium. The 'working class' continues to go backwards, to become more divided, to lose its way ideologically, to lose a sense of its own identity and mission. The end of ideology defines the space of class struggle, although for its part the bourgeoisie wages class war and continues to act in its own interests through restructuring, redundancies, pension reform, new labour laws and the ever more prevalent job insecurity. Through the 1990s the working class as a social subject, a reference point, became unrecognisable, lost, unreachable...

Communist Refoundation was forced to suffer this process of decomposition while remaining for many of these sectors the last charge, the final ship, even if a little leaky, in a sea infested by sharks and pirates as well as enemy ships. However, and here we return to our analogy, the PRC did not know how to deal with this difficulty and did not even put it on the agenda. It preferred to live on its electoral, institutional and party apparatus gains that the communist symbol allowed it to maintain. A layer of bureaucrats, elected representatives and other officials did not have their attention on that social disaster but rather on the political framework where they were trying to survive. Whereas the PSI had contributed to the demolition of the workers movement while working without any links with it, Refoundation shook up the ruins or rather began to 'surf' on them. It opted for the big manoeuvre rather than dedicating itself to the 'slow impatience' necessary for a real reconstruction. Over-tactical and eclectic choices were made in an attempt to survive the crises that its own past had presented it with. Above all it unproductively consumed its own patrimony rather than re-investing its resources in social struggles in order to develop a new force. The proof of its failure was, the progressive weakening of its social base; the constant loss of its links with society as a whole; its creeping marginalisation inside all the trade unions; the drying up of its own local groups and its own political vitality and a massive turnover that saw hundreds of thousands of men and women join Refoundation to then leave quickly afterwards. Gradually, and we saw this more clearly as the years passed and internal contradictions and antagonism exploded, Refoundation began to lose a sense of its *raison d'être* and the challenge it had posed, of refoundation. So it became the tired appendix of a story reaching its conclusion, the 'glorious' history of the Italian Communist Party which had left the scene, leaving behind an American style party and a few piles of rubble.

Nevertheless a political subject that fails to connect with its own roots can sail on in politics for many years and can even have partial successes, but in the end it will fold up at an unexpected and improvised speed. It could disappear from one day to the next and just leave a vague memory of itself.

A 'surfing' political line

A surfing political line can be identified in the permanent conflict characterising Refoundation's leadership. The first secretary, Sergio Garavini, resigned at Refoundation's first national congress following explosive differences with Armando Cossutta and a second congress was needed after about a month to defuse the conflict. After Bertinotti's triumphant election as secretary it took only ten months for the next showdown with the group led by Magri and Crucianelli which produced a significant split at the parliamentary level. Three years later we saw the most important split headed by Cossutta which however was preceded a year before by a tough stand-off between the two leaders during the first crisis of the Prodi government. Once Cossutta had left, the birth of the anti-globalisation movement provoked a sort of internal war between the ex-Cossutta people remaining in the PRC and Bertinotti's majority. Then we had the roller-coaster of the Venice Congress in 2005. The party was undergoing constant erosion, a rumbling earthquake, and it never managed to find a stable equilibrium, an action plan that lasted any length of time without it being blown off course by the tremors produced by the Italian political crisis. The crisis generated by the collapse of the Christian Democrats (DC) and the Italian Socialist Party (PSI), and the Italian Communist Party's change of name, tore into and overwhelmed Communist Refoundation (PRC) with such effect because of its political, programmatic and organisational weakness.

The electoral results, the effective communication skills of its leader and the need that the centre left had for the PRC which inflated its marginal value, led to the head of the party being put on a pedestal to the detriment of its arms and legs. True, from 1991 on the PRC had always been able to claim an average of one hundred thousand members with a high point of 150,000 in the first phase declining to 110,000 in 1998 and then falling below 100,000 after the Cossutta split. However it never stopped to reflect on the scale of an estimated turnover of more than 20% of its membership. This critical mass had not found the tools or structures to act effectively, to participate with conviction and to develop a homogenous politics. Those young people who came in with the anti-globalisation movement after only a few years underwent a process of passivity and of accepting that other people would make the decisions. They had no relevant role in the leadership structures and were not brought on.

Internal party procedures, putting forward political positions and the organisation of the PRC's intervention were largely given over to the leadership group and the central apparatus. In the beginning there was a real impetus of renovation and democratisation requested and imposed by the base. In fact at the first three congresses the federal and national political structures were elected in such a way as to respect the positions expressed in each area. The first national secretariat, called the national operational group (Gruppo Operative Nazionale) was elected member by member and not just as part of a slate. Each elected member of the group had to get more than 50 % of the votes. This rule produced some upsets as we will see. It so happened that I represented a minority position at the 1996 congress, but I was nevertheless elected to the Federal Political Committee of my city (Milan) which contrasted with the positions of the city leadership.

Little by little decision-making became delegated upwards, the national and local leaders took on the preponderant role and were often at the same time the institutional representatives of the party. The centre of power was solidly anchored at the Via Polichinico (party headquarters) apart from partial contradictions and counter-tendencies. The terrible thing was that the central apparatus knew little or nothing about how to lead a mass political intervention. Not just because of particular individuals but because in that sharp crisis of the workers movement the type of intervention you needed was above all one based on reflection, collective energy, elaborated together and tried out and tested in practice. The centre of gravity of this sort of intervention had to be not within the institutions but rather within a perspective of completely re-making our society. Such a perspective might not give immediate results but could achieve them in the medium term. Indeed hard work was needed and often it was not even considered. Things could not be limited to the electoral arena. On the other hand another phenomenon in the PRC was individuals' expectations of a career, seeing a party position as a stepping stone to a political representative role in the institutions and thereby gaining a salary, a personal income that may then be lost if you did not buckle down and conform. It is a perfectly understandable motivation but nothing was done to develop counter-measures that might hold back that tendency. It took time for this model to become the dominant one, and the period opened by the final turn to government helped institutionalise it. Also the reaction to this led to a slow withering away of militancy so that most activists who were left were to be found in the most traditionalist sectors, one thinks of the few, courageous sellers of *Liberazione* (the party newspaper).

Therefore we have a fundamental problem of political culture and strategy. Notwithstanding the contortions, the turns, the confrontations, the hoped-for renewals, the repeated calls for overcoming obstacles through sheer will, Refoundation essentially remained a neo-Togliattian type party. It was an historical offshoot of the PCI that had brought together and absorbed an attempt to build a new beginning. A grouping where the aspiration for the social compromise, in this sense in the 'Togliatti' line, had prevailed over those elements of liberation, of revolutionary radicalism that were indeed present even if this was often only in a virtual sense. However this aspiration was in *de facto* contradiction with the original formation of the group, when people spoke of a semantic break with historical continuity, and when in order to take off it enumerated a vast series of discontinuities with the past. Instead the PRC never succeeded in really going from the phase of simple 'resistance' to that of 'reconstruction' of a force capable of putting social transformation on the agenda again. In this way it went through continual sharp turns, apologetic changes of line, over-tactical manoeuvres and theoretical infatuations that lasted just for a short period. The party rank and file was tossed around, not really grasping what was going on and often incapable of developing a counter-tendency. Discontinuity with the past required critical and innovative thought but throughout its life the PRC never held a programmatic conference, it preferred simple presentations of its electoral programme. It needed to really shake up its own history to find an adequate identity, but when the taboo is finally broached, 'communism against Stalinism', it was immediately used to justify joining the government of the country. That is how the contrary effect was achieved, the communist identity had remained only glue that held things together. It was not defined in the modern context or illustrated within present reality so as to recuperate its internal rationality, including the lessons of defeats. Furthermore it was not even identified with a steadfast opposition to and distinctiveness from the two main political blocs. Consequently this identity became an empty shell.

The crisis of Refoundation, the latest events, the latest splits and the departure of its most important leader in all these years, can justly be defined as being the last act of this drama and process that began with the Occhetto turn of 1989. It was then that the definitive approach and symbolic commitment of the PCI to the Italian political system, its approval of the basic framework and the cancelling of its 'diversity', was decided. The journey to this end had started many decades earlier. It was characterised by so many 'compromises': Togliatti's in 1945, Berlinguer's 'historical' one in 1973, and the physiological one made by Occhetto and his successors in the 1990s. The political heart of Bertinotti's thinking can be found in the substantial degree of 'compromise', albeit more dynamic, within the agile logic of the ex-secretary of Refoundation. For many, many years the PRC tried to shield itself from the wind of political consensus blowing on its back. It tried everything, turning this way and that to find an escape from the flow of defeats and recriminations that the disappearance of the biggest European communist party had bequeathed it. In all this it kept its own vitality and truth. It looked down different paths but did not really go down them. The PRC had started speaking languages foreign to its tradition, Zapatismo, anti-globalisation radicalisation, ecology; and had even started to examine the critical, heretical consciousness of communist history, but in the end it was sucked back into the fundamental framework of its own political tradition. The taste of government was to be fatal.

These limits can also be seen in the absence of any real cultural debates. Intellectuals voted for Refoundation, they loved and supported it. There were always prestigious lists of supporters at elections and many *ad hoc* conferences were held. However over more than fifteen years Refoundation was not able to produce a theoretical or cultural review or magazine, it never had a serious publishing company, it never managed to set up a scientific committee and did not organise anything more than occasional, conjunctural debates. Evidence of a cultural desert was constantly disguised by the gifts of a party secretary who on the contrary was rather prolific in his published writings, although this was always in the form of interviews and never as a sustained, theoretical piece of work.

Was something else possible? Could another direction have been taken? Given the decomposition of the working class as a political or social subject in the course of the last twenty or thirty years you might well answer 'no'. It will be important with an historian's methods and a more detached perspective in the future to understand really how far, given the communist history of our country, it could have made that break, a logical rupture with its own past and with its own identity. In other words how much of both the orthodox and heterodox Italian communist traditions could be led to a 'new beginning'? In his last book Fausto Bertinotti– and we will come back to this in the final chapter, links the impossibility of this process to the defeat suffered in Prague in 1968 and to the incapacity of the then communist movement and the new mass movement to move beyond Stalinism from the left (even if some people at the time, to general derision, had in fact tried to do so). As we will try to argue in the following pages we, on the other hand, believe it was possible to keep alive the refoundation line. Once a critical mass had been won to this idea it would have been possible to develop a project able to establish a critical Marxism and intervene effectively in the new class struggle. Today we see theses and essays which radically contradict this possibility and map out a way forward that not only proposes the abandonment of communist refoundation but even eliminates the very idea of a left. It is maybe a suggestive idea on the polemical level but it is abstract and not very interesting in terms of a political hypothesis.

As for myself I have both loved and hated Refoundation. I am talking about the Refoundation party I lived from 1991 to 2007 when I left. I loved its potential, the glimpse of the future it represented and its capacity of resistance. Its existence was a platform for a constant criticism of 'existing reality'. I hated its continuity, its hierarchy, the rituals, the bureaucracy, and the verbal violence used on itself and its members and its notion of leadership. In writing this book I am not wearing an historian's hat, someone professionally trained. For me that would be both impossible and improbable. But I do wear the hat of a politician with a journalistic background and passion. I will be going through nearly twenty years in order to contextualise in time and space a history that even today is my longest single political experience. I am part of the in-between generation that came both too late and too early. I was too late to live the revolt of the 1970s and the protagonist role of that generation in the decade's social and civic struggles. I was too early to experience as a young person the exhilaration of the upturn in conflict and hope that involved a lot of people between 1999 and 2004. "Our time has passed and we weren't there" was the ironic remark made to me by an ex-colleague and comrade of *Liberazione* (the PRC's daily newspaper); A bitter statement that helps to understand my relationship with this party. Refoundation provided a real, concrete opportunity to give meaning and force to a subjective possibility; , to create a bridge between the past and the future. It partially did this, it organised a political, emotional and activist link between the political generation destined to live in the 21st Century and the one that grew up in the 20th Century. For somebody who was 13 in 1977 and was 40 at Genoa in 2001 Refoundation represented the space in which a willingness to rebel was played out. But the opportunity was lost and today we are in a full-scale crisis of the class struggle left, we have to work out ideas and ways forward to get back up the slope.

Perhaps today we don't need any more bridges unless we are talking on the cultural or ideal level. The way forward out of the long wave of the 20th century and the history of the failures of its left will take place exclusively in a wide open sea and will have to go beyond the intellectual and activist efforts that have gone before. We are not talking about the positive advantages of wiping the slate clean but rather the need to settle accounts, quite sharply, with the devastation caused by the bridges we have burnt behind us. We will need both time and a new language; nonetheless we still believe in maintaining some 'tender' relations with the past and its memories, if for nothing else but to take up what Benjamin called the need for a 'vengeful history'. An avenger for those who came before us, fought a battle and lost. Of those who have waited patiently so that, with the spotlight of the present, may be revived the images of a past that needs to be remembered.

....

Yes We Could

In the introduction, and we hope in the chronicle of these sixteen years, we have tried to outline our thesis, which is obviously partial but rooted in the direct and indirect observation of reality.[1] Refoundation failed because despite its best efforts the PRC had been tossed about in the tumultuous wake left by the dissolution of the PCI. When it tried to disentangle itself from that past in reality it only made a first step, hinting at an alternative but not being able to grasp it. Refoundation has the merit of giving birth to a resistance to the dominant ways of thinking, against the spirit of the time. Saying no to the turn of the Bolognina conference, to the dissolution of the PCI and the formation of the PDS was a moral and political subversion of the dominant political consensus that lasted some time as a political platform based on only two letters. Resistance has been a dominant feature of the PRC because the attempt to throw out the baby with the bath-water continued during the ideological offensive against the 'communists' and the domination of an insufferable and normalising two party system. Refoundation opposed, resisted and reacted for a long time against this constant pressure. But in the long term the pressure won out forcing this distinctive, aberrant party to conform to a political system in crisis. Resistance was broken up and swept away. Uniformity took over and was disastrous. In this way the cycle was

---

[1] *The second selection is the closing chapter of the book "La Rifondazione Mancata".*

over, the Bolognina turn has been symbolically recuperated with the move into the second Prodi government and then again with the hypothesis of the 'going beyond of communism' and its 'unspeakability' towards a new, democratic and generically alternative left. Above all it had been compensated for the failure of its refoundation hypothesis, for the vacuity of a political alternative and a coherent political line which in over fifteen years had never emerged nor been systematically explained.

In his book, 'We must be glad that the road will be long' [*Devi augurati che la strada sia lunga]* (Ponte alle Grazie, 2009) Fausto Bertinotti admits it is a defeat arising from the long period of crisis of the workers movement within which Refoundation has been smashed. According to Bertinotti the first defeat was in 1968 when Prague was left isolated:

"...with our attempt to keep left, to bring about a refoundation, we prolonged an experience we had inherited from the 20th century beyond the time it was historically justified within the communist and the anticapitalist left parties. We had extended an historical phase that had actually ended...the real potential for reform in the 20th century ended with the Prague Spring... From that time in Europe we saw the beginning of the crisis of a left which did not know how to take the dramatic opportunity to reposition itself by proposing a left wing exit from Stalinism. Prague was left alone not only by the PCI but also by the '68 movements... At that time they were looking too much to the east to Mao's China and did not recognise the Prague youth as brothers in liberty... The fall of the Berlin Wall was only the expression, the epiphany of something that had already been foreshadowed with the Prague Spring. It was the conclusion of a cycle."

Bertinotti maintains that '68 marked the end of the potential reform of communism, "the communist movement was finished as a fusion between class struggle and Marxist Leninist theory". Consequently was Refoundation a big illusion, ask Ritanna Armeni and Rina Galgiardi, co-authors of the book? "No," replies Bertinotti, "but today I realise how bold and acrobatic this operation was, how we had contributed to prolonging the dramatic problems facing us at the end of the last century beyond their natural, historically defined life... As a party we did not feel we could take the extreme step that would have brought the organisation to a politics totally beyond the communist tradition, something that would have allowed us to overcome the impasse we found ourselves in."

Bertinotti's epitaph contains some truth. It's true the "communist question" had links with the way Prague was abandoned by the communist left and by the new political groupings born out of

'68 who were on the march towards the glorious Chinese Cultural Revolution. This infatuation has still not led to any posthumous criticism because many of those leaders are sitting pretty in the heights of the establishment. In any case the invasion of Hungary by the Soviets and the repression of a mainly working class revolt already represented a missed opportunity. Even after Prague there was the Solidarność experience in Poland on the back of which Berlinguer launched his 'break' obviously not to refound but to declare the 'forward movement of the October revolution to be ended'. So it is true that the 1970s and 1980s saw a slow death to the crisis of communism and a related gradual resignation to its defeat. 1989 took everyone by surprise but it was only the epiphany of a process that had already begun. It is also true that this resigned adjustment had a negative effect on a political world made up of hundreds of thousands of activists, many of whom in the new left and the varied movements were expecting a sign of vitality, a shock and a response. Instead within the decay of a communism that was not renewing or reforming itself there was a growing erosion of ideas, language and willingness to change the world which put into jeopardy any sort of future hypothesis of refoundation. Ochetto and his leadership group must have been thinking of this when they decided it was better to cut off the links with its own past and its own identity by going 'beyond it all'.

However the holding firm of a third of the PCI and the willingness to look at the issues of refoundation was a defensive base from which to begin a new departure. The birth of the PRC was in itself an exit on the left and was an attempt to solve the problem. Choosing the word refoundation as the expression of this project meant that there was a possibility of thinking beyond an impossible reform of past history and not throwing away the still live potential of a Marxist conception of the world. Clearly at the moment of its formation within the PRC there were conflicting but collaborating forces some of whom wanted to revive its history and others which wanted to completely re-examine it; the latter were smaller and weaker. Also the comrades from Democrazia Proletaria, who came in after its congress of dissolution, did not perform very well. Instead of trying to develop an alternative political project they delivered themselves, hands tied, to the different leadership groups coming from the PCI, some with Garavini, some with Cossutta. Nevertheless the new political reality following the birth of the PRC was the start of a process whose single, positive trajectory involved putting the communist past up for discussion.

Original virtue

To use a current definition, the PCI had become a party of a social democratic type; in the 1980s even the stones in the road knew this. In reality the PCI has been an anomaly and its very moderate reformism has developed in a different framework from the history of European social democracy. In this way the party could have chosen, and this was the fundamental line of the leaders of the 'No' faction from Ingrao, Tortorella, Cossutta to Magri, a solution to the crisis that 'democratised' the communist identity within the framework of an unreconstructed Togliatti-style reformism: this was the fundamental line of the leaders of the 'No' faction from Ingrao, Tortorella, Cossutta to Magri. In other words the PCI could have continued to function as a reformist communist party fully integrated into the Italian political framework. It is not by chance that after the formation of the PDS there was a minority tendency led by Tortorella and Ingrao called 'democratic communists'.

When a movement of resistance to Occhetto's turn emerged and was pushing towards a split and the formation of a new party, and then when attempts to keep alive an umbilical cord to the PCI through the 'federalist pact' proposed by Cossutta were foiled, this was the time when the new entity had to emphasise even more its alternative role if it wanted to really thrive. Therefore it could not water down its own identity in a 'new form of reformism' similar to the one it had just split from. This was shown for example in the reaction Refoundation had to Cossutta's split which was clearly confronted only thanks to the rediscovery of conflict and the social movements, of the word revolution and the hypothesis of 'communism against Stalinism' contained in the 2002 Congress texts. We can also see this in the effectiveness and dynamism shown in Bertinotti's theory of the 'two lefts' which Cossutta unsurprisingly opposed silently right from the start. This point is further demonstrated in the way that Refoundation always reacted decisively and positively to significant rightist split-offs, for example the '95 split by the ex-PDUP and Cossutta's '98 one; whereas it retreated into its shell after the two small splits to the left, Ferrando's PCL split in 2006 and Sinistra Critica in 2007. This was not due to the effectiveness of these two small political groups but for the obvious perversion of its true nature and relationship to the working class. Communist refoundation cannot but be opposed to capitalism and its managers, including the centre left. It could only be revolutionary in terms of rediscovering the forgotten heritage of the workers movement. It could only be democratic in the sense of its members being involved and being protagonists at all levels of the party. On the other hand you could not 'refound' if you were going forward while looking back and admiring the past, trying to repeat the same practice in a new phase.

Obviously the big split was not illuminated just with a heroic halo. Refoundation was born on an emotional and dramatic upsurge expressing the determination of thousands, hundreds of thousands of Italian communists to not surrender to the Occhetto turn. If you examine that period of history it is absolutely clear how much passion and pathos coloured the political world. If you look at the initial events in the PRC journey you can understand how much that mood was decisive in the push towards the refoundation project. As Simone Bertolino in his book entitled 'The history and organisation of Communist Refoundation' [*Rifondazione Comunista, storia e organizzazione*] (Il Mulino, 2004) states, the PRC was formed as a 'system of solidarity' aiming to defend communist identity and its symbols. Further, at the base at least "the organisation was structured on two dimensions, slogans of the day and the communist community, and consequently on two types of combined participation. These were the social movement based on collective enthusiasm for the birth of a new subjective, transformative role...and the subculture based on the continuity of a system of closed relations defending an identity threatened by external events." This definition is interesting because it succeeds in placing the birth of Refoundation within its real human and material composition, with their expectations and the motivation that inspired over a hundred thousand people to take out membership in the Movement for Communist Refoundation in 1991. However this emotional, enthusiastic and community based support for the project over time produced a rather inert mass membership quite different from the role it played in the political process which created the PRC. For example the core of this membership played a real political role during the last phase of the PCI's life, at the 20th Congress, when the party was dissolved and the name changed. It forced the hand of hesitant leadership groups and pushed for the split option. Alessandro Valentini in his book entitled "The old mole and the Phoenician Arab" (*La vecchia talpa e l'araba fenice*, La Citta del Sole, 2000) is right when he notes the central role played by the Committees for Communist Refoundation in pushing Armando Cossutta's tendency to break the links which tied him to the 'old family' and to go for a split and the formation of a new political grouping. He is right because these events highlight a rank and file protagonism, a political determination that was a big part of the early life of the PRC even if it came to be quickly bottled up in the wrangles of the party leaderships and settling down process which would begin straight after its first electoral success in 1992. A very nostalgic community bound up with its own identity where, unsurprisingly pensioners had a significant influence within the membership (the biggest single category according to Bertolino's study at 30%). Although at the same time it drew on solid political resources and was able to have a real impact. During the first phase the PRC was able to be at the centre of the workers mobilisation against the negotiation policy of the CGIL,CISL and the UIL. Later after Cossutta's split and a very critical period in terms of election results and keeping the organisation together the party was able to play a decisive role in the 2001 to 2003 period when the social movements took off.

To summarise, our thesis is that Refoundation, through the way it was formed and due to the internal 'truths' it held on to, was able to bring about the necessary political discontinuity and counter the slow resignation and stupor that characterised the last ten to fifteen years of the PCI.

Sailing against the wind

It could have for example taken fully on board its first slogan, that of 'Heart of the opposition' that very quickly, as we saw already at the end of 1993, was sacrificed on the altar of government participation. Refoundation could have made the strategic, long term choice of being in opposition, not to carry out a crude, sectarian political line but in order to face up to the crisis in the workers movement, realising that it had been building up for years and it required a medium-term intervention. Theorising opposition as a fundamental political line meant, and still means, theorising the reconstruction of a subjective role in the heart of conflicts, by getting one's hands dirty and not by trying to get access to the levers of institutional power. It was about, and still is, drawing up a political strategy of conquering positions and making advances in struggles outside of the dominant political framework, while obviously not theorising the neutrality of the latter. During its first experience in government the PRC had succeeded in maintaining, in theoretical terms, its 'separateness' from the executive and its 'otherness' from the Olive Tree bloc, the Italian centre left, while of course contradicting itself in reality by approving the budget, the Treu economic measures and other similar government policies. It was evidence of its difficulty in dissolving itself within the centre left and of its hypothesis of absolutely maintaining its own political and strategic autonomy, this also explains the break with Prodi in 1998.

Support for opposition would not have automatically signified a disinterest in the question of the right wing forces and their danger but this threat could have been countered by 'technical' electoral agreements and deals about maintaining candidates in run-offs. The PRC would have been able to gain credibility in this way. But over and beyond the electoral arena it would have been able to position the head and centre of gravity of the party in a different place to the institutions and internal party bodies. It would have been more in contact with the problem of class recomposition. The latter was a specific problem that required analysis and practical, political knowledge that Refoundation did not display except in rare flashes. It seemed to be doing that in 1995 when there was a clear conflict with the rest of the moderate left which was 'kissing the toad', although this credibility was lost on the altar of Prodi's government.

Refoundation could have deepened its original actions, the political force of the 'No' roared at Ochetto and its establishment, by developing a long term political project that re-examined overall strategy and the communist hypothesis in today's reality. The perspective of 'going beyond capitalism', the partial formulation which is still today part of the PRC statutes, was never really properly discussed. To go beyond in which direction? How? With what forces? To do what? It is a hard, difficult discussion but it is the only one that would have allowed us to draw together the fundamental differences into a plan of political perspectives. It would have permitted us to understand if the PRC was really a party that wanted to go beyond capitalism in the hoped for long term or if it wanted to make this objective a programme that would inspire the concrete choices of today, informing its political line and the positions it takes. In fact the discussion on state power was not taken up at that time but was re-introduced only within the framework of the discussion on non-violence and the break with Stalinism. But it was done in an abstract way and did not lead to a useful discussion since the debate was framed in a way that you had to opt for the new theory supported by Bertinotti or for an improbable and incoherent 'Leninist' position.

Here I would like to point out another limit to Refoundation which foreshadows the successive splits. The political 'families' that had formed Refoundation had never really amalgamated or recomposed on the basis of a new framework. We can largely define these families in terms of two majority sectors and two much smaller groupings. The two major groups came out of the PCI and are the Cossutta people with its own internal tendencies (as we have seen earlier in my account in this book) and a more complex grouping growing out of a synthesis between the Ingrao supporters and the followers of Berlinguer which over time took on the name of Bertinottismo. Then we have the Democrazia Proletaria tendency (Proletarian Democracy) which is also made up of various sub groups but was mainly a small group of leaders who had maintained political influence to the extent of being able to hold down the post inside the PRC secretariat with Paolo Ferrero. Finally you have the Trotskyist tradition that was unable to unite at all and at the last congress in which it was present was represented in three documents, Malabarba, Ferrando, and the Hammer and Sickle group (which is the only one still in the PRC). The failure to recompose was demonstrated in the final act. At the time of the disintegration all the above families re-established their own autonomy, both political and organisational. The Bertinotti people have given birth to Sinistra e Liberta (Left and Freedom); Ferrando has the Partito Communista dei Lavoratori (Workers Communist Party); Malabaraba, myself and others are in Sinistra Critica (Critical Left); and the Democrazia Proletaria people and left Cossutta people are in charge of what is left of the PRC.

Refoundation could have also built up a new relationship with society, not determined exclusively by electoral politics. The Fifth Congress had tried to come to grips with its anomalous nature as a political party with the 34th Congress thesis "the necessity of moving away from the state, from the institutions to the dynamism of the social forces, the movements and the mass struggle... outside of the links we have inherited, even those important ones inspired by Togliatti's ideas". This thesis remained a dead letter. The PRC was configured, organised and structured exclusively in relation to elections. Life revolved around elections, it dominated internal battles and its big political turns. Elections, the number of votes and the ability to play an institutional role formed the overwhelming preoccupation of its leadership groups. This is the way it shaped itself, quite naturally and in good faith. If the objective is presence in the institutions, increasing your vote, then it is quite natural that over time the local branches, the circles would become election committees, the local leaders would find career paths in the institutions, and economic survival for the party would be based on state financing. The only motivation of the leadership group would be tied up with the institutions. Alliances, given the anti-democratic electoral laws, would take on an excessive importance. Intervention in society would be seen as instrumental only in electoral terms and the party organisation would always be preferred to the self organisation of the mass movements. On this issue it was possible for the PRC to bring about a thoroughgoing change in the political culture of the Italian left where the autonomy of the mass movements, their right to organise themselves on the basis of their social reality and needs has always been sacrificed to the needs of the dominant organisations whether these are the party, the unions or other civic associations. The only two exceptions in the history of the workers movement were the workers councils of 1919-20, which Gramsci placed so much hope in as a foundation for the workers' sovereign subjective role, and the councils of 1968-9 which opened a period of great social struggles. While there was no communist party during the 'red two years' of 1919-20 (it was founded in 1921) and the vacillations of the Socialist Party (PSI) of the time provided no reference point, the councils movement that emerged through the hot autumn of 1969 was slowly absorbed by the CGIL (main communist left trade union) and as a result of Togliatti shaping the PCI as a 'new party', sucking up and synthesising any movement of any type thrown up by social struggles. On no account were the movements allowed to be independently organised. Here was quite a different party to the one which raised the slogan 'All Power to the Soviets' and led the 1917 October revolution. The Bolsheviks based their whole philosophy on another thesis, part of the First International's manifesto drafted by Marx, according to which the 'emancipation of the workers will be the task of the workers themselves'. This central idea was generally not integrated into the thinking of the Marxist left and its terms were bastardised as a result of Stalinist orthodoxy, which remodelled the October revolution into its own version where self organisation was completely downplayed and a 'pure' Leninism was exalted. Lenin's conception of the party's 'guiding role' as an instrument of struggle within the self-organised structures of the working class was transformed in the Stalinist bible into the infallibility of the great leader very similar to the role of the Pope in the Roman Catholic Church. The role of the party in the mass movements swung between arguing for a false hegemony, which vulgarised Gramsci's conception and became totally arrogant, and merely using them for electoral ends. When it chose to get involved in the mass movements, and particularly the anti-globalisation one, Refoundation seemed to want to promote the idea of a left wing way forward but within an out of date framework corrupted by its own errors. In the social forums the PRC put itself 'on equal terms' with the other movements but in doing so bent reality to its own vision, it is not the same as a movement. It operated without any culture that understood the principles of mass self-organisation. It is also not surprising that this experience did not lead to forms of direct democracy based on the principle of 'one person, one vote'. Bodies of elected representatives subject to recall were not supported and we had to make do with cartels of pre-existing organisations with their own banners.

Another feature of this Communist Party was how the focus on elections also had a consequence for the central role of the leader. This model is completely in line with the history of so many communist parties originating in the Third International. Togliatti was the absolute boss, just like Stalin or Mao, or even Fidel Castro. Except that in those cases there is a heroic halo attached as a result of tragic and big events like wars and revolutions. In Refoundation's case there were no great dramatic events to justify any leadership excesses. The situation was much more prosaic. Above all there was a nostalgic continuity with a long history, this idea of 're-making the PCI' that inspired a large part of its founding members and above all most of its leadership group. It meant the old reflexes tended to emerge. So we see again the red roses presented by the young woman activist to the first secretary just after he finishes his big speech, the privilege of not having to give your parliamentary salary straight to the party, and the general sacred reverence. All of this borrowed from a way of doings things that was over and produced significant damage in the way the party was built. The word of the party boss became a shield behind which paid positions grew, with all the attendant privileges. It is important not to underestimate the effect of all this ritual on the leaders receiving such attention.

Alongside this inertia there is another aspect of the crisis and resistance within which the process is experienced, in an Italy dominated by an arrogant and voracious capitalism that is trying to survive the new global competition. Refoundation had to fight on two fronts:, against capitalism, its natural enemy; and against a left government which forced it into all sorts of contorted positions. Therefore we had huge pressure, a difficult context with workers being thrown out of their jobs while the unions went along with it all, negotiating with the bosses. At the same time activists became demoralised and those wanting to fight were isolated.

When you have a structural dismantling and weakening of the working class, and you are isolated ideologically, you can understand why sticking together closely behind your leader is a way of keeping the faith, keeping things together emotionally, particularly if this leader is a great, fighting communicator in the enemy camp, for example in the TV studios. It provided an antidote to the depressive feelings engendered by the daily difficulties of being a political activist. This was even recognised by people in the street and our enemies, how many times did we hear people say "we don't agree with your ideas but we must say we appreciate the coherence of your arguments". Of course these were the coherent arguments they had heard on TV from the eloquent Fausto Bertinotti. As the difficulty of political activism and the disintegration of Italian society continued, this collective identification and a sense of resistance nourished a general party euphoria which reached embarrassing levels.

In the end it is an aspect completely bound up with an excessive focus on elections. If your main representative is effective, incisive and good at scoring debating points this results in winning an electoral base around which your party shapes itself, and it is difficult for you to give this up. "You don't change a winning team". There was never any real criticism of Bertinotti or Bertinottismo within Refoundation, outside of the internal opposition groupings, until the latest election results came out. Once the electoral success ended then Bertinotti also bit the dust.

Refoundation therefore could have developed another model, a party prioritising social struggles rather than the institutions, a party that did not spend all its energy on paper membership drives, that valued youth members, made women welcome and organised its intervention on the basis of the number of social struggles it was involved in and supported rather than the number of votes at stake.

Furthermore Refoundation could have really carried out a 'communist refoundation'. It could have put the question of the historical failure of communism on the agenda and examined it from the point of view of its own historical project. A reconstruction of the left carried through via a loyal and honest debate without any pre-judging of the outcome.

We could have examined Stalinism without doing it in a way that was just a settling of accounts with its internal components, but rather through a study of the crucial historical turning points when Stalinism prevailed, when other roads might have been taken based on contemporary evidence. We could have put the political culture of the best of Marxism on the table, Lenin, Gramsci, Trotsky, Luxemburg but also Benjamin, Guevara and so many others, in order to really get to grips with it so that we could understand what is worth keeping from their political thought and philosophy. Surfing on the surge of the 'No' to the Bolognina Congress and the Occhetto turn, the PRC pretended not to understand how far the communist question was going to be examined and re-examined within Italian society. Instead it seemed that venerating the holy truths were enough to keep the faithful together and continue forward unperturbed. When Bertinotti understood the limits of this and began to look for 'innovation' it seemed more of an intellectual provocation that an area of research opened to the whole party, more of a timeless declaration than a serious and concrete engagement with the problem. The key issue was that the political thinking behind most of Bertinotti's leadership group was neither internally coherent nor did it have a precise objective. It was as if it was trying to innovate and rejuvenate itself, to be free of the name 'communist' without defining or really examining the question. It was an eclectic and shallow attempt. Even with the introduction of the debate on non-violence the target was not really attained because it was too mixed up with the turn to government, and was too far removed from a fundamental and intelligent discussion on the history and destiny of communism.

We should try and imagine the powerful impact that a profound reflection on the history of Stalinism could have generated in 1995 within the confrontation with the Dini government, at the heart of the struggle to defend pensions and inside workers struggles generally. Was it really the case that the events of 68, the isolation of Prague and the Maoist aberrations of the Italian New Left inhibited such a disruptive initiative? What would it have meant for the membership of a party still on the launch pad to examine the definition of revolution and mobilise its activists not around the wrangles of its apparatus or the role of its leaders but rather around political and historical analysis.

We are not saying that Refoundation would have been able to become an unusual revolutionary party, but by giving a voice to its own *raison d'être* it could have certainly strengthened its own anticapitalist identity. It could have brought together within its ranks reformist and revolutionary ideas, while at the same time maintaining clear independence from moderate political forces, keeping apart from any compromising project with Italian and European capitalism, and working within a long-term perspective.

The point is this, while a potential was there, the same that carried the PRC beyond the threshold of three million votes to become a real player on the political scene, what was needed was boldness and political agility from a leadership group who had to think through their own role and history. They would have had to be imbued with a spirit of refoundation, understanding that this meant discontinuity and not restoration. In reality the PRC's leadership group was not able to come to terms with the 'compromising' framework within which it had been formed, whether it came from the PCI or DP. It has been shown earlier that there was a tactical/strategic propensity which was dynamic and open to conflict, and capable of looking at these radical hypotheses; but the fundamental perspective of gradualism and social compromise was never really up for discussion. Not even, as we have seen, at the very important 2002 congress. It is no coincidence that the internal debate has almost exclusively taken place around the question of government: with the Progressisti (Progressive Bloc) in 1994, with the Ulivo (Olive tree bloc) in 1996, then a long pause from 1998 interspersed with some debate around the various local elections, and then again with the Union bloc in 2006. It cannot all be reduced to an obsession with Berlusconi, because in 1994 the perspective was clearly one of government and not confrontation with the right wing. In 1996 agreement to not stand against other left forces rapidly became a bargaining counter to get into government, with the consequent split. The same thing happened again in 2006 when 'alternating became the remedy for the alternative'.

So the key thing is to understand the fundamental approach, the overall strategy, which determines the secondary manoeuvres, the political means to be used and the allies to be chosen. A reformist strategy was incompatible with the internal logic of the PRC, whose political line could only be to sail into the wind and to be squeezed to the edge of the political.

The Wheat and the Chaff

The potential we have described up to now existed inside the party's membership and intellectual patrimony. The party was affected by significant internal contradictions. The most important one, to remain outside the system or to accept its political framework, exploded violently with Cossutta's split in 1998. On the one side were found the pro-governmental chaff that spawned the PDCI (Democratic Party of Italian Communists), on the other side the 'refounding' wheat that remained inside the PRC. But the separation of the two elements was not salutary and not only because Refoundation finished up becoming stricken with problems again. The showdown of 1998, the split, the fall of Prodi, meant that the complex and contradictory ingredients that up to now had kept the operation alive and well were getting weaker. Supporting the government and then pushing it over, radicalising its slogans and then swelling the ranks of institutional post-holders, building up a lovey-dovey dual leadership and then stabbing each other in public, these contradictions should have been discussed in depth in order to reach a synthesis of the diverse sensibilities and perspectives in Refoundation that would have consolidated its overall project. Instead what happened was a split that was largely within the apparatus and was covered up for more than a year from the party bodies where there could have been a broad, democratic and educational debate.

So what happened was that moderate party structures stayed loyal to those who broke with the government and the recycled radicals and hard-liners went off with the split. The first phase of Refoundation finished like this, with pictures of Cossutta and Diliberto on the benches of Montecitorio (parliament) giving each other a hug and exchanging kisses while the rejected Bertinotti looked on with head bowed. It ended with two communist parties both competing for votes in the European elections. It ended in the demoralisation of a party membership which had put itself on the line to begin things again, bringing with it the strength of the 1970s experience yet would now become ever more worn out, silent, distant and absent. The 'strong impulsion' generated from the formation of Refoundation as a basis for reform, to quote Bertinotti, was burning itself out in these events and from now on the question was raised in terms of a semantic reconstruction. Here we agree with Bertinotti when he claims that "Refoundation had an historical opportunity that had raised hopes. These hopes were encapsulated in the anti-globalisation movement". We also agree when he adds: "...we did not feel able, as a party, to take the extreme step that would have brought us to intervene politically beyond and outside of the communist tradition, something that would have helped us break out of the impasse we were in." Indeed these were the two lost opportunities, Refoundation failed twice: in how it used the enthusiasm and power of its original launch and in making the leap to a new type of political formation.

There were some of us who supported this position in 2001, 2002 and 2003 as we have seen above in earlier chapters. However Refoundation did not take that step. There was an opening when the PRC had the choice of two possible ways forward: either to grasp the new upsurge of the movement and present its activists with a new type of radical, anticapitalist political activity, or to take up the offer made by Manifesto, the Association for the Renewal of the Left, perhaps also from the left of the DS (Democratic Socialist party, formed from ex PCI majority) for a broader organisation with more of a cutting edge, the famous 13% vote share that Magri talked about in his article bidding farewell to the PRC in the Rivista del manifesto, which would pressure the DS from the left. Refoundation chose neither one nor the other option and theorised its self-sufficiency albeit within the elastic formula of the Sinistra Europea (European Left). In the end also this chosen option had no legs because it had already been tried and had failed.

The anti-globalisation movement should not of course be mythologized. It was a political explosion that took off within the space left free by the failure of the governmental left and within the worldwide movement critical of globalisation. However its positive dynamic hinted at a refoundation of politics and of the left, if only the latter had been more courageous. Going beyond the communist tradition was necessary then because it would have taken place on the wave of a mass radicalisation and would have been distinguished by going forward towards the left rather than being a renunciation of it. It would certainly have been a complicated operation which would have further violently shaken up the PRC, it would probably have still insisted on the separation between the wheat and the chaff, but it would have been a turn with international breadth and not just resistance as usual. Instead the split was only postponed, carried out amid-the ruins with an empty language with no future, defending the communist identity on one side and a vague support for 'newness' on the other. Politics is all about timing, a good political line that is too far in advance or behind of reality rapidly turns into bad politics. Refoundation was born at the right time, in opposition to the liquidation of the PCI, but in a few years had lost it way. It turned again to criticising globalisation but did not have a credible political project for it.

Today we find ourselves smashed by too many defeats and now deprived of the tools we had at our disposal to move into the 21st century without surrendering.

Return to the 19th Century

If we can gather together the forces and ideas we have to imagine a new beginning on a long road with a 'slow impatience' that will need a strong ideological strategic framework that Refoundation had basically always lacked. We can no longer accept the emotional impatience that characterised the history of the PRC, the superficial analysis made possible by the enthusiastic upsurge of the Refoundation membership. It is no longer useful either to raise the banner of continuity with a 'little old world' that has to be consigned to the archive of our memory. While we must look through communist eyes the project has to take on the form the present time and history gives it. We know that the substance of the objective is to guarantee a new fusion between the ideas of critical Marxism and the future path of the class struggle.

A communist party in Italy has served its time, it has done what it could and any attempt to simply replicate another one risks becoming a farce. The various parts have been acted out by everyone, also by the opposition, and the 'audience' now needs a new play altogether. That we need a party has to be a concept we defend and not abandon particularly given the complexity of the political situation we face. We need a party as a collective tool and not as a 'church', as a carrier of memory and of a collective wisdom able to 'understand the world' but clearly respecting the democracy of the subjects of that transformation which is an essential condition for conceiving a systematic alternative. What we call this party and the political project will be down to the subjective forces which can bring about this transformation. But if the name comes before the thing itself, to paraphrase Ochetto's phrase at the time of the PCI turn, the project will not take off at all. If we had to define such a project freely without any type of external constraints we could only continue to call it communist. But if the term communist takes on such significance that as a signifier it confuses what it is signifying then it is of no use. It is no surprise that this sort of debate about the communist name tends to take place in socially ineffective layers.

There is a desperate need for a class struggle left, and 'dropping the whole idea of a left' does not seem a better programme than the work involved in its reconstruction. Building it without a thoroughgoing reflection on the errors of the historic left would also be useless. To make a step forward we need above all solid thinking, ideas, an ability to understand reality and to steer a course within it. We will need autonomy from capitalism and its mediations to develop a political subject apart from the current governments of the world, free from gimmicks and able to produce another type of political discourse. A new class struggle left party can also function with diverse political cultures having different perspectives, even a radical reformist perspective alongside a revolutionary one, but within the framework of a shared anti-capitalism that necessarily keeps it autonomous from governments. Fundamentally that is how the workers movement in the second half of the 19th century was born, with socialist or social democratic parties formed after the development of the Leagues, co-operatives, mutual/friendly societies which existed as independent and alternative to the bourgeoisie. This is an invaluable lesson for us in the light of the way the present bourgeoisie uses more parties and political forms, including the social democratic parties who for some time have lost any sense of being an alternative to it.

We will need democracy, understood as a culture of conflict and an invitation to participate, and above all we will need a new generation, not only made up of youth, with a desire to rebuild. The old political generation is tired and defeated even if its memory and points of view, if generously offered, could become supportive in a project of reconstruction. However it will be a new political generation that will rebuild a class struggle left in this country. Even if in Italy today there is a low awareness of the need for a class struggle left there is an urgent need for one.

Appendix: Italian political timeline from end of Second World War

Post-war Italy to the 60s: Christian Democrats establish hegemony helped by PCI reformist line and the CIA

1946 - Referendum votes for republic to replace monarchy. Despite armed CP led forces controlling significant parts of Italy, particularly in the North, Togliatti leads Italian CP to accept compromise with bourgeois parties, dubbed the Salerno turn.

1948 - New constitution. Christian Democrats (DC) win elections and rules Italy alone until 1980s. Italian CP (PCI) allied with Socialists (PSI) get 31% of vote. US through CIA intervened massively to support DC. Assassination attempt on Togliatti, PCI leader.

1964, Togliatti dies and his chosen successor Enrico Berlinguer becomes leader. At this time the PCI had about 1,350,000 members (4.2% of working population), the biggest CP in world. Post-war boom leads to massive changes in Italian society.

Years of lead, Historic compromise and red terrorism

1969, Hot autumn following May 68 in France Italy sees a long period of strikes and social mobilisation on many fronts. Big forces to left of CP emerge. Downturn and a significant minority adopt left terrorist position of Red Brigades.

1972 - Giulio Andreotti (Christian Democrat) becomes prime minister - a post he will hold seven times in 20 years.

1976-78 - Communist election gains (34.5% in 76 general elections) lead to voice in policy making, the consequence of historic compromise line developed by Italian CP leader, Berlinguer.

1978 - Former Prime Minister Aldo Moro kidnapped and murdered by left terrorist group, the Red Brigades. Abortion legalised.

1980 - Bombing of Bologna station kills 84, linked to right-wing extremists.

The Craxi years

1983 - Bettino Craxi becomes Italy's first Socialist prime minister since war- successfully manoeuvres CP from government influence as it rules with Christian Democrats. New media empires, particularly Berlusconi's, are built up during this period.

Berlin wall falls and PCI splits

1991 - Bologna Italian CP Conference ('La Bolognina') Communists rename themselves Democratic Party of the Left (PDS). Party of Communist Refoundation (PRC) formed in December with a third of the membership who refused to follow the new Occhetto-led PDS. Sergio Garavinni (its first national secretary) and Armando Cossutta are the main leaders.

Corruption probe and break up of main governmental political parties

1992 - Revelations of high level corruption spark several years of arrests and investigations. Right wing populist/separatist Northern League benefits from corruption scandals and develops strongly. PRC wins 5.6% of vote and 35 seats in parliamentary elections and 6.5% and 20 seats in senate.

1993 - Bribery scandal leads to Craxi's resignation as leader of Socialist Party. Christian Democrats and Socialist Party implode. Major political recomposition takes place. Garavini moves aside for his former ally Fausto Bertinotti to become new national secretary.

First short-lived Berlusconi government 1994 then Dini and technocrats to 1996

1994 March - Newly formed Freedom Alliance wins election. Berlusconi is prime minister for the first time. The coalition, which includes Silvio Berlusconi's Forza Italia, the Northern League and the neo-Fascist National Alliance, collapses by end of year following clashes with anticorruption magistrates and a battle with trade unions over pension reform.

1995-96 - Lamberto Dini heads government of technocrats. Austerity budget. PRC votes no in confidence vote on this and helps bring down government. Garavini, with Lucio Magri and others does vote confidence to Dini and leads a 'reformist' split off which becomes the Movement of Unity Communists (MCU).

First Prodi Centre-Left government 1996 to 2000

1996 - Centre-left Olive Tree alliance [including PDS] wins election. Romano Prodi becomes prime minister. PRC wins 8.6% of the vote and supports new government.

1998 - Prodi government loses confidence vote after PRC breaks with government. Cossutta refuses to support party line and splits forming the Party of Italian Communists.

Massimo D'Alema [of PDS, formerly CP] becomes prime minister and Cossutta's people join it. PDS becomes Democrats of the Left (DS) merging with some small reformist parties and finally removes the word socialism and the small hammer and sickle from its logo, replacing it with the red rose.

2000 April - D'Alema resigns as PM after poor regional election results and is replaced by Giuliano Amato who leads technocrat's government until 2001 elections.

Berlusconi comeback
Second Berlusconi-led government 2001 to 2006

2001 May/June - A centre-right coalition, led by Silvio Berlusconi of the Forza Italia party, wins the general elections. Berlusconi forms new coalition government which includes the leaders of two right-wing parties, Gianfranco Fini of the National Alliance and Umberto Bossi of the Northern League.

2002 February/March - Controversy as parliament approves bill enabling Berlusconi to keep control of his businesses.

2002 October - Lower house of parliament passes controversial criminal reform bill which critics allege is intended to help PM Berlusconi avoid trial on corruption charges.

2003 June - Berlusconi's trial halted after parliament passes law granting immunity from prosecution to five holders of key state posts, including the prime minister.

2004 January - Constitutional Court throws out law granting Berlusconi and other top state post holders' immunity from prosecution. Berlusconi's trial resumes in April.

2004 December - After a four-year trial Prime Minister Berlusconi is cleared of corruption.

2005 - Government coalition collapses after suffering a crushing defeat in regional polls. Berlusconi resigns. Days later, he forms a new government after receiving a presidential mandate.

Second Prodi government 2006 to 2008 - Prodi in, then out

2006 April - Centre-left leader Romano Prodi wins closely-fought general elections. He is sworn in as prime minister in May. PRC joins government, Bertinotti is named President (Speaker, UK) of parliament (like the Speaker in the British or US parliaments). Other leaders such as Ferrero become ministers.

2007 February - Prime Minister Prodi resigns after the government loses a Senate vote on its Afghan foreign policy. Franco Turigliatto and Salvatore Cannavo, leaders of Critical Left and of Refoundation, were the two key voters against the government and their party. The president asks Prodi to stay on and Prodi goes on to win confidence votes in both houses of parliament. Small groups from the left of the PRC such as the Marco Ferrando-led Communist Workers Party, Critical Left and the Communist Alternative Party (Francesco Ricci), split in this period.

2007 December, PRC joins the Rainbow Left coalition with, among others, Cossutta's Party of Italian Communists and the Greens. No election agreement between PRC and the DS/Centre Left.

2008 January - A no-confidence vote forces Prodi's government to resign.

Berlusconi back again
Third Berlusconi government 2008 to today

2008 April - Berlusconi wins general elections, securing a third term as premier after two years in opposition. Disaster for the Rainbow Left which only wins 3.1% of the vote compared to the 10.3 % won by same parties in previous general elections. All members of parliament were wiped out since they failed to reach the threshold. Refoundation implodes. Bertinotti withdraws from political activity. The faction led by Paulo Ferrerro wins a slim majority at the July congress and inherits the name. The losing faction, Nikki Vendola, leader of ex-Bertinotti group sets up Movement for the Left (MpS)

2009 October - Constitutional court overturns law which granted Premier Berlusconi immunity while in office.

2009 December - Prime Minister Silvio Berlusconi is assaulted at a rally in Milan. In the European elections the anticapitalist left coalition of groups representing the PRC, Cossutta's PDCI and others got only 3.4% of the vote and no MEPs.

2010 March - Prime Minister Silvio Berlusconi's coalition makes strong gains from the centre-left in regional polls.

Dave Kellaway

Portugal
Interview with Francisco Louçã

"Somehow, we filled a space that did not exist, a political space that had not yet been recognized"

Interview with Francisco Louçã[1] by Miguel Romero[2]

For some years, the political space to the left of "social democracy" has been shifting in Europe. Not always in the right direction: the crisis of Rifondazione in Italy or the Scottish Socialist Party or Respect platform in Britain are clear signs that the road is still steep and it is easy to stumble. But there are also stimulating experiences that appear to open breaches in a very prolonged phase of disorientation and political deadlock: the NPA in France, Die Linke in Germany and the Bloco de Esquerda in Portugal are those that have achieved the widest audience and, accordingly, are reference points for other ongoing projects.

We plan to give an account of these experiences through conversations with political leaders who are open to reflection on the practice of their organisations. We are not interested in ideological issues; we want to know the ways these organisations practice politics, their problems and their results.

What most attracts us about these experiences is their diversity, the different or even contradictory options that arise. We believe that every reader will find in them aspects that match and aspects that diverge. This is a good vaccine against "models". There are no parties which are infallible guides. We need instead a practical internationalism that seeks to know about other experiences of anticapitalist politics and understand them so as to learn from them.

---

[1]   Francisco Louçã is an economist and a Left Bloc member of the Portuguese parliament. He was the candidate of the Left Bloc in the presidential election of January 2005, when he won 5.3% of the votes.

[2]   Miguel Romero is the editor of the Madrid-based journal 'Viento Sur', a journal sharing the general stance of Izquierda Anticapitalista, section of the Fourth International in the Spanish state. *The interview was carried out in March 2010.*

We do not have a timetable for the publication of interviews. We will try to not delay too much. We began the series talking with Françisco Louçã about the Bloco de Esquerda in Portugal, the least known organisation of the new anticapitalist left in Europe, perhaps because it is the most "unorthodox". This is in itself a good reason to take an interest in it.

Miguel Romero: Let's start with the origins of the Bloco.

Francisco Louçã: There was a social process of defeat of the left in the referendum on abortion in 1998. It was a situation in which the whole left was present with an expectation of winning which ended in a defeat, a tangential defeat, but an unexpected defeat with a great moral impact. It is true that this led the leadership of the UDP [Unión Democrática Popular, a group of Maoist origin] who at that time already had less electoral presence though more of a militant base than the PSR [the Fourth international organisation] to think about making a proposal to the PSR to create a new political force that completely reconfigured the field of the socialist left. And it presented this proposal. When it did so, there was not a tradition of strong unitary relationship of militant perspective; there had been an electoral convergence in 1983, six years before, which had failed, and the results were not significant.

MR: Was there a unitary campaign for the right to abortion?

FL: Not only between the UDP and the PSR. Within the framework of the campaign all currents were involved, people from the Communist or Socialist Parties or Catholics or even right wing people who did not accept that women were criminally punished for having an abortion. In the tactical options of the campaign there was some relationship between the PSR and UDP, but also with many others. There was a relationship of social movements with political parties, the expression of a movement in a unitary framework, but finally, nothing that created a political culture of relationship to a new party.

You are right: the proposed establishment of the Bloco was the decision of a political leadership. When I met Luis Fazenda [leader of the UDP], after a few early meetings between representatives of both parties, we knew very little. We knew each other from afar, we had met once or twice at some meeting, but we had never had a conversation in depth. In this approach an important role of linking up was played by some people: for example, Fernando Rosas, a well-known political figure of the Portuguese left intelligentsia from the generation prior to ours, who came from the Communist Party and afterwards the extreme Marxist-Leninist left, and had already worked with the PSR for many years.

There was a general perception that an era was over. The moral effect of defeat in the abortion campaign was a sense of failure and the end of the period of April 25. The traditions of each party were such that most of the activists admitted that they needed something new; it was accepted, in the PSR, the UDP and PXXI [Política XXI, an organisation originating from a split in the PCP] which was another current associated with the process, but in principle it was thought that a coalition would suffice. Then a precise, daring proposal was made: not a coalition, but a new political movement. There were no conditions for a unification of the parties which would require a convergence at the ideological level; this road lacked interest but what was possible, and much more important, was to create a political organisation, whose strength and whose unity was established beyond ideology. To have a solid and stable political agreement we do not need to agree on the interpretation of the 1917 Revolution or the Chinese revolution in 1949. We had to concentrate on the definition of the political tasks and the formation of the political culture of the new movement, from the base. This proposal initially encountered difficulties within the UDP and inside of the PSR. But after initial resistance it was affirmed. I think that it was crucial to raise that option, although it was the most difficult.

MR: All this reminds me of the situation here after the defeat in the NATO referendum. You were more intelligent than us, more "political" in the best sense of the word. You understood you had an opportunity to convert a defeat into a step forward for the anticapitalist left and not to let it escape. Here in 1996 we didn't see that, and when we believed we saw it a few years later it was an illusion.

FL: The risk is that when in a phase of retreat, building a new organisation is something dangerous. We had a political proposal which attracted many people who were not from the PSR, the UDP or of PXXI. Attracting many independent leftists was a very important aspect. In a few months the Bloco became an organisation of 1,200 or 1,300 members, most of whom were not members of the founding organisations. But above all, the Bloco was a political force with a capacity to act. In politics opportunities arise that are taken or not taken; these opportunities are built or they disappear. We faced significant challenges quickly: e.g. the movement for independence in Timor in 1999 after the foundering of the occupation by Indonesia, which had great force in Portugal. Also the mobilisations in response to the wars in the Balkans. That same year there were European parliamentary elections. The Bloco was present for the first time; we didn't get anybody elected.

MR: But the results were better than those previously obtained by the PSR and the UDP?

FL: We got more votes than the sum of those obtained previously by the organisations. Enough to understand that this vote in Lisbon would elect a deputy in national parliamentary elections. As it was shortly before the parliamentary elections, that created a capital of positive hope and expectation which was what upset the electoral balance. So we got two members in Lisbon which in successive elections became 3, 8 and 16. These successive electoral victories had an immediate impact on public and social intervention and all this in a very short time. It was possible to quickly see that the project to create a political force had strong ideas: the fight against globalisation, then was the period of the great rise of this movement, against war, against capitalism.

We provided immediate answers and that allowed us to do something that had never happened in Portuguese politics. Portuguese institutional politics consisted of two left wing parties and two right wing parties with few oscillations; there were internal changes but without structural changes in these parties. The UDP had a single deputy in 1976. There were splits in the Socialist Party re-absorbed later; the Communist Party had as many as 45 deputies at one stage (now 13). Nobody had outstripped the Communist Party in electoral terms. The emergence of a fifth national party is a unique case in a very stable structure. And we are talking about 25 years after April 25.

MR: I understand that you had sidelined ideological issues, but how were the political bases for agreement formalized? I imagine that there would be a common reference document.

FL: The Bloco began with a political text entitled Começar de novo (Starting Anew), a brief reference text that we later transformed into another more programmatic document, once we had verified the strength of political agreement on the attitude to society. The text was a natural result of the evolution of organisations, currents and independent persons, who had an important role in our leadership. It included our responses to actually existing capitalism, financialization, globalization, unequal exchange, mechanisms of exploitation and their social extension, the institutional question of the European Union... and other issues that had to be dealt with:

social delinquency as exploitation, the vision of war... Political development was very much consolidated around these questions.

Somehow, we filled a space that did not exist, a political space that had not yet been recognized. This was possible thanks to the decisive role of the leadership, because any organisation with institutional influence is under great pressure, any political organisation that starts from a small group of hundreds of people is subject to enormous tensions of differentiation. Either a leadership is capable of managing this process, absorbing, creating public authority... or the process fails. Authority is very important, mass political authority, let's call it. The consolidated organisation should see that its leadership represents an alternative to the existing parties and is working to create such an alternative in the social struggle of the masses.

For many years comrades had known that a party only has political influence when it is a compulsory reference point in all national debates; in any important matter that is being discussed, it must be a compulsory reference. I firmly believe in this. On issues such as the Treaty of Lisbon, the stability programmes, the fundamental choices of economic policy... debate is intensive and this is where the ability to influence, create polarization comes into play.

MR: There is one aspect of your experience that I find particularly interesting. I assume that prior to the creation of the Bloco, there was a basically stable political map in Portugal as in most European countries. The appearance of the Bloco unbalanced and destabilized the map, because a political force appeared that was present in the institutions, but was not subject to the rules of "governability".

FL: Yes, certainly. When we elected two deputies, it appeared as an electoral surprise. It was clearly a strong electoral base which reflected, to some extent, "abrilismo" ["Aprilism"], the political resistance of April 25. But it later responded to a left, socialist, radical, culture which struck a chord with militants of other parties.

The basic idea was to reject the idea that the Bloco was a mere "updating" of the far left and, on the contrary, place it as a force that competed for the leadership of the left. This was the case from the beginning, but it was gaining strength, because objectives must be based on what you can do. We knew that the key to our intervention was not to dispute a similar ground to that of the Communist Party. We could only gain strength in comparison to the Communist Party if our goal was far beyond that, pursuing a comprehensive recomposition of the left. This led us from the beginning to have a very unitary position towards the CP, which initially attempted, as you would expect, to belittle and ignore the existence of the Bloco, to then have a relationship with two aspects: a parliamentary relationship which was very unitary, negotiated, and intense, and at the same time, much dispute in terms of social viewpoint and political reference. The more aggressive the CP was from the political point of view, the more it lost. This allowed us to attract sectors coming from the history of the CP and win a huge confidence from the popular base which identified with the CP, in the fight against the austerity or for a combative trades unionism.

However, the key was the way in which we could respond to the challenge posed by the Socialist Party, as the ruling party and the regime of "alternation". We were able to have a very strong political momentum when the Socialist Party lost the elections to the right in 2002; then the Bloco could have a very active policy in the alternative and in confrontation with the government and have a very unitary policy with the CP and the Socialists, something that the CP did not do. It always argued that there was a symmetry between the Socialists and the right. One government is the same as another. It is true that the policies that are applied may be even worse under a Socialist government as we see today, with the labour legislation of the Socrates government, but from the social point of view there are different bases. Therefore we developed a very active role in dialogue with the Socialist social base, which is an important part of the population, while presenting our criticisms and alternatives: this was our true dispute for hegemony and that is what we did. At that time there was in the leadership of the Socialist Party Ferro Rodrigues who was a leader of the Movement of the Socialist left (MES) at the time of the April 25; I have known him since I was 14 years old. We could do many things with them, in spite of major differences in economic policies, but in the fight against poverty and for social security we took valuable initiatives. This leadership was decapitated by a judicial proceeding, a legal frame-up. Afterwards came José Socrates, who is a liberal technocrat.

What became clear at the time was that the Bloco de Esquerda should have two concerns: one, to build a movement with mass influence to represent an important social force with an anticapitalist consciousness, a socialist politics, there can be no doubt about that. But at the same time, we had to develop a centre of tactical intervention, a capacity for tactical relations that could be very effective in confrontation with neoliberal policies. I think that this is the main difference between the Bloco de Esquerda and many other European revolutionary organisations that we know of. Tactical intervention is very important to us. There is an "identity-based" space of affirmation of a political culture, an ideology, but the political action of the organisation is not the affirmation of identity, but the relationship with other sectors to create convergence, because if there is an attack on social security, or concerning the retirement age, an attack on wages, that requires a left organisation with mass influence, which is important in the fight to stop this attack. This is a way of practicing politics to win: we must be strong where Governments are weak; we need to create convergence where there is more support for socialist policies.

MR: is this a criterion of the leadership or a party culture among the activists? Some time you hear it said in educational sessions that a revolutionary policy "being correct" does not have much value: what matters is to intervene to change reality. But to change reality it seems the initiative of the party is not enough; there is a need for a close relationship with the social movements and that may give rise to conflicts between the "political" and the "social".

FL: These conflicts exist. In general, social movements in Portugal are very little organised. The strongest and more structured is the trade union movement which has a rate of unionization of only 15 or 18%, and is very limited in its capacity of organisation, of social intervention, although capable of promoting some big political actions with a strong impact, demonstrations of 100,000 or 200,000 people on issues like education, health, unemployment, or "austerity".

But there is no structured feminist movement, the environmental or counter-cultural movements are weak, although there is a significant internationalist movement. We are developing pioneering work with our members, and this sometimes influences our relations with civil society. Already some years ago, about four years ago, we decided to involve ourselves in the work of the social organisation of young people in precarious work, collaborating with some trade union organisations, but also meeting some hostility from other unions, and with non trade union organisations. We developed our own policy initiatives: mobilisations, legislative initiatives, create associative networks and so on. But it is political initiative which creates these movements and our activists try to occupy the greatest possible political space.

MR: I understand, but I think that this situation must create tension, or at least risks of tensions between the "political" militants of the Bloco and the "social" activists of the movement...

FL: But this is something inevitable, natural in a mass movement. And on the other hand, it must be considered that the Bloco has the characteristics of a "political movement"; we have some 8,000 adherents with very uneven levels of militancy. What fundamentally defines our political identity is public dispute, a very strong confrontation with the government in Parliament, which is the centre of political debate in Portugal. There are very tough debates with the Prime Minister every fortnight, in which we present alternatives, with important consequences including for the governing party, every fifteen days. In the previous parliament, in which the Socialist Party had an absolute majority, our policy of alliances with critical Socialist sectors led several times to the government's parliamentary defeat: in two cases, the government won by two votes, because several members of the Socialist Party voted against their government on important topics: privatisation, health education, and above all labour legislation. This represents a serious break from the political viewpoint in Portugal; hence came our relations with Manuel Alegre, who led this process of political and parliamentary insubordination and who will be a major left candidate in the upcoming presidential elections. We have a very broad convergence with many sectors that can defend the public sector against privatisation or against greater flexibility and new labour legislation. This improves our ability for expression in the mass movement, hinders the government offensive and could politically unbalance this conflict.

We create social space for political struggle, thus increasing the chances of convergences. Our line is this: the centre of activity for the Bloco de Esquerda is the defence of public services, our main battle is fighting liberalization and privatization, the defence of public services of education and health, the protection of economic democracy against inequality. We want people to understand that we are useful, that we can decide and from that point of view serve to change their lives. And we want this impact in the dispute with the government and the Socialist Party.

MR: It seems that this policy depends a lot on immediate results, let us say obtaining "successes", not simply electoral, but at least partially attaining the objectives proposed. But in the situation in which we live is very difficult to obtain those "successes". Sustaining the long-term construction of an anticapitalist organisation on tactics and their short-term results seem very problematic.

FL: A pressure for "results" exists, but I think that it is not the decisive aspect. Faced with social despair what we have is a reform without reforms, a social democracy without compensation. This leads to social tensions with consequent fear of unemployment, insecurity, isolation of wage-earners and so on. The perception of injustice is accentuated by our ability to act. This is in itself a result: people know that there is someone who fights for them, who is prepared to expose this insane, economic system, to explain, to show what injustice is in itself something mobilising and organising.

For example, something we often do is respond very directly to the financial scandals, the functioning of the banking system. This is something which has also led to many judicial processes on the part of managers, entrepreneurs, many attacks from them. The best-known employer in the country Belmiro de Azevedo, recently made a violent attack against me. This strengthens us much... And these employers know why we threaten their power: there was a case of collapse of a bank in a crisis of 2008, several banks had problems, but one of them went under; a parliamentary committee of inquiry on this bank was created, where we were present and we denounced all the details of offshore trading, commissions... We held public meetings explaining how these processes worked; this created an anticapitalist education, a concrete perception of what the economy is, a very strong perception from the point of view of the indignation, the politicization, the mobilisation of people and their response.

MR: How do these public meetings work?

FL: We hold them regularly all around the country to give an account of our parliamentary work and discuss with people. In addition, two years ago, we started to organise in August a series of street meetings, in public squares in the open air, for people passing by, which last year attracted more than 20,000 people. Always on these specific issues, where there is a great social concern. The audience is very interesting: pensioners, Socialist Party voters, teachers, some young voters. We have a reverse of the Communist Party age pyramid: the CP has few young voters and many elderly, while in our case it is the other way round. Now we start to recompose that relationship. It's about having a strong political impact while simultaneously perceiving the need for specific, practical changes and also their difficulty. Not to create illusions about what can happen, not promise people a pay rise, but show how wages could rise if there were measures of economic justice. This gives anti-capitalism a much greater force than any anticapitalist, propaganda proposal because it allows a specific expression of what injustice is, why some companies do not pay taxes, why in one hour commissions of 30 million Euros are paid to a banker, why a manager can earn seven times the salary paid to an employee, and so on.

MR: The Bloco has been a highly pluralistic organisation since its foundation. How do you work in such conditions? A system of seeking consensus? How do you manage disagreements?

FL: At the last Congress, last year, there were three lists: the majority which won 81% more or less, a minority motion with 11% and the other which was 8%. So on a directly proportional basis we elected 80 members to the National Committee which is the governing body: therefore, there are 16 or 17 members of minorities, who present their viewpoints. There is a minority that is part of the Trotskyist current known as "Morenistas" and maintains a systematic opposition, do a kind of "entry" work, which is not very relevant; they have some people, some young people, but are not important in promoting the political thinking of the Bloco. There are other currents in the second minority who collaborate and have partial agreements with the majority. The majority itself is very diversified, also because we have regional organisations that are already strong enough in themselves. The differentiation of the country is extensive, so that in each region different perceptions are posed, a different work from the point of view of political synthesis. This is expressed in congresses, meetings, regional and sectoral conferences (trade union, ecology, youth, mayors and councillors, who are about 350, most participating in municipalities without direct responsibilities; only in rare cases we are part of a governing majority). We have little implantation in local institutions; in proportion, far less than at the national level.

MR: Sorry to insist on this, but democratic management of differences arising out of its own practice in a large party seems very complex. There is a culture that comes from the social forums, and that has permeated many organisations, establishing consensus as the sole criterion. But it tends to convert disagreement into a disease, rather than something normal in a free and healthy collective.

FL: In a structure such as the social forums consensus is possible because it works with common minimum denominators and freedom of action: outside of the consensuses everyone does what they want. In a party that cannot be true: a party has to work with the maximum possible agreement and not the minimum possible agreement. What is decisive in politics in the long term is the strategic coherence of a leadership, which knows where to go how to act.

MR: Yes sure, but these are objectives that are extremely difficult to achieve and they cannot be achieved without debate.

FL: All the elements are important: but having a leadership with a very clear consciousness and rejecting leadership methods which create division are central. A party like the Bloco simultaneously has a strong public presence, an important institutional presence and a great social diversity. The leadership must be very capable of interpreting all the signals and making decisions that strengthen the Bloco. The level at which decisions are taken in a leadership of this type is an everyday, permanent level. But they are important decisions. We now have, for example, a confrontation with the government on a regional finance law, a confrontation, very sharp moreover, with public implications, threats of resignation from the government, and so on. We have a conflict on labour legislation, a major problem concerning a large multinational factory which is going to close, lay off workers... The ability to act is highly dependent on very precise, very tactical decisions.

As we live in a universe where politics is communication, "tactical and precise" also refers to the choice of words: the form of conducting politics is largely around image, through the proposal made, the conflict of ideas, the presentation of alternatives, the social organisation that is recognized and creates impact. This involves choosing very precisely: a leadership does not speak with many voices, speaks in highly concentrated terms, which involves having a very high level of confidence and a high degree of consultation. When I need to make immediate decisions, I consult the key persons on the subject concerned, the other parliamentarians, people with more experience and knowledge in this field; and at the same time if I know that someone is to make a speech that can politically affect the image of the Bloco, we jointly discuss the exact manner in which that should be done. It is not just about politics in general, but matters of detail, knowing exactly how each view is expressed. For example: the Prime Minister gives an interview on the political situation on Monday. All broadcasters transmit the live response of the various parties. Therefore it is very important that our response is extremely accurate, not what a leader thinks at that time. Before responding, we take a few minutes to consult. Because the political conception of an organisation relies heavily on communication.

MR: Let's see, develop this a little more.

FL: This is one of the major changes made by the Bloco, and not only derives from this institutional presence that we won, but cannot lose. This is a strategic choice that we have made in the past five years: transforming our model of communication regarding left traditions left as we know them.

MR: This is an important issue. Can you explain what your system of press is? In particular, to consider one of the oldest traditions of left communication: what role does the newspaper of the organisation play?

FL: Ever smaller. We have a monthly newspaper that is sent to the members of the Bloco and distributed on newsstands. But perhaps in the future it will no longer exist, because the centre of our communication is the internet. We have a web portal where a professional team works that is already very large, about ten people, working in radio, television, and media consulting. We also intervene in social networks. It is a highly developed information system with an ambitious goal. We would be happy if we had about 100,000 people, 1% of the population following the information we produce daily.

MR: You are very far from that?

FL: We are already close to 40 or 50,000 people counting all forms of communication we use: social networks, internet access, broadcasting on YouTube and similar things. We also have several people working as press consultants with the leadership with the Bloco. The relationship with the press is a difficult one.

MR: It sounds weird that you have "media advisors" in a militant organisation...

FL: These people are great professionals in communication, and are also among the best political cadres that we have. We need skilled people, with a capacity of communication with the directors of newspapers, the television editors, with those responsible for news, to respond appropriately.

We are in a world in which we focus on communication. The dominant communication is a world of manufacture of rumours as a political weapon, of communication agencies formed by "spin doctors". We have to overcome them. There is an intensive debate about that, and we have to be the most capable in this debate, creating ideas that mobilise and inform social mobilisation. So we had to decide on a major change in our system of communication, which will be increasingly important in our policy.

MR: OK, let's move on to another topic. Suppose that you consider that an objective is correct but have no capacity for mobilisation in the short term, because it is too radical: for example, the prohibition of layoffs. If so, do you discard it?

FL: We are introducing a programme that is consistent from the point of view of a socialist idea. We are not interested in the paralysing distinction between maximum and minimum programme. When we introduce a proposal for action, of response, immediate intervention on the situation, we try to be understood by people, and we can therefore expand our ability to influence in this area, starting from this response.

For example, turning to your question on the prohibition of layoffs, this as you know, is a subject of discussion with comrades from other European countries. We advocate an idea that seems to me just, difficult and provocative: prohibition of layoffs in companies that make or have made profits. If you have made a profit in past years, the idea is that it is returned to society, maintaining employment. People understand that it is a strong position but not part of the tradition of the labour movement on this issue. I think it is an understandable and correct position. On the other hand, the general idea of banning layoff, outside of this context, would I think be empty. It would mean automatic nationalization of all companies in bankruptcy by a neoliberal government, which has no sense or credibility. It does not correspond to the level of overall perception of the working population or the capacity to implement a socialist model. A left government with a socialist culture cannot emerge immediately and therefore this cannot be regarded by the generality of workers as a concrete answer to unemployment. It is mere political poetry: it doesn't help, or mobilise, or give rise to an important battle for the consciousness of people. I understand that it is among alternatives arising in the political and social struggle. But we cannot choose the proposals that are the most radical, but those that respond best to the question that arises and, therefore, achieve a greater impact.

MR: I have the perhaps mistaken notion that the more success a party obtains the more it is "nationalized". On the other hand it seems clear that the conditions to take forward anticapitalist politics are increasingly international. To go to specific issues: frankly, I do not see in the Bloco much interest in issues outside of Portugal.

FL: No comment!

MR: I was afraid of that...

FL: Now to be serious. Today a socialist programme would undoubtedly be strangled by the European Union. Any active socialist policy has to deal with the EU institutions to transform the conditions of European politics. It is obvious. We, however, still have no chance of victory in this area. We are still in a context of initial political construction of a European intervention. On the other hand, the stronger a party or movement is in a country, the more it depends on national politics, the more absorbed it is in national politics. Even a global or European coordination of the left must be based on strong national parties rather than minority organisations which are coordinated for ideological reasons. We need to attempt a relationship of very diverse currents, a little as Trotsky did in the 1930s with the British ILP, Dutch SAP, the POUM,... a relationship of different currents with much more variety than what we can imagine today.

We must do this with great naturalness. There is a certain nationalization of politics when this is decisive, that is true. A political organisation with mass influence is the subject of claims which do not arise in other circumstances and this is why it has these priorities. It is also true that a form of international coordination is lacking, we are in a phase of reconstruction of the left and there will be here and there successes and failures. It is also true that Portugal is not, for example, France: France is the most politicized country in Europe and is a central European country. Perception of political relations is very different in France than it is in Portugal. It is perfectly understandable that is so, because France has another place in European construction, as do Germany and Italy, even Spain. Portugal is a country which is very peripheral from this point of view.

MR: Let me ask you a question on a topic which will probably be controversial on the European left. At the presidential elections to be held in January the Bloco will support the candidacy of Manuel Alegre, a prominent member of the Socialist Party left. Can you explain the reasons for this decision?

FL: Manuel Alegre was a presidential candidate five years ago. The PS ran Mário Soares and he was presented as an alternative candidate. He launched a movement which surprised us, because he had many more votes than Soares. He swept the Socialist electorate and added many independent leftists who were critical of the then Socialist Government: it was the first indication we had that it was possible to have a dialogue with a distinct sector of the Socialist electorate. From there our tactical vision became more precise and we had a direct goal, namely to establish a permanent dialogue with this sector.

Dialogue was launched, particularly with Alegre, who moreover radicalized his differentiation from the Socialist Party, for which he was a deputy as well as being Vice-President of the Assembly of the

Republic. Alegre voted against the government on important economic issues, often agreeing with us; this led to a major crisis in the PS.

Dialogue and convergence established this political base allowing the holding of two major forums, one on democracy and left politics and one on public services. Actions were carried out in Lisbon and had a strong political impact because never had a leader of the Socialist Party supported a meeting convened by very different forces, involving also trade unionists, leaders of the CGTP and others from the social left. This was seen as an act of transformation of Portuguese left politics.

Alegre then decided not to be a candidate for Parliament for the PS because of disagreement with the reform of the labour code, but he remains a member and has participated in initiatives of his party. Now he has decided to be a candidate for the Presidency. This candidacy has created a huge division in the Socialist Party. So far the government has said nothing. The problem currently is that no Socialist leader wants to put themselves forward because they would get fewer votes than Manuel Alegre. A significant part of the centre and right Socialist sectors have spoken out against Alegre, accusing him of being a person very close to the Bloco. The CP has already announced it will present a candidate and has also criticized Manuel Alegre for his relationship with us, but announcing that their votes would go towards the election of a candidate from the left.

MR: Have you have considered the possibility of taking a similar position: your own candidate with the destination of their vote announced from the beginning?

FL: In these elections a candidate of the Bloco would have no meaning; they are elections that will be decided in the first round. The right is unified around President Cavaco Silva, so either he wins in the first round or a left candidate does. No President has ever lost in a bid for re-election, but a President running for their last term of office has never had a strong challenge. This means that the electoral polarization will be total.

If we had a candidate, it would be insignificant from the electoral viewpoint and sectarian from a political viewpoint. But that is not the reason why we will not be present. Our choice is part of the policy we want: i.e.to develop to the maximum a current that can raise inside the broad electoral space of the Socialist Party the contradiction of a strategic discussion on neo-liberalism or public politics, neo-liberalism or socialism. And this is what Alegre represents. His discourse has been very strong on insecurity, unemployment, the labour code and he clearly belongs to a sector to the left of the Socialist Party. Recently, his speech against the stability and growth programme presented by the Socrates government and condemning privatization, wage policy and the degradation of the public services, was one of the positions with major impact on society and the political debate, and led to responses from the Government. Incidentally, the Bloco was the only party that presented an alternate text to the programme, which was voted on in Parliament, with alternatives to the wage freeze, privatization, tax policy, showing how public services and social security should be funded.

Creating a majority party requires the development of these differentiations over time and the political change that they represent. On the other hand, we have a government with a relative majority; the government wants to bring the elections forward. It has constitutional difficulties around this, but wants to overcome them as soon as possible to try to regain an absolute majority, taking advantage of the fact that the drama of the budgetary adjustment has not yet taken place in 2010; they know the social problems which will accompany such a reduction of public spending and wages and pensions.

The Socialist Party lost the absolute majority because of the increase in the vote for the Bloco de Esquerda. And this rise in the vote of the Bloco is explained, largely, because of our relationship with critical Socialist Party voters. Disgruntled Socialist voters felt that there could be an alternative and that bridges of dialogue on the left existed. That changed the perception of hundreds of thousands of people. And the government knows. If it calls early elections, it will seek to fight the Bloco in order to regain the absolute majority.

The only left party that is in dispute with the Socialists is the Bloco, because what is decided here is whether there is an absolute majority. A policy of isolation in the presidential election was the worst mistake that we could commit. What interests us specifically is situating the contradiction and the difficulties on the side of the Socialist Party and we have the strength of a policy of convergence. Therefore for the decisive dispute which is that of the government, the more able we are to have convergence, dialogue and broadening , the stronger we and we will deprive the Socialists of an instrument of isolation us that it could benefit from in that context.

MR: Well, we are already finished. In his last article, Daniel Bensaïd proposed recuperating the "communist" idea as that which best corresponds with what we want to do, even recognizing that it is contaminated by Stalinism. We should not lose sleep over names, but I think it is true that we have no words to satisfactorily explain who we are and the society that we are fighting for. What do you think about

this topic?

FL: It is true that more and more activists are recuperating the word communism, since the tragedy of the Soviet Union or China. In the sense of common property, a society transformed radically (but this process unfolds strictly in terms of ideas) it is a militant reference point for some very politicized layers. As a form of social identification that produces sympathy for our project, I do not think that we succeed in overcoming in the short term the brand that marked the Soviet tragedy. It is true that the Soviet century ended with the fall of the wall and that ended the centrality of the history of the Soviet Union for all formations on the left. We have to face this history in the 21st century, as also in China which will be still more important for the future, very differently to how we did in the 20th century, in that there are now other emancipatory movements which can make important contributions. I think we need to have a very open mind on this question.

However, in social intervention, defining ourselves as "socialist left" feels better and more straightforward in the struggle for hegemony with people who call themselves socialist and whose policies are often the most aggressive against the working population.

MR: Finally, I think that the greatest achievement of the Bloco in recent years is its reliability, the political-moral link it has established a significant part of the "people of the left"‚ beyond even of their own constituents. Have you sought specifically to strengthen this relationship or is it a consequence derived from political intervention?

FL: What we want is to be as independent as possible to have direct relations with a portion of the population, but it is clear that the decisive aspect of communication is the way in which we construct a discourse with impact on millions of people and that is part of the creation of a social movement of struggle. The kernel of this is being highly politicized, very prepared and attentive to detail. The detail must always be rigorous. It must always be to the millimetre in terms of what is being done and what is said. Modern communication is a regime of clips: political discourse is 25 seconds. It therefore has to be very direct and mobilising against the "pacifying" and alienating discourses.

How to construct credibility in the context of this relationship? Especially with policy coherence. For example on fiscal matters, a matter on which we have worked for ten years, we work on tax inequality, combating evasion, the protection of the financial system... we are trying to build a public perception about this. In a situation of injustice, it is important that people know how injustice works, how they are robbed.

On the other hand, is the ability to accumulate trust. People follow our interventions in discussions with the Government. The Prime Minister is a very aggressive man, particularly with the Bloco because he feels that our policy is inconsistent with his. This is a huge advantage for us. Firstly because the media focus on conflict and not consensus. The first news is that of confrontation between the Government and us. This builds over the years the idea of a left that disputes, which is not afraid, that teaches things as they are. We have already brought about the fall of a member of the Council of State, a banker who was a trusted aid of Cavaco Silva. We showed his responsibility in the failure of a bank. We managed to force the resignation of a director of the main Portuguese private bank for fraudulent handling of offshore accounts. We managed to defeat them.

There is a strong class hatred transmitted also on the other side: action creates reaction and there is class hatred from our social adversaries and the government class also, who are aware that we are at a turning point for the country's political future. This creates credibility, creates strength. It largely explains why we have more votes than the CP, despite the fact that this party has an intense history in the anti-fascist struggle, a continuity of activists over several generations and still has a social base, strong, organised, still with more social intervention than us. We have a lot to do, but this is what explains this difference.

MR: One more. A few months ago, in a statement to the newspaper "Diagonal", Jorge Costa, a leader of the Bloco with whom I have the impression that you get on quite well, said: "the struggle of the Bloco is for the destruction of the traditional political map of the country ". It is a strong formula which leads directly to the question of government. But what can it mean to govern from the left in the world we inhabit in Western Europe?

FL: We used the expression "destruction of the traditional political map" in the most precise meaning of the terms, namely that the existence of the Bloco de Esquerda will transform Portuguese politics and, in particular initiate a battle for hegemony so there is a dominant force in the Portuguese left able to opt for socialism. This is exactly our challenge to the Socialist Party. The Socialists have 40%, the CP 10%. Our problem is the 40% of the Socialist Party. While alternation is situated between the Socialist and the right with essentially continuous politics, the social organisation of the workers is overdue. The Bloco is not intended to be a marginal party for government alliances, coalitions or support as others might think, but a party whose objective is to fight for hegemony, to be dominant, because it is a dominant force. This means also raising the question of government.

This party wants to govern and that is what people understand. People are not currently waiting for an organisation that raises the strategic conditions of socialism as an immediate solution, but a government that can immediately respond to economic disaster. That is why the question of neo-liberalism is so important from a tactical point of view. We have to gain hegemony within the fight against neo-liberalism. If confused Keynesians and similar people have intellectual hegemony among politically active people conscious of what neo-liberalism means, we are lost. The same is true with human rights: if the left is not able to raise the banner of human rights, it is not a political reference point.

To win, the left must be capable of gaining hegemony within, and leading, the fight against neo-liberalism, because that is the actually existing capitalism. We do not accept a distinction between capitalism and neo-liberalism: neo-liberalism is the form of capitalism, the effective form of its updating and the transfer of income inside modern societies. It is here where the relations with other sectors arise, so as to gain hegemony for a governmental alternative regarding this policy. Our goal is not resistance; our goal is to win, to be a strong majority, to have the majority, to determine policy. The process of political recomposition of reconstitution of class representation is a condition to make this possible. This will not happen without having achieved hegemony, and without having attracted a large part of the national "intelligentsia". We must be able to manage national projects, direct the financial system, to carry out a decisive project of a decisive socialist rupture. It will take a long time yet to get there; time for implantation and class organisation, the structuring of a popular and workers' movement, which is the only possible axis for a combat for socialism.

The enunciation of this policy objective must be our starting point. At each decision which is practical, immediate, for us to show what a socialist government would do as opposed to a neoliberal government. We must ensure that people feel that difference. Today it is only a minority: it is necessary to broaden the number of people with this perception.

March 2010

Translation by International Viewpoint

Starting anew with the Left Bloc

by Alda Sousa[24] and Jorge Costa[25]

Starting anew

This chapter does not aim to be a political or social essay on the history of the Bloco de Esquerda (Left Bloc). Neither is it a journalistic account or report. Both authors are founding members of the Left Bloc and have belonged to its leadership from the start. We are in fact an active part of this story: the way we look at and write about 12 years of existence of the Left Bloc comes from our personal commitment.

We accepted the challenge proposed by the editors. In the last 12 years several articles have been written on the Left Bloc or by Left Bloc members in various anticapitalist newspapers, mainly in Europe.

However, with this chapter, we present further information which allows the reader to get a clearer picture of how and in which political climate the Bloc was founded and how it has developed. Why was the decision taken to launch a new organisation instead of an alliance or coalition? How was it done? How did the former organisations relate to this process? Did they fuse in the Left Bloc? How do you become a member? How are the leaderships elected? Who chooses the comrades who will eventually become MPs or councillors if they are elected? What does our parliamentary work look like? How do we use our strong presence in Parliament? What does our political and social work outside Parliament look like? Do we define ourselves as anticapitalists? How do we relate to other political forces on the left? Are we clear about forming a government with social democracy or not? Which were the major and more difficult choices the Left Bloc had to face?

Actually, these are some of the core questions which both of us have been asked over the years when talking to members of other European anticapitalist organisations.

---

[24]   *Alda Sousa is a lecturer of Genetic Epidemiology at the University of Porto. She joined the LCI/PSR in 1975 (the Portuguese section of the Fourth International). She is a feminist activist in pro-choice campaigns and a founder member of the Left Bloc. She was an MP between February and July 2004.*

[25]   *Jorge Costa has been for many years a member of the Political Committee of the Bloc and was an MP. He is also a member of PSR. He is co-author with Francisco Louçã of "The Armed globalisation" (2004) and of "The owners of Portugal - 100 years of economic power" (2010). He was a MP for the Bloc in 2010 and 2011.*

A success so far.... very much due to the initial choices

From the start, and especially after, or just before, another success of the Left Bloc, many political commentators, journalists and politicians from other groups have predicted and announced its imminent demise. The "caviar left", the "impossible union between Trotskyists and Maoists", a bunch of "trendy intellectuals aside from social reality", were some of the epithets we have been awarded. When the Left Bloc won 3% of the votes some commentators predicted that it had reached a peak from which it could only fall. But the Left Bloc continued to grow, to 6.8% and 10%. Not only did the Left Bloc not disappear, it became an inescapable political force which changed the political landscape. It has became a party that counts, able to prove in practice that we are not doomed to be smashed by neo-liberal capitalism and that some small victories are possible even in the context of a fierce capitalist offensive. This is particularly relevant in a defensive period, since it is important to show that struggle pays. Today it is impossible to imagine Portuguese politics without the Left Bloc. As to the criticism of being just a bunch of trendy intellectuals (as opposed to the Communist Party who is supposed to be "the" working class party, even for right wing commentators), one just has to attend any of our national conferences or public meetings, to realize how plural and diverse the Left Bloc is in terms of jobs, culture, generation, political experience.

People of all ages, retired, casually employed youth, unemployed, service workers, factory workers, rural workers, intellectuals, university teachers, students, immigrants, people who lived underground or left the country before 1974 and people for whom the Left Bloc is the first politically organised militancy, the Left Bloc has many colours.

Nearly 12 years after its foundation, we are convinced that the "key" to the success of the Bloc rests on the initial decision to set up a new party, instead of a coalition or an alliance of forces. This new party was not founded on the basis of historical or programmatic affinities and a priori ideological cohesion, but rather on a common understanding and analysis of the current global political situation, the role of capitalism and imperialism and therefore on the basis of the political confrontations which would shape our activity.

The possibility of building this regroupment in a very defensive situation, with people from different political origins and traditions, implied that we had to be able to formulate concrete political proposals and to have an impact on society. That is why started by discussing not a programme of historical reference, but a programme of political intervention.

One of the consequences of this decision was, over the years, the building of a new and strong political leadership.

The workers' movement and the Portuguese political parties

It may be difficult to understand the changes that the Left Bloc brought about without setting it in the context of Portuguese society and its specific political and social history. The Portuguese bourgeoisie had been weak in the 19th and 20th centuries compared to other European ones. The late industrialization of the country gave rise to a working class which was still embryonic at the end of the 19th century. In 1910 the monarchy was overthrown and the Republic installed.

From 1910 to 1926 (when the fascist coup took place), the major current within the workers' movement was the anarchists. Their newspaper "A Batalha" (The Battle) was the most read paper in the country. The Socialist Party (SP), social-democrats linked to the Second International, was already weak. After agreeing with the decision of Portugal to enter the First World War, their credibility declined to the point that they virtually disappeared, only re-emerging as an organisation again in 1973, a year before the fall of the dictatorship. Today the SP is a quite inorganic force within the labour movement, in spite of the number of votes it gets among sectors of the working class and the poor.

The Communist Party (CP) was founded in 1921. It was not, as in most countries, a split from social democracy, but rather a convergence of anarchists, anarcho-syndicalists and other sectors of the working class. In fact the CP was the only political force to survive the strong and severe repression that the dictatorship imposed on the working class, intellectuals and society as a whole after 1926, although later some other organisations were created under dictatorship.

In the mid-1940s, the CP adopted a strategy of entering the national trade unions created by the Salazar regime. To some extent it proved to be useful, as they were able to influence the leaderships and call for some strikes in very difficult repressive conditions. A large confederation of trade-unions, the CGTP-Intersindical, was created in 1970, when the regime had somewhat softened.

Together with the prestige of the CP leaders (who endured many years of prison, torture, and of living underground), this has allowed the CP to have control of the organised workers movement when the dictatorship was overthrown in 1974 and thereafter. This partially explains why the workers' movement, dismembered by the repression and without a public existence, was not able to stand autonomously. Moreover, even during the pre-revolutionary years of 1974/5, only a minority of advanced workers raised the question of taking power.

The working class and the left parties at the fall of the dictatorship

25th April 1974 marked the end of a 48 year dictatorship and the start of a pre-revolutionary process which was to last until November 1975. On 30 April Álvaro Cunhal (the CP General Secretary) returned from his long exile in the former USSR and Mário Soares (the SP leader) comes back from Paris. A huge crowd greets them as their trains arrive at Lisbon Central Station. 1st May 1974 saw the largest ever demonstration in Portugal, 1.5 million people gathering at a football stadium with the two leaders side by side speaking to the crowd.

Of all the organisations that became open and legal after April 1974, the CP was obviously the largest and best organised. But other organisations, especially with a Maoist origin (coming from a 1964 split of the CP, following the impact of the Sino-Soviet conflict), were also very important. União Democrática Popular (UDP) had, at one time, several thousand members and managed to elect one MP in Lisbon on several occasions (in 1975 for the Constituent Assembly, in 1976 for the first elected Parliament and again in 1979). Also organisations like Movement of the Socialist Left (MES), with its origins among Left Catholics, students and intellectuals, played an important role against the colonial war before 1974. The Proletarian Revolutionary Party (PRP) was a split from the CP who turned into armed struggle in last years of dictatorship. The Communist Internationalist League (LCI), the Portuguese section of the Fourth International, was founded only a few months before April 1974 but it also played an important role in that period, not only in its mistrust of the large alliance of classes with the military advocated by the CP but also in contributing to an independent organisation of workers and of the soldiers. Soldados Unidos Vencerão (United Soldiers will Win) (SUV) were very much influenced by the LCI who later became the Partido Socialista Revolucionário (PSR) in 1979.

In May 1974, Ernest Mandel was the invited speaker at a very large meeting held in Lisbon, called by several organisations besides the LCI. The question of independence of the former colonies was central.

However, with the normalisation following November 1975 most of these organisations collapsed or were incapable of resisting the capitalist offensive that followed. Some, like MES, even dissolved into a large talking shop. The UDP and PSR were the organisations most able to fight back and resist. Even though that first experience was not very successful, the UDP and PSR made an electoral coalition in 1983 in Lisbon and Porto.

Throughout the 1980s the PSR was engaged in several important activities like feminist work, student work against the fees, anti-racist work, anti-militarist work (for which we paid with the murder of José Carvalho, one of our leaders, by a band of skinheads in 1989). The end of the 1980s and 1990s were also marked by several experiences of opening up and relating to other currents and individuals. In 1987, *Combate*, formerly the PSR monthly newspaper, turned into a much wider project where several journalists and intellectuals formed the majority of editorial board although they were not members of the PSR. That allowed for a much wider audience and the collaboration of different sectors of the Left who were certainly not prepared to join the PSR but who played a major role in these years of resistance and strong debate.

In 1991 an important group left or was expelled from the CP. While some of them quickly joined the SP, others, like Miguel Portas, were to set up a new group called Política XXI. By the end of 1997, the PSR and Política XXI formed a coalition in the local elections in Lisbon and Porto.

The question of abortion: from a taboo to the 1998 referendum

The 1886 Portuguese Penal Code considered abortion a crime and women could be sentenced to from two to eight years in prison. In 1974, some small but radical women's groups raised the question of legalizing abortion. A small group of doctors even organised a clinic where early abortions could be performed within a safe setting. This clinic was to be closed later on, during the normalization years. The LCI was the first political force to also stand for abortion rights. But as late as 1978, several years after the fall of the dictatorship and when abortion was already legal in many European countries, the CP claimed that it was not a question felt by working-class women who, according to them, were only worried about the rise in the cost of living and not interested in abortion rights.

In 1979, the National Abortion and Contraception Campaign (CNAC) was set up, petitioning for a change in the law. Later that year, Maria Antónia Palla, a journalist, was taken to court and was accused of incitement to abortion, because she had produced a TV programme on backstreet abortion in 1976! In the same year, Conceição Massano, a young woman from a village in Alentejo, was denounced by a neighbour who had read her diary where she had written about an earlier experience of abortion. The solidarity movement was so strong that none of the judges convicted them.

Only in 1984 did the law make its first change, proposed by the SP: abortion became legal in case of rape, where the mother's health was really in danger (up to 12 weeks of pregnancy) or in case of malformation of the foetus (up to 24 weeks). In all other cases, that is, when a woman decided to terminate a pregnancy because she did not want to have that child, abortion remained forbidden; the penalty also changed, reduced to up to three years of imprisonment.

In 1998 the SP was in government with a relative majority in Parliament. A group of young socialist MPs introduced a bill to decriminalise abortion on demand up to 12 weeks of pregnancy. It was passed by three votes. Under the pressure of the conservatives, and being himself quite conservative on this issue, the Prime Minister António Guterres proposed a referendum on "Do you agree with decriminalising abortion when requested by women, up to ten weeks into pregnancy, and performed in an authorised health institution?"

It was held on 28 June 1998: only 31.9% voted, a massive abstention for Portuguese standards: the NO result had an extremely narrow victory, 50.07% to 48.28% who voted YES. So, the penal code which criminalised abortion, with the threat of up to three years in jail, did not change then. It had to wait until the new referendum which took place in 2007.

The aftermath of the referendum and the founding of the Left Bloc

Profound defeats often contribute to the dismantling of political organisations. But they may also be an opportunity to learn from its lessons and to build new alternatives. That is precisely what happened in Portugal after the first referendum on abortion, which came in a period of political retreat, after an accumulation of right wing offensives and a series of defeats for the working class.

Most of the present leaders of the Left Bloc as well as many members of the three founding organisations were then engaged in the campaign, either in their former party's campaign or in a broad umbrella movement which campaigned for decriminalisation, together with feminists, members of the CP and members of the SP (very divided internally on that question). The broad pro-choice movement did not really have a strategy to win. It both underestimated the offensive of the Catholic Church and of the right while making its campaign too self-confident.

The weakness of the radical left then became more apparent, leading to debates within each of the three organisations that later founded the Left Bloc. What is the value of a left organisation if we are neither able to stop the attacks of the ruling class nor to win a referendum on abortion?

It was Luís Fazenda, at the time the General Secretary of UDP, who took the initiative to contact first Fernando Rosas, a well-known and respected historian, a former CP militant and a former leader of the Movimento Reorganisativo do Partido do Proletariado (MRPP) who became a fellow traveller of the PSR in the 1980s. He then contacted Francisco Louçã who contacted Miguel Portas from Política XXI. In a video produced at the Left Bloc's tenth anniversary, Fernando Rosas recalls his first meeting with Fazenda: "His idea was very clearly to go forward in creating a new political project, not just an electoral coalition". The four of them started to meet regularly to discuss their analysis of capitalism, imperialism, the political forces in Portugal and the political answers that were so badly needed.

At a later stage, meetings took place not just among the four of them but of delegations from each of the three organisations and also some independents who became very enthusiastic about the possibility of creating a larger left platform. When a quite broad political agreement was reached, the next difficult decision was whether to create just an electoral coalition or an alliance or else to found a new party

Founding a quite unorthodox new party

After several months of meetings it became clear that an electoral coalition or an alliance would show little ambition. It would have been too short a project leaving many left militants with the impression that they were together just to secure seats in Parliament and not necessarily to make the much needed changes.

This proved to be right. The fact that the Left Bloc was set up as a new party made it possible for many activists from the left -trade-unionists, members of workers' committees, feminists, ecologists, activists from other social movements, along with many well-known left intellectuals, to take part in the process. So we brought together very different traditions, coming from the CP, Maoist or revolutionary Marxist (Trotskyist) currents, as well as people from independent social movements.

At the end of 1998, start of 1999, each of the three organisations held a conference to explicitly discuss and vote on the question of making just an electoral coalition or launching a new party. Although at each conference there were militants who just wanted a coalition, the vast majority of delegates voted enthusiastically for the proposal of setting up a new party.

The Left Bloc was deliberately not a homogeneous political force with a defined ideological profile. Besides being a pluralist organisation, its definition stemmed more from the concrete needs of intervention, the political confrontations that were bound to shape our activity than from an a priori ideological cohesion. So, the appeal that brought together the founding members of the Left Bloc was at the same time vague and very ambitious.

Bloco de Esquerda foundation: the appeal "Starting Anew" (1999)

"Bloco takes over the great traditions of popular struggle in the country, learning from other experiences and challenges. Bloco renews the legacy of Socialism and incorporates the convergent contributions of several citizens, powers and movements that have throughout the years been engaged in searching for alternatives to capitalism. This is the starting point to build a popular, plural, effective, influential and militant Left able to rebuild Hope."

Between February and April 1999, many public meetings took place in the main urban centres of Portugal, having as speakers not just one of the leaders of the three organisations but also independents such as Fernando Rosas or José Mário Branco. These meetings were always packed, they attracted many people, not just the organisations' rank-and-file but also many young people who had started to radicalize, and older militants from all left currents, "orphans" of former left organisations who had never given in to reformist ideas. Since affiliation to the Left Bloc is on an individual not on a collective basis, this allowed many left individuals and activists to join without having to make a choice between each of the three currents.

Fernando Rosas commented recently: "I think that a very important factor was the political and personal trust that was established between the four founders and the commitment that was established among us that the Bloc was more important than the sum of each of its components. Therefore we agreed that different political positions could be overtly expressed, but also that no public declarations should be made BEFORE we had attempted to have a common position on the subject."

A document was signed between the organisations in early 1999. Besides the rule quoted above, it established that the three founding organisations would continue to exist as long as they felt the need for it, and also contained details such as who would be the first candidate in European elections and the first candidate in Lisbon. These safeguards proved to be useful in later years.

How are leaderships elected?

We have often been asked this question. The best way to answer is to explain the preparation of our national conferences, which take place every two years. Any group of 20 Left Bloc members may present a political platform to be discussed and voted on. Each platform has equal rights: the organising committee of the conference (composed by some members of the outgoing leadership plus one representative per platform) ensures the publication and diffusion to all members of a bulletin with the various platforms and contributions, as well as the calendar of debates between the platforms and the dates for election of delegates. At the conference, the platforms present a slate for the leadership, which has to include parity between men and women. Slates not linked to one of the political platforms are not allowed, since for us a leadership should not be a sum of individuals but the result of the expression of concrete political points of view.

The Mesa Nacional (National Leadership) of the Bloc, about 80 members, is elected at the national conference, in direct proportion to the votes that each platform scored. At its first meeting, the National Leadership elects a Political Committee of 15-20 members that takes major political decisions in between meetings of the National Leadership which are held every two months.

Since the Left Bloc's foundation, the three organisations that founded the Left Bloc and the majority of independents have always been part of the same platform. In the early years, independents had a quota of 50% and the remaining 50% were distributed equally among the three currents. It is still an unwritten rule that the three founding organisations have the same number of members in the National Leadership.

A peculiar and innovative way of being anticapitalists

Soon after its foundation it was clear that the Left Bloc was much more than the sum of its initial parts. A "shared hegemony" in the leadership, together with an extraordinary skill in creating political responses and a high level of political confrontation gave the Left Bloc a wide audience, built trust and many hundreds of people joined the party, which now has around 9,000 members.

The Left Bloc has always been able to combine its presence in Parliament with an intense contact with workers, students and intellectuals. While this happens all year round, it becomes more intense and visible in summer, when the Left Bloc holds public meetings in popular places, near the coast and the beaches. Over the summer of 2010, for instance, these meetings attracted some 20,000 people.

The Left Bloc is no longer seen as just a protest party, but a party posing an alternative. Even in Parliament the Left Bloc has succeeded in getting several proposals approved, the first, in 1999, being to consider violence against women a public crime. Many more could be cited. The Left Bloc is therefore seen as a party which can lead to some, albeit sometimes small, victories.

From its early days, the Left Bloc has allowed political representation of its initial components. So far there has not been a fusion of the founding organisations, they have changed into political associations with their own websites and educational activity, without competing with the initiatives of the Left Bloc.

The Left Bloc is an anticapitalist force, heterogeneous but with a strong and cohesive leadership, plural and with diversity in its membership and leadership. There are Marxists and non-Marxists. But the Left Bloc has learned from the very beginning that plurality may be expressed as polyphony, not as cacophony as Luis Fazenda likes to say. We do not measure our anti-capitalism by the number of times we use the word anticapitalist or revolutionary in our resolutions or leaflets. We are not a party that makes abstract propaganda for socialism. In our opinion, the idea that most demands can only be fulfilled under socialism may turn out to be dangerous and demobilising. We have sometimes been accused of not having a strategy and of relying too much on tactics. From our point of view this is both unfair and wrong. The interview with Francisco Louçã explains this point very well.

Present and future challenges

This chapter was not supposed to deal with the current situation. But what we are living now in Portugal is not a "normal" situation. The consequences of the economic crisis and the rejection by the Portuguese Parliament of PEC-IV (the proposed austerity package) on 23 March 2011 led to the immediate resignation of Prime Minister Sócrates and to new national elections which will take place on 5th June.

At the beginning of April Sócrates asked the European Commission for help concerning the Portuguese debt. Shortly after, a troika composed of a representative of the International Monetary Fund (IMF), another from the European Central Bank and also a European Union commissioner came to Portugal to assess the situation. They met with the right-wing parties: Partido Social Democrata (PSD) and Centro Democratico e Social (CDS) and with the SP. Both the CP and the Left Bloc have refused to meet with entities that nobody elected and refused to pretend that they were open to negotiate with them.

At the start of May, the Portuguese troika of PS, PSD and CDS signed an agreement with the international troika accepting the conditions imposed on Portugal in order to get a loan of 78 billion Euros. The content and consequences of the agreement are devastating: of the 78 billion, 54 billion will be used in paying back those who have lent us money, 12 billion to recapitalize the banks. There will be only 12 billion Euros left. It is predicted that in two years' time we will be an additional 100,000 unemployed, adding to the already existing 700,000, social benefits will be reduced dramatically, company taxes be diminished and VAT will go up.

Besides opposing this agreement and its consequences, The Left Bloc has concrete proposals:

1) An audit of the debt, so that we know exactly to whom we owe and why we owe. As Francisco Louçã said, when we go to a restaurant we do not pay the bill before we have checked it. In fact we propose that the part of the debt that results, for instance, from corruption be taken out from the debt.

2) Immediately initiate a process of renegotiating the debt, payment deadlines and interest rates

3) Create a bailout fund with money coming from taxes on transfers to off shore accounts, and taxation of stock market operations

Obviously the results of the elections are difficult to predict. We live in a period of strong and deep crisis and recessions do not favour the Left. A small party would not have the capability of facing the present situation. But a party like the Left Bloc speaks for millions of people in TV debates and will be in contact with many others during the campaign.

The crisis and the debt are a challenge. We aim to take the challenge and transform it into a new opportunity to build a larger left. Our strategy is clearly to become a new leadership for the left, alternative to the SP's leadership.

Alda Sousa and Jorge Costa
17 May 2011

Chronology of important events for the Bloc

1999 Up to the end of February, the project of the Left Bloc is presented in public meetings by its founders. These meetings are always packed and a new enthusiasm and hope is felt. End of February, the Bloc becomes a new political party.

In May the Bloc takes part in the mobilisations against the NATO intervention in Kosovo. In June European elections take place. Miguel Portas is the 1st candidate on a national slate. The Bloc has its first electoral experience of many to come. The result was only 1.79% but very promising.

By the end of August a referendum on independence took place in Timor-Leste a former Portuguese colony occupied by Indonesia since 1975. The outcome is a massive victory for the pro-independence movement but the pro-Indonesian paramilitary forces do not accept the defeat and spread terror and horror in the population. In Portugal the largest solidarity movement ever seen takes to the streets with daily initiatives and the Bloc plays a major role in it.

In October National elections take place. The Bloc elects two MPs: Francisco Louçã and Luís Fazenda. When the parliamentary session opens, they stand up for 2 full days, until the other parties accept that one of them is to sit in the first row, (as the leaders of all parliamentary forces do). A fifth party is represented in Parliament, something the other forces find hard to accept. Moreover, the Socialist Party, with the most votes, elected 115 MPs, exactly one half of Parliamentary members, which obliged it to make alliances either with its Left or with the right.

2000 The first bill that the Bloc proposed in Parliament, that violence against women is considered a public crime, is approved.

The Bloc starts to change the political landscape of the country, not only by its cutting-edge proposals in Parliament but mainly because its two MPs and other leaders are present in every important struggle: whether it is a factory that is about to close, or a member of the Roma community that is beaten to death at a police station, the Bloc is always present in solidarity. Also, the existence of two MPs gives them a much wider audience in the media, particularly on television. The concrete proposals of the Bloc, in particular in what concerns the tax reform system and social security become widely known

In March the Bloc hosts the 1st meeting of the European Anticapitalist Left, where the Scottish Socialist Party, the Ligue Communiste Révolutionnaire and the Red-Green Alliance are the other participating organisations.

2001 Presidential elections take place at the end of January. The Bloc presents Fernando Rosas as a candidate. He scores 2.98%.

The G8 meets in Genoa. The Bloc is present at the anti-G8 demonstration with a delegation. From then onwards, the Bloc will always be present and establish links with the anti-globalisation movement.

When Bush occupies Afghanistan, the Bloc starts to build a long term anti-war movement.

Local elections take place in December and the Bloc is present for the 1st time. Although the result was rather modest as compared to the National elections, it has meant the beginning of a slow organisation and political intervention at the local level.

2002 The disastrous result of the Socialist Party in the local elections, in particular in large cities, leads to the Prime-Minister's resignation and the call for new National Elections, which take place in March. A coalition between the conservative party (PSD) and the Christian-democrats (PP) wins by comfortable majority. The Bloc elects 3 MPs: Francisco Louçã and Luís Fazenda are again elected in Lisbon and João Teixeira Lopes in Porto (the 2nd largest city). This was a major breakthrough that no organisation of the radical left has ever achieved before.

The coalition government led by Prime Minister Durão Barroso (now President of the European Commission) initiates a series of attacks on working class rights, by changing the laws existing since 1975/76. The hot debates in Parliament between Francisco Louçã and Durão Barroso became widely popular. The Bloc fought this new Working bill in Parliament and in society. In December a general strike takes place and the Bloc is very involved and its leaders are most welcome at any workplace.

2003 The Bloc takes a major role in organising initiatives against the forthcoming invasion of Iraq by Britain and the USA. Traditionally, the CP has organised a "Peace movement" which was a sort of umbrella for its satellite organisations, therefore limiting the participation of a wider audience. Besides holding several public meetings across the country, the Bloc was also able to organise a huge public meeting in Lisbon with speakers ranging from Francisco

Louçã, one MP from the Communist party, Carvalho da Silva (the leader of CGTP), Maria de Lourdes Pintasilgo (catholic, former candidate to the presidency in 1986), the former president Mário Soares, and even some Conservatives who were against the war.

Moreover, when Bush, Blair, Aznar and Durão Barroso met in the Azores and signed the agreement to invade Iraq, the Bloc organised a demonstration outside the military basis of Lajes, with 300 people and the presence of Francisco Louçã.

2004 A petition for a new referendum on abortion gets to Parliament. The law requires 35,000 signatures, the broad movement created along 2003 and 2004 reaches 121,151. The right wing coalition refuses to call for a new referendum.

The exhaustion of Barroso's government increases as shown by the results of the European elections held in the beginning of June. Soon afterwards, Barroso is chosen to become President of the European Commission and resigns as Prime-Minister. The Bloc calls for new elections, but President Sampaio chooses Santana Lopes (from Barroso's party) as Prime-Minister. The disaster goes on and by the end of November the Parliament is dissolved and new National elections are called for February 2005.

By the end of 2004 and beginning of 2005, the 3 founding organisations of the Bloc ceased to exist as such, turning into political associations.

2005 In the February elections the Socialist party wins with absolute majority. The Bloc elects 8 MP's (4 in Lisbon, 2 in Setúbal and 2 in Porto, 4 men and 4 women). A new and very difficult political period starts then, with Prime Minister Sócrates implementing all the anti-working class reforms that Barroso did not achieve.

At its 4th Conference, the Bloc clearly defines itself as anticapitalist force.

2006 Presidential elections take place in January. Francisco Louçã stands as a candidate. End of 2005 and January 2006 a very strong and militant campaign runs throughout the whole country. This campaign shows the popular roots of the Bloc while also reinforcing it. Francisco Louçã scored 5.3% of the votes. Mário Soares (former president and the official candidate of the Socialist Party won 14.3%, while Manuel Alegre, a Socialist party member and vice-president of the Parliament won 20.7% presenting himself as an independent candidate and passing Soares to his left.

After the presidential elections, Bloco underwent an internal debate about the strategic course: it assumed/defined the aim of becoming an alternative to the Socialist Party, in order to debate the majority within the Left.

In September the Bloc organised a March or Jobs that crisscrossed the country: two to three public meetings every day, with many workers present. Sometimes, the workers of companies that were going bankrupt or threatened with closure contacted us or we went to these companies.

A general protest against Sócrates' policies takes place in October. The Bloc supports the trade-unions mobilisations against cuts in pensions, jobs and public services.

2007 In February a new referendum on decriminalization of abortion takes place. The YES wins. The Bloc campaigned in the most difficult areas of the country (where the NO had won in 1998) and also helped boost the plural and broad civic movements who determined a victorious political line.

At its 5th Conference, the Bloc clarifies its participation in political activities at International level. It also defends climate justice and ecological revolution as part of the socialist transformation process.

In September the Bloc organises a March against precariousness which affects over one million workers in Portugal, mostly (but not exclusively) young people.

2008 Government attacks on education bring over 100,000 teachers to demonstrate twice that year.

2009 At its 6th Conference, the Bloc discusses the participation of some left parties in governmental coalitions in Europe, concluding that they led to very serious defeats.

Three elections take place in 2009: for European Parliament, where the Bloc scored 10.3% and elected 3 MEPs; national elections where we went from 8 to 16 MPs, not only electing one more MP from Lisbon and one more from Porto but also broadening the regional representation (1 MP from Braga, Aver, Coimbra, Elyria, Santarem and Faro); and local elections where we elected several members to local parliaments.

2010 The Bloc decides to support Manuel Alegre as candidate for the presidential elections which will take place in January 2011.

The political and social situation is worsening. Besides all legislation already approved by the government, which takes social benefits from the poor and does not touch the banks and the rich, the situation is to become even worse with the 2011 Budget. November the 24th a general strike takes place, called by the two main trade-union confederations. It is estimated that 3 million people went on strike.

At the end of November, a NATO summit takes place in Lisbon and the Bloc is much involved in anti-NATO activities, either with other forces or with a concert against NATO organised by the Bloc.

2011 The Left is defeated at the presidential elections hold in January, since Cavaco Silva, the historical leader of the right, is elected in the first round. Manuel Alegre scores only 20% of the votes, the same as 5 years before.

As the government of the Socialist Party hardens its attacks both on working class and the unemployed and retired, the Bloc sets in Parliament a censure motion against the government, which was discussed (but defeated) on March 10th.

The rejection by the Parliament of PECIV (Stability and Growth programme), presented by Prime Minister José Sócrates March 17th led to his resignation and the call for new General Elections which will take place 5th June.

In April the IMF settles down and starts to impose its conditions for a loan to Portugal.

Meanwhile, the Bloc started the preparation of its VIIth National Conference to be held May 7-8th. The developments of a strategy against precariousness as well as a programme for a Left Government able to defeat the IMF are at the centre of the debate.

Alda Sousa, April 2011

Appendix:
Role and Tasks of the
Fourth International

Resolution adopted at the 16th World Congress,
March 2010

1. We are in a context marked by an unprecedented combination of a global economic crisis and a worldwide ecological crisis, a multidimensional crisis without precedent, which puts capitalist and patriarchal civilisation into crisis. This is a major turning point. This dual crisis shows the failure of the capitalist system and puts on the agenda the reorganisation and reconstruction of an anticapitalist workers' movement.[26]

The social and economic attacks and neoliberal counter reforms against the popular classes are going to increase. These attacks will particularly affect women, given that their situation is worse to start with (much higher rates of poverty, unemployment and casualisation than men) and they will have to compensate for the cuts in public services and social allowances increasing their unpaid work within the family. There will be more wars and conflicts.

Religious fundamentalism will be increasingly used as the ideological underpinning both for attacks on the popular classes, targeting notably women's control of their own bodies, and wars and conflicts between nations and ethnic groups. A non-Eurocentric approach to sexual oppression and emancipation is important to opposing both Islamic fundamentalism in particular and the Islamophobic ideology of 'clash of civilizations' that helps fuel it. Ecological catastrophes will hit millions of people particularly in the poorer regions making the situation of women who are heads of family disproportionately worse.

A new historical period is on the horizon. New relationships of forces between imperialist powers in the world economy and politics are taking shape, with the emergence of new capitalist forces like China, Russia, India and Brazil. The combination of the weakening of US

---

[26] *The original, authoritative translation of this resolution is online at http://bit.ly/ratot4i It was was edited for this volume.*

hegemony and the sharpening of inter-capitalist competition between Europe, Russia, Asia and the USA also has geo-strategic effects in new political and military configurations, with an increased role for NATO, and new international tensions. In recent years American imperialism has compensated for its economic weakening by redeploying its military hegemony in the four corners of the world. The social and economic contradictions have led even in the USA to the discredit of the Republican team around G.W. Bush. The election of Obama is a response to this discrediting as an alternative solution for US imperialism, even if his election also responds to a desire for change on the part of a section of US society which will be disappointed but is real.

In conclusion, the crisis makes obvious the failure of neoliberal ideology although the relationship of forces remains favourable to capital. As an ideology, it shows itself incapable of offering a solution, which is why the G-20 proposals are a return to the past that blew up with the crisis, wrote an end to the Washington Consensus, but placed the IMF in the decision-making centre with its clearly neoliberal priorities. All the contradictions inherent to this social system are going to are going to come under stress without social democracy and the centre left being able to offer an adequate response. Even neo-Keynesian measures, which have not been adopted anyway, would not be enough to resolve the crisis. In this way the gap between the discourse, the pretensions of the ruling class and the reality of the suffering and catastrophes which are inflicted on the peoples and workers, the building up of pressure on them, create the conditions for exacerbated social tensions and political crisis.

The crisis has a particularly harsh impact on women and on sexual minorities that are excluded from the family (or choose not to live in it), and are thus cut off from its resources. The crisis is driving many of the most marginalized people, such as transgender, into even deeper poverty. This is true especially in dependent countries where a welfare state is weak or non-existent.

2. Social fightbacks are continuing to rise on a world scale but in a very unequal fashion and remain on the defensive. The global justice movement lost the dynamism that it had had up to 2004. The Belem WSF showed, nevertheless, the need and the possibility for international convergences, but in a framework where struggles are more fragmented and dispersed. In Europe the success of the mobilisations against the G-20 and NATO give an indication of a renewal of the global justice movement. The Istanbul ESF could be another important occasion. The World March of Women offered the possibility of organising joint initiatives in 2010 which could have become a step in rebuilding and strengthening this international feminist movement.

In certain European countries, France, Greece, Germany, Poland, Italy, social struggles have a central impact on the political scene, but these struggles are not sufficient to block or turn around the underlying trends in the capitalist offensive and the effects of the crisis. They have not succeeded in overcoming the process of division and fragmentation of workers. These struggles remain defensive. They have not yet found an expression in terms of anticapitalist consciousness. In this framework, in the absence of an anticapitalist left reactionary, even xenophobic and racist alternatives and trends can get stronger.

In the Middle East, peoples are continuing to resist Western and Israeli occupation and aggression, in Palestine, in Iraq and in Lebanon. The murderous aggression waged by the Zionist government in Gaza, two years after that in Lebanon, has not been able to defeat the resistance. Although Hamas and Hezbollah are now the main political references in this resistance, apart from these organisations there are left currents that act not only with a perspective for national liberation but also for social liberation, which reject human exploitation and which reject categorically the segregation of women. This is the position that we want to strengthen.

Latin America continues to be the centre of resistance to neo-liberalism and the continent with the most explosive situations, even though these are uneven from one country to another. Venezuela, Bolivia and Ecuador are experiencing the most radical processes, with partial breaks from imperialism that have meant some important advances at the levels of government and/or social movements. There are others where the prognosis is unclear, like Paraguay, and all these find in Cuba a point of reference. Some others maintain versions of neoliberal policies, with neo-developmentalism in Argentina, or social liberalism in Uruguay and Brazil. The latter, in spite of its sharp contradictions with the US, especially over defence policy, its membership of UNASUR and its agreements with Venezuela, nonetheless collaborates with fundamental policies of Washington and aims to achieve regional leadership. For their part, Colombia, Peru, Chile and Mexico remain clearly neo-liberal.

Nonetheless, a new political situation is emerging, with the renewed imperialist threat in the region, with the presence of the Fourth US Fleet, the coup in Honduras, seven new US military bases in Colombia, the direct intervention of the US embassy in the most important trade union conflict in Argentina for years, the political and military interference in Haiti. All these aim to roll back the political advances and develop an international response.

This means that the class struggle will intensify in Latin America in the coming period. The governments of Venezuela and Ecuador are moving back from their most radical proposals, showing two aspects in particular that cause concern: the orientation towards the extraction of natural resources and the limited democratic participation of social sectors. In Bolivia, there is a radicalisation of the processes of change, which rests directly on the social movements.

Although these processes are in dispute, with advances and retreats, they run the risk, in the course of their evolution, of not advancing to anticapitalist positions, unless there is a strengthening of the self-activity of wage earners, indigenous peoples and other oppressed social sectors, and greater pressure from these sectors on the governments of Venezuela, Bolivia and Ecuador.

At the same time, the radicalization of social movements, especially the struggle of indigenous and peasant movements, is putting pressure on these governments and at the same time posing a clear anticapitalist perspective, in defence of natural resources, land, water, biodiversity, etc., and a change in the development model, as was expressed in the Declaration of the Assembly of Social Movements at the Belem WSF, and the recent assembly of Alba TCP, which in its final statement denounced capitalism and called for its overthrow. The national, regional and international meetings of the social movements demonstrate the radical potential contained in the southern part of Latin America.

One urgent political task for the organisations is to stimulate the self-activity of the masses, generalising workers' control and the creation of bodies of popular power; otherwise, in Venezuela, Bolivia and Ecuador, there is a risk of a definitive reverse and a consolidation of capitalism in these countries, where it is currently challenged.

The activity of the sections and groups of the Fourth International in Latin America need to take into account these tendencies, the national question in the region and the connections between anti-imperialism and anti-capitalism, and define a tactic for intervention in a process characterized by the inter-relation between the states that make up the ALBA and social movements with strong histories of self-organisation and self-management. These two forces sometimes converge and sometimes enter into contradiction. This implies promoting demands for unitary struggles in defence of the rights of indigenous peoples, against the criminalization of protest, privatizations, extractivism of natural resources, machismo and the economic and ecological crisis, thereby stimulating the strategic political debate about power and hegemony in our societies.

In a series of what are usually called emerging capitalist countries or those resulting from capitalist restoration,, China, Russia or the former eastern bloc, the whirlwind of globalisation is tending to proletarianise hundreds of millions of human beings. But this new social power, which can play a key role in the coming years, has not yet formed mass independent organisations, trade unions, associations, and political organisations capable of facing the challenge of this global reorganisation.

The pillaging of resources in Africa to the benefit of big capitalist multinationals is increasing with the complicity of the existing governments. The continued growth of GDP in recent years in sub-Saharan Africa does not benefit the population, only social inequality in increasing. Faced with the deterioration in living conditions, there have been major struggles, such as the general strikes in Guinea, the demonstrations in Togo, the general strike in the public sector in South Africa. The food crisis at the end of 2008 sparked many demonstrations. However, the absence of a political alternative is a heavy obstacle to the success of these struggles, such as in Guinea or in the Cameroons. They are either diverted towards bourgeois political formations as in Madagascar or they lose themselves in religious dead-ends as in Nigeria or Congo (DRC) or worse in ethnic or racist ones like in Kenya or South Africa.

The building of democratic peoples' and workers' organisations' remains an absolute necessity for the success of struggles.

In Asia, the ongoing fast development of capitalism in China and in India and in most of South-Asian countries raises crucial political questions. Around half of the global working class lives in Asia and the necessity to create or strengthen revolutionary parties in this part of the world is critical. The situation is very different from one country to another:

• China is of the outmost importance. Decades of repression explain why the creation of a revolutionary party in China has to start from scratch. Bringing the experience and tradition of the international labour movement to China will be necessary to stimulate the creation of a revolutionary party as well as international solidarity. The Fourth International will have to pay special attention to the social and political developments that the present international crisis could bring about in the near future.

• In India, where the population will be larger than that of China's by 2050, and where faster industrialisation has increased the number of workers and the rural crisis is deepening, the political situation and our tasks are different. The labour movement is very well developed and organised but dominated by Stalinist or Maoist political parties. The construction of a revolutionary party defending our programme cannot just ignore them.

• In South-East Asia, the situation is very uneven. In some countries like Thailand and Burma, the labour movement is very weak. In these countries there is neither social democracy nor radical left parties. In these countries our task is to establish stronger links with the social movements that are active in the defence of farmers, women and workers when trade unions exist. Indonesia and Malaysia are in an intermediary situation. There are some small revolutionary parties with whom we can engage a constructive political debate and collaboration.

• In the Philippines and Pakistan, the Fourth International has strong organisations which can be a basis of our political activity throughout Asia.

In these countries we are confronted with Islamic fundamentalism. We oppose the Taliban in Afghanistan and the Muslims extremists in the Philippines like the Abou Sayaf because they are reactionary forces. We cannot make any agreement with them in the name of anti imperialism. In other countries like Indonesia or Malaysia, we also could be confronted with Islamic fundamentalism and the FI has to strengthen its analysis.

• In Sri Lanka, after several decades of war, the government has defeated the LTTE militarily but the root cause of the Tamil question has not yet been addressed. Besides, the Rajapaksa government uses open and brutal repression to silent his opponents and the media. The FI should be part of the international campaign of solidarity with the Tamil people. In all Asia, the FI defends the rights of ethnic groups and indigenous peoples and support their struggle for self-determination.

• In Japan, the process of fusion of the two organisations linked to the FI is underway. They have published a common newspaper since September 2009.

In South Korea too, where the labour movement is strong, there is also a convergence of different forces toward the creation of a New Anticapitalist Party. Because this country has a strong tradition in the working class struggle, the Fourth International has to follow this event closely. Furthermore, the FI should organise solidarity campaigns to support the militants of revolutionary parties who are now repressed by the State.

3. The dynamic of capitalist globalisation and the current crisis have also changed the framework of evolution and development of the traditional left. Reformist bureaucracies have seen their leeway considerably reduced. From reformism without reforms to reformism with counter-reforms, social democracy and equivalent forces in a series of dominated or developing countries are experiencing an evolution towards social-liberalism; that is these forces are directly underwriting neo-liberal or neo-conservative policies. All the forces politically or institutionally linked to social-liberalism or to the centre left, including the women's movement, notably in the institutionalised forms of NGOs, women's aid associations, etc, are to varying degrees being dragged into these qualitative changes in the workers' movement and are incapable of formulating a plan for getting out of the crisis. What is more, we are seeing policies, such as that of the Lula government in Brazil, which are making the ecological crisis worse. The clash with these parties is more difficult since they maintain their control, particularly electorally, of part of the workers movement, and it is therefore necessary to build a real, credible political alternative.

The traditional communist parties are continuing their long decline. They try to break this decline by grabbing onto the coat tails of the leading forces in the liberal left and the institutional apparatuses or falling back on their nostalgic and self-affirming positions. While there are sectors or currents who wish to build the social movements with anticapitalist forces, such as Synaspismós in Greece, they are doomed to have contradictions and divisions because of their reformist nature. In effect, the decision to build anticapitalist parties does not mean we are not aware of the existence of radical, anti-liberal, left reformist currents that play a role and have electoral credibility. Therefore, they continue to be competitors and-or political adversaries. Their position can be reinforced by occasional tactical shifts, generally electoralist, to the left, by social-liberalism, often to re-establish its consensus among the working class and popular sectors. This poses the challenge for us of implementing a united front offensive capable of responding to the needs of men and women wage earners. At the same time, when on the basis of clear political conditions we decide to intervene inside anti-liberal, reformist left parties (such as in the case of Die Linke), we do it with no illusions about the nature of these parties, and we build anticapitalist tendencies linked to social movements, that fight electoralism, institutionalism, and any attempt to compromise with capitalism.

4. We want to get involved in this reorganisation to create a new left that is capable of meeting the challenge of this century and rebuilding the workers' movement, its structures, its class consciousness, its independence from the bourgeoisie at the political and cultural level.

• An anticapitalist, internationalist, ecologist and feminist left;

• A left that is clearly alternative to social democracy and its governments;

• A left which fights for a socialism of the 21st century, self-managed and democratic and which has a coherent programme for getting there;

• A left that is conscious that for this goal it has to break with capitalism and its logic and thus that is cannot govern with the political representation with which it wants to break;

• A pluralistic left rooted in the social movements and the workplaces which integrates the combativeness of the workers, the struggles for women's and LGBT liberation and emancipation and ecologist struggles;

• A non-institutional left which bases its strategy on the self-organisation of the proletariat and the oppressed on the principle that emancipation of the workers is the task of the workers themselves;

• A left that promotes all forms of self-organisation by workers and by the popular classes; that encourages thinking, deciding, and doing things for itself and on the basis of its own decisions;

• A left which integrates new social sectors, new themes such as those expressed by the World Social Forum in Belem, and above all the new generations because you cannot make new things with old material;

• An internationalist and anti-imperialist left which fights against domination and war and the self-determination of the people and which lays out the framework for a mass democratic international;

• A left able to link the precious heritage of critical and revolutionary Marxism with developments of feminism, ecosocialism and the indigenous movements of Latin America;

• An independent and class-struggle left which fights for the broadest united action against the crisis and for the rights, the gains and the aspirations of the workers and all the oppressed.

These are the criteria and the general content of our orientation for building new useful anticapitalist instruments for fighting the current system.

5. This is the aspiration in which the problems of building the Fourth International and new anticapitalist parties and new international currents are posed. We expressed it in our own way, from 1992 onwards, so in the last two world congresses, with the triptych "New period, new programme, new party", developed in documents of the International. We confirm the essentials of our choices at the last World Congress in 2003 concerning the building of broad anticapitalist parties. The Fourth International is confronted, in an overall way, with a new phase. Revolutionary Marxist militants, nuclei, currents and organisations must pose the problem of the construction of anticapitalist, revolutionary political formations, with the perspective of establishing a new independent political representation of the working class that takes into account the diversity of the working class, in gender, race, residence status, age, sexual orientation, in defending a resolutely class-based programme.

Building broad anticapitalist parties is the current response we offer to the crisis in the workers' and left movement and the need for its reconstruction. This project is based on mass struggles, bringing mass movements to the forefront and the emergence of a new generation. Of course, this does not eliminate our revolutionary Marxist, ecologist, feminist internationalist identity and our basic aim of defeating capitalism to create a new ruling order based on democracy and direct participation: that is, a real socialist democracy.

That is true on the level of each country and at an international level. On the basis of the experience of the class struggle, the development of the global justice movement, defensive struggles and anti-war mobilisations over the last ten years, and in particular the lessons drawn from the evolution of the Brazilian PT and of Communist Refoundation in Italy and from the debates of the French anti-liberal left, revolutionary Marxists have engaged in recent years in the building of the PSOL in Brazil, of Sinistra Critica in Italy, of the New Anticapitalist Party in France, Respect in England. In this perspective we have continued to build the experiences of the Bloco de Esquerda in Portugal and the Red-Green Alliance in Denmark.

The common goal, via different paths, is that of broad anticapitalist parties. It is not a question of taking up the old formulas of regroupment or revolutionary currents alone. The ambition is to bring together forces beyond simply revolutionary ones. These can be a support in the process of brining forces together as long as they are clearly for building anticapitalist parties. Although there is no model, since each process of coming together takes account of national specificities and relationships of forces, our goal must thus be to seek to build broad anticapitalist political forces, independent of social democracy and the centre left, formations which reject any policy of participation or support to class-collaborationist governments, today in government with social-democracy and the centre left, forces which understand that winning victories on women's rights, like in the abortion referendum in Portugal, strengthen the radical anticapitalist forces.

It is on the basis of such a perspective that we must be oriented. What we know of the experiences of differentiation and reorganisation in Africa and Asia point in the same direction. Nevertheless in the countries of Latin America the construction of broad anticapitalist parties should integrate from its beginnings a clear stand for socialism. It is through this complex and diverse process that we can make new advances.

Where we are working inside such broad political forces, it is important to fight for the right of self-organisation within these parties by women and LGBTs, and on this self-organisation's being reflected in the parties' programmes and practice. This self-organisation is a means of resisting pressures towards electoralism and institutionalization. In new radical political formations in several Latin American countries, the right to self-organisation is important to fighting for a 21st-century socialism from below that rejects authoritarian tendencies and the temptation to repeat 20th-century errors. In general within such broad forces, we start from an understanding, as an indissoluble part of our socialism, of the necessity for a collective and resolute response to all manifestations of prejudice including sexism, racism, Islamophobia, anti-Semitism, homophobia and transphobia. We also fight for specific attention to organising by youth; for the integration of black, immigrant, women's and LGBT issues into the party's public statements and daily interventions; and for representation of specially oppressed comrades in the party leadership and among its spokespeople and candidates for office.

6. This is the framework in which we must approach the question of the relationship between the building of the Fourth International and a policy of anticapitalist coming together at the national, continental and international levels. We must discuss how to strengthen and transform the Fourth International in order to make it an effective tool in the perspective of a new international grouping. We already have started, with limited results it has to be admitted, conferences of the anticapitalist left and other international conferences. On the international level, we have initiated, on this political basis, many conferences and initiatives of international convergence and coming together: the constitution of the European Anticapitalist Left (EACL), with the Left Bloc in Portugul, the Red-Green Alliance in Denmark and the Scottish Socialist Party. We worked with organisations like the SWP in Britain. Other parties, even left reformists who had at one time or another a political evolution "to the left", like Communist Refoundation in Italy, or Synaspismós, also took part in these conferences. We also held international conferences of revolutionary and anticapitalist organisations, on the occasion of the World Social Forums at Mumbai in India and Porto Alegre in Brazil. On this level, we created bonds of solidarity with the Brazilian PSOL in its break with Lula's PT. We have supported the efforts of our Italian comrades to build an anticapitalist alternative to the policies of Communist Refoundation in Italy. These few elements show the type of orientation that we want to implement. The different conferences this year such as those in Paris or Belem show the necessity and the possibility of joint action and discussion by a large number of organisations and currents of the anticapitalist left in Europe. It is now necessary to continue a policy of open meetings and conferences on topics of strategic and programmatic thinking and joint action through campaigns and initiatives of international mobilisation.

7. The Fourth International and its sections have played and still play a vital road in defending, promoting and implementing:

- a programme of demands that are both immediate and transitional towards socialism;

- a united front policy that aims for mass mobilisation of workers and their organisations;

- a policy of working-class unity and independence against any type of strategic alliance with the national bourgeoisie;

- opposition to any participation in governments that merely manage the State and the capitalist economy having abandoned both all internationalism and the fight for an end to inequality and discrimination on gender, racial, ethnic, religious or sexual orientation grounds.

The Fourth International has played and still plays an important role in keeping alive the history of the revolutionary Marxist current, "to understand the world", to confront the analyses and the experiences of revolutionary militants, currents and organisations and to bring together organisations, currents and militants who share the same strategic vision and the same choice of broad convergences on revolutionary bases. The existence of an international framework that makes it possible "to think about politics" is an indispensable asset for the intervention of revolutionaries. Consistent internationalism must pose the question of an international framework. But for historical reasons that it has itself analyzed, the Fourth International does not have the legitimacy to represent in and of itself the new mass International that we need. So when it is a question of taking a step forward in the bringing together of anticapitalist forces, these new organisations, in particular in Europe and Latin America, cannot relate to and join this or that current identified with the Fourth International, and this is true whatever the reference point, the various Morenoites, the Lambertists, the SWP or other variants of Trotskyism.

Let us note, nevertheless, that a major difference between the FI and all these tendencies, over and above political positions, which is to the credit of the International, is that it is based on a democratic coordination of sections and militants, whereas the other international tendencies are "international-factions" or co-ordinations based on "party-factions" which do not respect rules of democratic functioning, in particular the right of tendency. The historical limits of these international "Trotskyist" currents ", like other ex-Maoist or ex-Communist currents, prevent us today from advancing in the crystallization of new international convergences. Chavez's call to found a Fifth International poses other questions about its origins, its framework, that is to say, its viability. The Fourth International declares that it is willing to participate in the debates and preparatory meetings that may be organised. We will contribute our historic gains and our vision about what a new international and its programmatic foundations could be. A genuine new international can only be born if its members share a programme, an ability to intervene in society, a democratic, pluralist form of functioning, as well as clear independence from governments in order to break with capitalism.

In the present relationship of forces, the policy for advancing towards a mass international must rather take the road of open and periodic conferences on central political questions, activity, specific themes or discussions, which make possible the convergence and the emergence of anticapitalist and revolutionary poles. In this sense, the Fourth International is in favour of the proposals from revolutionary Marxist currents and/or groups who share with us a common understanding of the international situation and our aspirations for building new international frameworks.

In the new anticapitalist parties which may be formed in the years to come, and which express the current stage of combativeness, experience and consciousness of the sectors that are the most committed to the search for an anticapitalist alternative, the question of a new international is and will be posed. We act and we will continue to act so that it is not posed in terms of ideological or historical choices, which are likely to lead to divisions and splits. It must be posed on a double level, on the one hand real political convergence on tasks of international intervention, on the other pluralism of the new formations, which must bring together currents of various origins: Trotskyists of different kinds, libertarians, revolutionary syndicalists, revolutionary nationalists, left reformists. So in general, when there have been concrete steps towards new parties, we have proposed that the new broad anticapitalist party functions with the right of tendency or currents, and that the supporters of the Fourth International in these new parties organise themselves in ways to be decided, according to the specific situation of each party. Our Portuguese comrades in the Left Bloc, our Danish comrades in the Red-Green Alliance, our Brazilian comrades in the PSOL, are organised, in particular forms, as a Fourth International current or in class struggle currents with other political tendencies.

8. In this movement we are confronted with de-synchronizations between the building of parties on a national level and the construction of new international groupings. There can be, in the present situation or in the next years, new anticapitalist parties in a series of countries, but the emergence of a new international force, and all the more so, of a new international, is not, at this stage, foreseeable. A new international will only be the result of a prolonged period of joint action and common understanding of events and tasks for overthrowing capitalism. While we affirm a policy of international convergence, this confirms the particular responsibilities of the FI, and thus the need for its reinforcement. We can and we seek to represent an organisational framework that is attractive and, democratic, for revolutionary organisations which share the same political projects as ours. It is in this dynamic that the Filipino comrades are situated, the Pakistani comrades and the Russian comrades are situated, and that can be the case tomorrow of, for example, the Polish or Malian comrades.

9. We have, in fact, a particular role that is recognized by a series of political currents. We may be the only ones who can make political forces of various origins converge. This is for example, what in Latin America the Venezuelans comrades of left currents of the Bolivarian process say to us. It is also the case in Europe, in the framework of the relations of the EACL and of other currents. So, the next world congress must be an important step for the meeting of all these forces. This Congress will be a congress of the FI and there will be no organisational growing over at this stage. But we want the FI to play the role of a "facilitator" of convergences in the perspective of new international groupings.

10. As a result, in order to strengthen ourselves and play this role all the bodies of the FI must be reinforced: regular Bureau meetings, International Committees, specific working commissions, travel, and exchanges between the sections. It is necessary to reinforce the activity that the International has deployed over the last few years in regularising and strengthening EPBs meetings and the efforts of coordination between the Latin American sections. The meetings of the International Committee (IC) which are held every year representing about 30 organisations must ensure the organisational continuity of our international current.

Lack of resources as well as the decline in the presence of women, notably in our leading bodies, in the last period (a result of the decline in activity of a strong, autonomous women's movement which has had an impact on our national organisations and thus the International), have meant that we have not sustained an active women's commission and a corresponding network of regional meetings and international schools. Three women's seminars have been held since 2000 as well as meetings of the women comrades present at each IC. These have maintained a limited and fragile but nevertheless real feminist internationalist perspective. In the next period, given the centrality of our understanding of women's oppression and the strategic nature of the fight against it and the struggle to build the autonomous women's movement in an anticapitalist perspective, we must find the necessary resources to ensure that this question is developed as a central element of the anticapitalist perspective we propose. In this framework we must at the same time strengthen our internal commission and be on the offensive in proposing discussions to our partners, including participation in seminars and schools in our Institute. This process must also find a reflection at national level.

At the same time we must ensure that the women in our organisations, and in the new parties we are building, find their full place and that the simple adoption of parity or quotas for leadership bodies or electoral lists is not considered a sufficient answer to the obstacles to women's full participation in the political process. The range of measures constituting a positive action plan was presented in the 1991 World Congress resolution on positive action.

The youth camp which is held every year with around 500 comrades must have a central place for the youth work of our European sections, in the perspective of forming young internationalist cadres. As more and more of our organisations in Europe are within broader anticapitalist formations we continue to encourage our comrades to invite youth from the broader organisations to the camp, and to participate in the preparatory seminar held in Amsterdam every Easter. The camp is also an important occasion for young comrades from Europe to meet comrades from other continents, and the efforts made by organisations outside Europe to send comrades to participate in the camp are very important. As the only regular public initiative of the FI, the camp also plays a role as a place to which younger people from organisations with which we are building relations can be invited, as was the case with camp in Greece in 2009 with the presence of small delegations from Russia, Ukraine, Belarus, Poland and Croatia

The Amsterdam educational institute has taken on a fresh impetus. We now have to ensure that the schools and seminars are held and ensure the equilibrium of its management and its organisation. The FI must also open up its meetings and its Institute. The Institute occupies a central place, not only to educate the cadres of the section but also to contribute to the exchanges between currents and to various international experiences. The seminar on climate change, open to a series of international experts, is a good example. Like other meetings it indicates the necessity and the possibility that we are a crucible for programmatic elaboration of essential questions that anticapitalist and revolutionary currents are tackling.

The existence of an international school in the Philippines is a tool of great importance to form new generations of revolutionary militants coming from all parts of Asia and to share their experiences. In the near future, there will be a new school in Islamabad in Pakistan which enlarges our capacity to educate militants and organise political debates in South Asia. The FI has to give full support to the IIRE in Manila and in Islamabad.

Our schools have always been an occasion for inviting participation from organisations with which we are building relations. This role must be strengthened and broadened in the coming period throughout the IIRE network.

To sum up, in the coming period, and on an orientation aimed at building a new international force or a new International, the FI as an internal framework, represents an essential asset for revolutionary Marxists.

March 2010

About Resistance Books and the IIRE

Resistance Books

Resistance Books is the publishing arm of Socialist Resistance, a revolutionary Marxist organisation which is the British section of the Fourth International. We publish books jointly with the International Institute for Research and Education in Amsterdam and independently under the name of Resistance books. Socialist Resistance also publishes a bi-monthly magazine of the same name and occasional pamphlets.

Socialist Resistance is an organisation active in the trade union movement and in many campaigns against the war, in solidarity with Palestine and with anticapitalist movements across the globe. We are ecosocialist, we argue that much of what is produced under capitalism is socially useless and either redundant or directly harmful. Capitalism's drive for profit is creating environmental disaster, and it is the poor, the working class and the global south that are paying the highest price for this.

We have been long standing supporters of women's liberation and the struggles of lesbians, gay people bisexuals and transgender people. We believe those struggles must be led by those directly affected, none so fit to break the chains as those who wear them. We work in antiracist and anti-fascist networks, including campaigns for the rights of immigrants and asylum seekers.

Socialist Resistance believes that democracy is an essential component of any successful movement of resistance and struggle. With Britain and the western imperialist countries moving into a long period of capitalist austerity and crisis, deeper than any since the Second World War, Socialist Resistance stands together with all those who are organising to make another world is possible.

Further information about Resistance Books and Socialist Resistance can be obtained at www.socialistresistance.org.

International Viewpoint is the English language on-line magazine of the Fourth International which can be read at www.internationalviewpoint.org.

The International Institute for Research and Education

The International Institute for Research and Education (IIRE) is an international foundation, recognised in Belgium as an international scientific association by Royal decree of 11th June 1981. The IIRE provides activists and scholars worldwide with opportunities for research and education in three locations: Amsterdam, Islamabad and Manila.

Since 1982, when the Institute opened in Amsterdam, its main activity has been the organisation of courses in the service of progressive forces around the world. Our seminars and study groups deal with all subjects related to the emancipation of the world's oppressed and exploited. It has welcomed hundreds of participants from every inhabited continent. Most participants have come from the Third World.

The IIRE has become a prominent centre for the development of critical thought and interaction, and the exchange of experiences, between people who are engaged in daily struggles on the ground. The Institute's sessions give participants a unique opportunity to step aside from the pressure of daily activism. The IIRE gives them time to study, reflect upon their involvement in a changing world and exchange ideas with people from other countries.

Our website is constantly being expanded and updated with freely downloadable publications, in several languages, and audio files. Recordings of several recent lectures given at the institute can be downloaded from www.iire.org, as can talks given by founding Fellows such as Ernest Mandel and Livio Maitan, dating back to the early 1980s.

The IIRE publishes the *Notebooks for Study and Research* to focus on themes of contemporary debate or historical or theoretical importance. Lectures and study materials given in sessions in our Institute, located in Amsterdam, Manila and Islamabad, are made available to the public in large part through the Notebooks.

Different issues of the Notebooks have also appeared in languages besides English and French, including German, Dutch, Arabic, Spanish, Japanese, Korean, Portuguese, Turkish, Swedish, Danish and Russian. For a full list visit http://bit.ly/IIRENSR or subscribe online at: http://bit.ly/NSRsub. To order, email iire@iire.org or write to the IIRE.

Forthcoming books

Capitalism - Crisis and Alternatives, Özlem Onaran, Michel Husson, John Rees, Claudio Katz et al., September 2011 (€8, £7, $11).

Marxism and Anarchism, Karl Marx, Frederick Engels, Leon Trotsky, September 2011 (€8, £7, $11).

Fascism and the far right in Europe, September 2011

Introduction to Marxist Economic Theory (Third Edition), Ernest Mandel, Özlem Onaran, Raphie de Santos, November 2011.

The thought of Leon Trotsky, Denise Avenas, Michael Löwy, Jean-Michel Krivine.

The Transitional Program for Socialist Revolution, Leon Trotsky, Daniel Bensaïd, John Riddell.

Dangerous relationships: marriage and divorces between Marxism and feminism, Cinzia Arruzza.

Titles from Resistance Books

Militant years - car workers' struggles in Britain in the 60s and 70s, Alan Thornett, February 2011 (£12, €14, $19).

The Global Fight for Climate Justice, Anticapitalist responses to global warming and environmental destruction, Ian Angus ed., June 2009 (£10, €14, $18).

Ireland's Credit Crunch, Kearing, Morrison & Corrigan, October 2010 (£6, €8, $10).

Foundations of Christianity: a study in Christian origins, Karl Kautsky (£12, €18, $25).

The Permanent Revolution & Results and Prospects, Leon Trotsky (£9, €15, $18).

My Life under White Supremacy and in Exile, Leonard Nikani, February 2009 (£10, €12, $15).

Cuba at Sea, Ron Ridenour, May 2008 (£8, €12, $15).

Ecosocialism or Barbarism (new expanded edition), Jane Kelly ed., February 2008 (£6, €9, $12).

Cuba: Beyond the Crossroads (new expanded edition), Ron Ridenour, April 2007 (£10, €15, $20).

Middle East: war, imperialism, and ecology, sixty years of resistance, Roland Rance & Terry Conway eds. and Gilbert Achcar (contributor) et al., March 2007 (£12, €14, $19).

It's never too late to love or rebel, Celia Hart, August 2006 (£8, €15, $20).

Notebooks for Study and Research

Revolution and Counter-revolution in Europe from 1918 to 1968, Pierre Frank, May 2011 (€10, £9, $14), NSR 49.

Women's Liberation & Socialist Revolution: Documents of the Fourth International, Penelope Duggan ed., October 2010 (€8, £7, $11) NSR 48.

The Long March of the Trotskyists: Contributions to the history of the International, Pierre Frank, Daniel Bensaïd, Ernest Mandel, October 2010 (€8, £5, $8), NSR 47.

October Readings: The development of the concept of Permanent Revolution, D. R. O'Connor Lysaght ed., October 2010 (£5, €6, $8), NSR 46.

Building Unity Against Fascism: Classic Marxist Writings, Leon Trotsky, Daniel Guérin, Ted Grant et al., October 2010 (€6, £5, $8), NSR 44/45.

Strategies of Resistance & 'Who Are the Trotskyists', Daniel Bensaïd, November 2009 (€8, £6, $10), NSR 42/43.

Living Internationalism: the IIRE's history, Murray Smith and Joost Kircz eds., January 2011 (€5, £4, $7), NSR 41.

Socialists and the Capitalist Recession (with Ernest Mandel's 'Basic Theories of Karl Marx'), Raphie De Santos, Michel Husson, Claudio Katz et al., March 2009 (€9, £6, $12), NSR 39/40.

Take the Power to Change the World, Phil Hearse ed., June 2007 (€9, £6, $12), NSR 37/38.

The Porto Alegre Alternative: Direct Democracy in Action, Iain Bruce ed. (€19, £13, $23.50), NSR 35/36.

The Clash of Barbarisms: September 11 & the Making of the New World Disorder, Gilbert Achcar (€15, £10, $16), NSR 33/34.

Globalization: Neoliberal Challenge, Radical Responses, Robert Went (€21, £14, $21), NSR 31/32.

Understanding the Nazi Genocide: Marxism after Auschwitz, Enzo Traverso (€19.20, £13, $19.) NSR 29/30.

Fatherland or Mother Earth? Essays on the National Question, Michael Löwy (€16, £10.99, $16), NSR

Resistance Books
London

International Institute for Research & Education
Amsterdam, Islamabad & Manila

September 2011

CPSIA information can be obtained at www.ICGtesting.com
Printed in the USA
LVOW06s2159250614

391665LV00001B/181/P